THE
LAKE
HOUSE

COOKBOOK

THE LAKE HOUSE COOKBOOK

TRUDIE STYLER
&
JOSEPH SPONZO

CLARKSON POTTER/PUBLISHERS
NEW YORK

Published by Clarkson N. Potter/Publishers, 201 East 50th Street, New York, New York 10022.
Member of the Crown Publishing Group.

Random House, Inc. New York, Toronto, London, Sydney, Auckland.
www.randomhouse.com

CLARKSON N. POTTER, POTTER, and colophon are registered trademarks of Random House, Inc.

Originally published in Great Britain by Ebury Press in 1999.

Library of Congress Cataloging-in-Publication Data is available upon request.

ISBN 0-609-60412-0

10 9 8 7 6 5 4 3 2 1

First American Edition

THIS BOOK IS DEDICATED TO THE GERSON INSTITUTE, A NONPROFIT ORGANIZATION DEDICATED TO THE HOLISTIC TREATMENT OF DEGENERATIVE DISEASES — **TRUDIE STYLER**

TO JULES & JIM AND STING & TRUDIE, DREAMCATCHERS — **JOSEPH SPONZO**

Contents

An
Introduction
to Lake
House

The House & Garden

In 1991 our family moved to a small village in Wiltshire, only the sixth family in 450 years to have lived at Lake House. The recorded history of the house begins in 1550, when Robert Taylor and Andrew Salter, merchant tailors of London, who had owned Lake House for less than a month, sold it to John Capelyn, merchant. In 1578 George Duke, Esquire, bought it, and the house stayed in his family for over 300 years. The Reverend Edward Duke, who died in 1852, inscribed his initials on a tree that still stands in the garden today. In 1897 Mr. Joseph Lovibond took over from the Reverend's great-grandson, Robert Duke, followed this century by a Lieutenant-Colonel Bailey.

Suddenly to find ourselves the most recent in the line of such a heritage is somewhat daunting. Simply by living here we have become part of the history of Lake House and its surrounding area, and this has added a whole new dimension to our lives. Where once we were city dwellers, with all the transience that so often entails, now we find ourselves part of a rural community, imbued with a sense of continuity.

We have spent the last six years transforming the house and its original 60 acres of land into the place it is today. The work on the house will doubtless prove to be a continuous cycle of maintenance and repair. The work on the land is also by its very nature cyclical, dictated by the seasons. But Lake House is so beautiful that it is with love as well as duty that we labor in this task.

How we came to Lake House is, with hindsight, such a simple story considering the financial and emotional investment it was to involve. We were looking for a house in the country that we could use for weekend breaks, a place where our growing brood could spread out a bit and get back to nature. Lake House was the first house we were shown – in fact the first that I was shown, as Sting was touring in the U.S. at the time.

HOW WE CAME TO LAKE

HOUSE IS, WITH HINDSIGHT, SUCH A SIMPLE STORY

THE SPIRIT OF
THE HOUSE
WAS WARM AND
WELCOMING

The spirit of the house was warm and welcoming, its history positive and life-affirming. It had survived the Civil War and two major fires, one in the 1830s and one on the Good Friday of 1912. King Alfonso XIII of Spain had once stayed there. And during the Second World War it had been used as a convalescent home, its ornamental gardens ploughed up to grow much-needed food.

Anyone who has ever bought a place to live in will know that, perhaps subconsciously, you effectively make your decision within the first few moments of seeing it. Despite the enormity of the commitment – or perhaps because of it – your heart almost always speaks louder than your head. You might really want a garden and a big kitchen but once you've seen that skylight in the hall and the stained-glass window in the living room, you're hooked. After all, you tell yourself, there is a park nearby, and you don't really cook much anyway.

Lake House was bigger than we had planned and it needed a lot of work but there were two things about it that really attracted me. The hook was the majestic 300-year-old copper beech tree dominating the back lawn. That tree – you couldn't put a price on it. Also, only two miles away stood Stonehenge – ancient, mysterious, silently beckoning. Ley lines are said to pass through the land. Every year crop circles appear nearby as if by magic – or, if you're a non-believer, by elaborate hoax. On that clear, cold, late-autumn day when I first saw Lake House, I was captivated by the romance of it all.

The problem was that offers were closing that same day and Sting had not seen the property yet. Photographs didn't do it justice. And the size and beauty of Lake House meant that we were no longer thinking in terms of a weekend retreat, we were contemplating a major upheaval from city to country living. I must have been very persuasive when I spoke to Sting that day, or maybe he could sense my certainty. But whatever it was that convinced him, with a tremendous leap of faith he agreed, and our lives were changed forever.

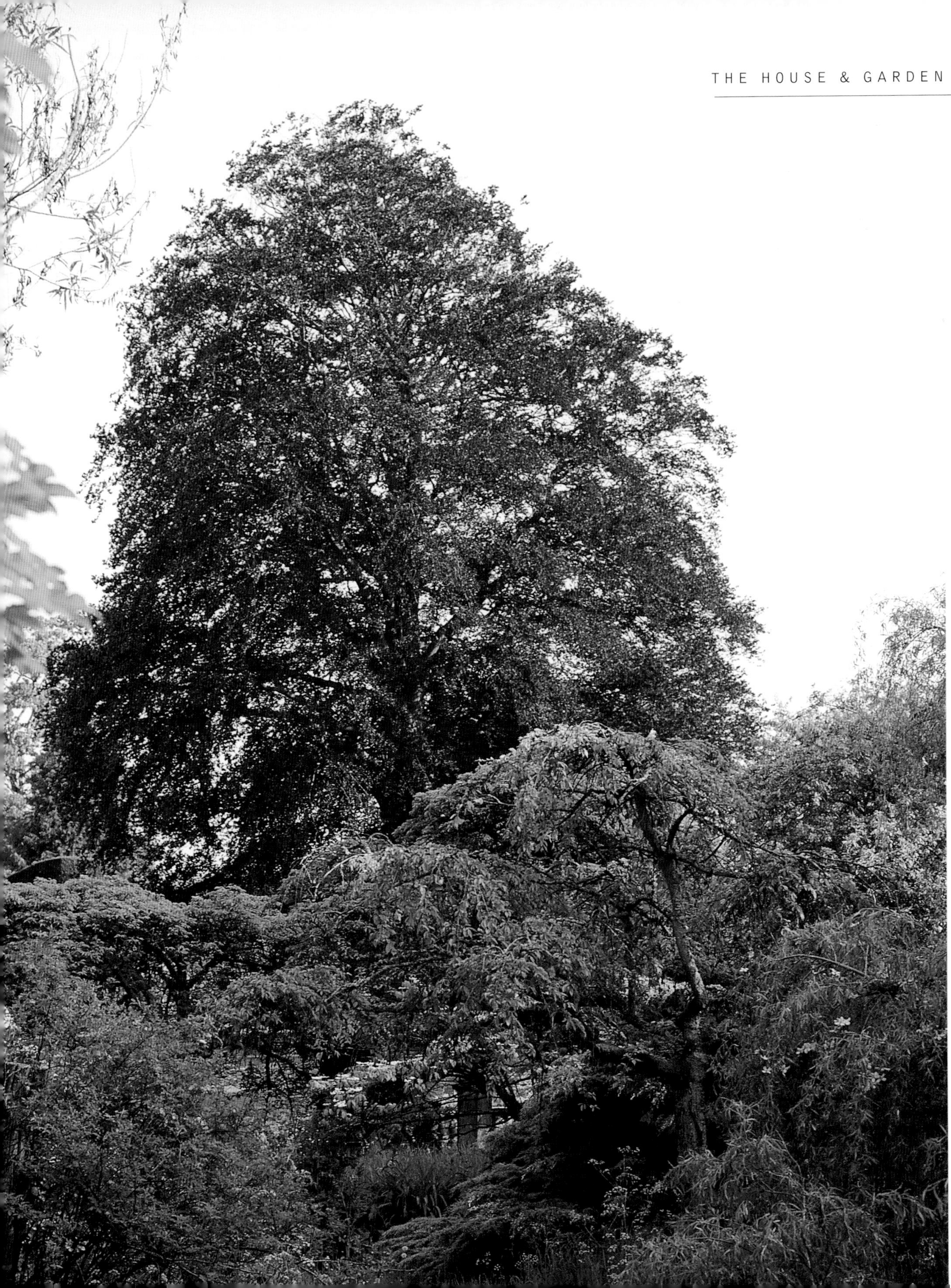

A few months later the sale was completed and the children and I made the big break, even though Sting was still away on tour. Our first night was an adventure in itself. The previous owners seemed to have lived in just two rooms, so the house felt less than cozy and we were all freezing cold. My son Jake and I slept where King Alfonso had once slept – which we now call The King's Room, partly out of respect for the history of the house and partly because it is an irresistible name-drop! I woke up in the middle of that first night totally disorientated and managed to fall out of bed and smash my face on the bedside table. I fumbled my way to the bathroom in shock and put the light on. My face was covered in blood, my front tooth shattered.

I have to admit that by this time I was beginning to doubt my sanity in bringing my family to this place in a freezing February. At that dangerous 2 A.M. low point it didn't seem so

romantic. We were "townies," out of place rattling around the big rooms. The children, however, rose to the challenge. I'm not sure if they thought I was completely mad and decided to humor me or if it really was a great adventure for them, but their excitement and sense of freedom quickly became apparent. My belief that we had done the right thing was soon restored.

It has taken the vision and expertise of many craftspeople to tap into the heart of Lake House and bring out its homely atmosphere. Thirty-five builders more or less moved in with us, becoming so much a part of the extended family during the five years they spent here that when they finally left it seemed quite empty. There were times, though, when Sting and I despaired of ever having the place to ourselves. Sometimes everyone would stay overnight, so you were never quite sure who you would bump into on your way to the bathroom in the morning. The results of the marathon makeover, however, have made it all worthwhile.

One of the most striking successes has been the kitchen, which is a prime example of how Lake House has been transformed from country manor to family home. The previous occupiers had installed a small kitchen on the ground floor, with no dining area. But we discovered that the original kitchen and butler's pantry had been in the basement. Boarded up and abandoned probably since the War, all that it contained was a wrecked old Aga and plenty of cobwebs. For me it was a dream of an opportunity and I couldn't wait to get my hands on it. We ended up gutting the area to make a practical U-shaped space, comprising a good working kitchen with Aga and gas stove, plenty of work surfaces and connecting pantry space. This leads through to a dining table running alongside the casement windows facing the back lawn, which in turn leads round to a TV area with comfortable sofas and a cozy fireplace. It is the heart of the house. People tend to congregate there long before mealtimes, hovering around the Aga in anticipation of Joe Sponzo's delicious creations. It is satisfying to know that the original function of this space has been restored.

PLANTED WITH 5000 TULIPS, PEONIES, ROSES AND

In other parts of the house, the success of Lake's transformation lies in the details. Wherever possible we have used fabric on the walls rather than paper, particularly in the bedrooms. We have also enhanced the house's individuality with friezes, the authentic recreation of stucco ceilings, and painstaking renovation of period details such as paneling and fireplaces. We have relied consistently on the talents of our friend the designer Alain Mertens, whose conservative approach when restoring historic buildings always respects the environment. All this work has been time-consuming but it is no more than Lake House deserves.

Outside the changes have also been extensive. The driveway is now cobblestoned rather than tarmac, the stables have been rebuilt and the cottages within the grounds have been converted into a recording studio. When we arrived there were ornamental gardens, a neglected kitchen garden, beautiful water gardens and a water meadow. The upper River Avon also runs through the land, not a hundred yards from the house, a stepped pathway leading down to a Palladian-style bridge. Replanting this was the first project we undertook outdoors. With memories of the municipal parks of my childhood, their too-neat borders with small, tidy flowers and their "keep off the grass" mentality, I was inspired by the generous scale and vibrant colors of Monet's garden at Giverny. After many squabbles with the gardener, my desire for wide flower borders either side of this pathway prevailed (despite their proximity to the trees) and they are now planted with 5,000 tulips, peonies, roses, clematis and tissue poppies. The effect is large-scale, wild and dazzlingly colorful.

The water meadow was too damp to use as grazing land so we decided to transform part of it into a small lake with an island in the middle. This has had the bonus of drying out the remainder of the water meadow so it is now suitable for grazing. We have been paid the highest compliment

TISSUE POPPIES, THE EFFECT IS DAZZLINGLY COLORFUL

WE COULD NO LONGER TAKE FOR GRANTED THAT THE FOOD WE

since then, as the swan family that inhabited the stretch of the river going through the garden has now made the island and lake its home.

However, now that we had all this land the most exciting prospect was growing our own food on a large scale and achieving some measure of self-sufficiency. Moving to Lake House brought back to me my childhood dream of living on a farm. Although Sting and I are both from urban working-class backgrounds, it is with some sense of going back to our roots that we have come to Lake and are trying to live off the land. My father and Sting's father were both keen vegetable-growers, and as a child I had always taken flavorful, home-grown produce for granted.

We moved to Lake House at a time when some disturbing facts about the food industry were coming to light and it seemed we could no longer take for granted that the food we bought in shops would be wholesome, nutritious and safe to eat. In 1995, for example, unexpectedly high residues of toxic chemicals were found in carrots and the Ministry of Agriculture issued a recommendation that they should be peeled before use. Similarly we were told that apples, despite their pristine and shiny appearance, should be scrubbed thoroughly, and preferably peeled before being given to children. Then, as the British meat industry plunged deeper and deeper into the BSE crisis, questions were raised over the safety of beef. Like many other parents, we became increasingly concerned about what we should feed our children. In the end I decided that I would only be satisfied if I knew exactly what we were putting on our plates. And the best way to do this was to produce the food ourselves. We were lucky enough to be in a unique position to do this.

We have had the help of two organic gardeners at Lake House. We started by growing green leafy vegetables, potatoes, apples and pears, while on the livestock side we kept a couple of milking cows, some hens and goats. The farm has expanded enormously since then: we now also have pigs, chickens, turkeys, ducks and trout. We grow tomatoes, melons, peppers, chillies and eggplants in large greenhouses, and we produce our own cheese and honey.

At Lake House we grow the things we enjoy eating, and between what we all like and what grows well we have achieved a good variety of foods without abandoning our organic principles. Everyone working at Lake House is totally committed to this way of farming and it is a matter of great pride to us that we hold the Soil Association certificate of organic status. It takes a minimum of two years' conversion to be awarded this status, and the standards are extremely strict.

We do produce a lot of vegetables at Lake but, apart from the occasional surplus which is given away to visitors and neighbors, it really does all get eaten. From the day we moved in, Lake House has been host to a constant stream of visitors, to the point where it often feels as if we are running a small hotel. First there were the builders, then Sting's band and crew (two albums have been conceived and recorded here), plus video crews, family, friends – people from all walks of life. Lake House has also hosted two family weddings, our children's christenings and several birthday celebrations. When we have parties here, we really make the most of it. The house comes into its own on these occasions and we always try to include some extra element of entertainment.

Lake House is a special place and Sting and I feel very lucky to have found our own little corner of England. During summer evenings we can often be found sitting outside on the front step, just as we did as children. The doorstep might be a bit more grand but basically we are the same. It is as if we have finally found our real home.

BOUGHT IN SHOPS WOULD BE WHOLESOME AND SAFE TO EAT

Why Go Organic?

IT'S BETTER FOR OUR HEALTH, BETTER FOR THE ENVIRONMENT AND BETTER FOR THE ANIMALS

The simple answer is that it's better for our health, better for the environment and better for farm animals. Yet despite these benefits, deciding to go organic is still seen by many as an "alternative" lifestyle choice. This is ironic, since until about fifty years ago all food was produced organically – there was no other way. So-called conventional methods of food production have been with us only since the 1940s, when the idea took hold that traditional farming would never produce enough food to provide for a growing population. So intensive farming practices that resulted in much higher yields were developed. Unfortunately they also resulted in plants and animals that were more vulnerable to disease because they were no longer protected by their natural environment – hence the massive boom in agrochemicals in an attempt to correct the situation. Now we have an array of pesticides designed to kill or control insects, weeds, fungus, mites, snails, slugs, eelworms, rats and mice. There are substances to remove water, sprays to remove leaves, fumigants, insect-repellants, insect-attractants and growth-regulators. Some of these biodegrade but others persist on and in the crop, which means they are consumed by all of us on a widespread scale. The cumulative effects of ingesting this chemical cocktail over a lifetime have never been properly assessed.

Although the big players in the food industry would have us believe that we have no alternative to modern farming methods if we want a ready food supply, there is another way and that is the organic one. Doubts about whether organic farming can yield enough food for an entire population are being dispelled as organic produce steadily increases its share of the market. So what exactly is organic food? How does it differ from the other foods on our supermarket shelves?

Most people are aware that organic food is produced without using chemicals but there is much more to it than that. Organic farming works with nature rather than against it, in order to produce healthy food from healthy soil and from animals reared on a natural diet and kept in humane

NATURE IS A DELICATE BALANCE THAT WORKS BEAUTIFULLY

conditions. Whereas conventional farming methods deplete the soil and the environment in the interests of the maximum possible yield, in organic farming the quality of the food produced is as important as the quantity, and putting goodness back into the land is as much a priority as taking from it.

The first aim of all organic farmers is to be as self-sufficient as possible: At Lake House this means we produce much of our own animal feed and provide our own fertilizer from recycled waste and animal manure. This is basic good husbandry and makes much more sense than expensive artificial fertilizers and animal feeds (which cost conventional farmers $161.00 an acre on average).

The second aim is to use farming methods that help sustain the environment. "Going back to nature" is a cliché but in truth that is exactly how organic farming works. It is not a battle against nature, with an armory of chemicals to boost growth and kill the enemy. Nature is a delicate balance that works beautifully when all the necessary elements are in place. Organic farming recognizes the importance of each element in maintaining that ecobalance. For example, crop rotation is used as a means of ensuring sufficient nutrients for each crop and to help control weeds, pests and diseases. Rather than killing pests with chemical sprays, their natural predators are encouraged. Hedgerows and trees are maintained. Biodiversity – a mix of traditional varieties and breeds best suited to the climate – is favored. And, in general, everything is done on a smaller scale on mixed farms. All these measures add up to the healthiest possible environment for plants, animals and people. This is virtually impossible to achieve with conventional farming methods, because of the widespread use of chemicals and the sheer scale of modern farming which has completely changed the landscape.

Intensive farming may have started with the best of intentions – to produce cheap food for all – but somewhere along the line it went drastically wrong and now we are pay-

WHEN ALL THE NECESSARY ELEMENTS ARE IN PLACE

ing the hidden price. It has wreaked untold havoc on the environment, taken a gamble with our health and condemned millions of animals to live in conditions of appalling cruelty. It has also been responsible for what may, on the surface, be a lesser crime: the prodigious loss of flavor in our food. Many of the older generation complain that food doesn't taste like it used to and they are right. This is because many traditional varieties have been replaced by ones with a high yield, uniform appearance, good resistance to disease and a long shelf life – but very little taste. How many children now know what a strawberry in season should taste like, or an apple ripened on the tree rather than in an artificial "controlled-atmosphere" chamber, or a chicken that has pecked its way happily around the farmyard rather than one confined to a battery cage for its short but miserable life? The loss of flavor has impoverished us all.

ORGANIC FOOD AND OUR HEALTH

Eating healthily used to be a relatively straightforward affair. You just avoided the foods that were bad for you – saturated fat, sugar, salt, and so on – and ate plenty of those that were good for you – fruit and vegetables, lean meat and fish, whole grains such as whole-wheat bread, pasta and rice. But now it seems that even the "good" foods carry risks to our health, and that this is a direct result of the way they are produced. Spot checks have shown that fruit and vegetables may exceed even the official "safe" levels of pesticides. Salmonella is rife in our poultry and eggs. Milk is contaminated with chemical residues, especially lindane, which has been linked to higher rates of breast cancer and abnormal fetal development. The BSE crisis was a horrifying illustration of how contamination can spread right along the food chain. Added to this are more general concerns about the use of routine antibiotics in cattle and poultry farming and, more recently, genetic modification. The list of potential food hazards seems to get longer by the day.

My views on the importance of eating an organic diet are uncompromising. I believe that the food industry has betrayed the public's trust. When you examine all the processes our food goes through before it arrives on our plates it becomes obvious that much of the goodness has been destroyed. Even the gentlest of cooking can affect the nutritional value of food. Prepacked, precooked processed foods are all the more depleted. Yet even before the preparation stage, conventionally grown produce and intensively farmed animals are bombarded with chemicals.

There are several groups of pesticides used in growing fruits, vegetables and cereals, the two best known being organochlorines and organophosphates. Organochlorines (OCs) were the first synthetic pesticides to be developed and were widely used from the 1940s to the 1970s. Now mostly banned in the West, they are still permitted elsewhere in the world. OCs accumulate in body fat, where they remain for many years. They have been found in breast milk, can

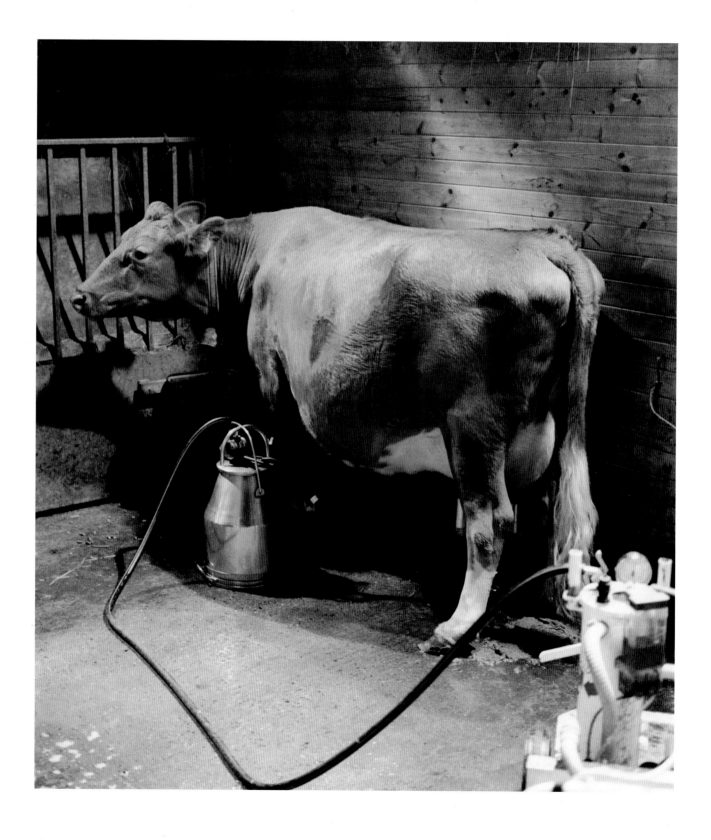

transfer across the placenta to the unborn child, kill wildlife and poison the farmer who handles them.

Organophosphates (OPs) are now the most widely used pesticides, developed during the Second World War as a by-product of nerve gases. This provenance immediately rings alarm bells in my head, despite all the assurances about their safety. OPs biodegrade much quicker than OCs – in a matter of months rather than years – but they are extremely poisonous substances capable of causing major damage to the human nervous system. They are used on wheat, vegetables and fruit and in sheep dip. The dangers to farmers in regular contact with these pesticides are well known: they have been linked to increased rates of cancer, allergies, infertility and depression.

Pesticide residues are legally permitted in food and tests are conducted to try to establish safe levels of intake. However, these tests are carried out on only a small proportion of the foods we consume and do not cover all of the pesticides in use. The Working Party on Pesticide Residues (WPPR) has calculated that the average daily diet contains traces of thirty different pesticides, including two of the most dangerous, DDT (an organochlorine) and lindane (gamma-HCH). Although DDT was banned in the UK in 1984, the 1996 WPPR survey found traces of it in beef, lamb's liver, bacon, chicken, white fish, margarine, eggs and yogurt. The continuing presence of this chemical can be explained by its use elsewhere in the world and also by its extreme persistence in the environment. Traces of lindane were found in cereals, chicken, chocolate, milk and yogurt. Lindane is an organochlorine that is still used in the U.K. (and in the U.S., where its use is more restricted), despite the fact that it is banned elsewhere in Europe and is considered to be one of the most dangerous pesticides in existence. In the U.K. it is used on cereals, oilseed rape, beans, green leafy vegetables and fruit. It is also widely used on sugar beet, which is fed to cattle. Since, like DDT, it accumulates in body fat and transfers to breast milk, it is not surprising that traces of lindane have been found in cow's milk and other dairy products. It is

surely no coincidence that the U.K. has the highest rate of breast cancer in the world and that in Lincolnshire, where lindane is used freely on sugar beet, the rate is 40 percent higher than the national average.

Of course we can wash and peel our fruit and vegetables. But this removes only about 15 percent of chemical residues. The rest remain in the food. It is difficult to predict the long-term effect on our health of regularly consuming minute amounts of all these different chemicals. The official government line is that there is no cause for concern. However, several recent studies have shown that a combination of pesticides may be hundreds of times more powerful than the individual pesticides alone. All the chemicals used on our food are toxic to some degree and many are potentially carcinogenic. There is little comfort to be had from so-called "safe" levels when you consider that many chemicals that were regarded as safe for years were eventually banned after being proved dangerous.

The ludicrous thing is that healthy crops do not need to be drenched with chemicals any more than healthy animals need routine doses of antibiotics and growth promoters. One of the most reassuring facts about organic farming is that the use of artificial fertilizers and pesticides is not permitted. Furthermore, farmers manage very well without them. Besides being free of chemical contamination, organic produce appears to have several intrinsic health benefits. This may be partly because it is grown in better-quality soil and takes up nutrients from the earth. It contains fewer nitrates and less water and is often richer in vitamin C, iron and magnesium than nonorganic produce. The Camden Food and Drink Association has shown that organic potatoes contain 25 percent more zinc and tomatoes 25 percent more vitamin A than their conventionally produced counterparts. Although there is no official evidence as yet that an organic diet is significantly better for your health, many organic devotees argue that their sense of well-being, both physical and mental, has been greatly enhanced by it. Alternative practitioners are convinced that organic food has an important role to play in building up the body's immune system and fighting illness.

One of the most extraordinary examples of this is the writer Beata Bishop. Her book, *A Time to Heal*, chronicles her battle against malignant melanoma and her decision to take her health into her own hands. Faced with what she saw as a choice between crippling conventional therapies and an unconventional nutrition-based regime, she chose the latter. The Gerson Therapy, devised by Dr. Max Gerson in the 1930s, is based on a diet of organically grown vegetables and fruits, usually taken in juice form. The treatment is grueling and extremely rigid but after following it for 18 months Beata Bishop's cancer, which had already spread to the lymph nodes in her groin, had been contained by her body within a hard, calcified shell, which was then surgically removed. She believes that her immune system had been strengthened to such an extent that it had imprisoned the malignant cells to stop them spreading further through her body.

While it is impossible to draw general conclusions from one case study, and I certainly would not suggest that cancer patients should abandon conventional treatments, Beata Bishop's experience demonstrates that organic food may play an important role in preserving and even restoring health. It certainly brings home to me that if I want to look after my body it is important to give it the best-quality food, and that means organic food.

As a mother I also want to give my children the best possible start in life by providing them with healthy, nutritious food. Children, particularly babies and toddlers, are a special case when it comes to organic food. Their immature immune

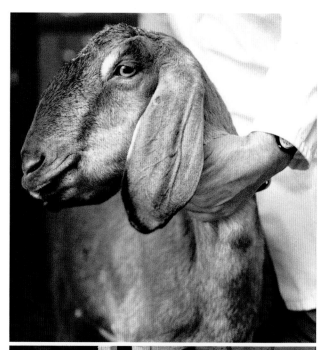

systems are particularly sensitive to toxins in the diet and they eat proportionally more food for their body weight than adults. Furthermore, the "safe" limits of pesticides are calculated according to average adult body weights, not children's, so their intake of chemical residues is proportionally higher. Babies who are being weaned eat a limited number of foods such as puréed fruit and vegetables plus dairy produce, all of which are vulnerable to pesticide residues.

The obvious conclusion is that if anyone needs organic food, children do. In the modern world, persuading children to eat well is not always easy. At school, for instance, they will consume nonorganic produce. And they tend to want the type of food their friends have, even if that is the worst type of junk. All you can do is try to ensure that at home, at least, they eat only what is good for them. When they are babies and toddlers it is much easier to control their diet. Take advantage of this to get them used to good, nutritious food right from the start. Organic baby food is readily available now, offering convenience and high quality. However, do bear in mind that it is cheaper to prepare your own from organic produce.

With my youngest child, who is now three years old, I have been able to raise an almost entirely "organic baby." At Lake House we have been eating mostly organic since Giacomo was born and I have noticed that he has thrived much better than my older children.

ORGANIC FOOD AND THE ENVIRONMENT

While the health benefits are most people's main reason for choosing organic food, a bonus is that it has been produced without any detrimental effects to the environment, local wildlife or the health of the farmer. Indeed, these are equally important considerations. One of the central principles of organic farming is to keep environmental pollution to a minimum. We had already learned the importance of this through our work with the Rainforest Foundation. Seeing for

ourselves the destruction of the rainforests and the devastating consequences for their inhabitants hammered home to us the necessity of caring for our planet. It is vital to try to hold on to that ideal in our own backyard as well as working for it in the Amazon and elsewhere in the world. Protecting the earth's resources is intimately bound up with our future health and that of our children, and goes hand in hand with the sense of responsibility toward the land that we have gained since living at Lake House.

Organic farming not only avoids polluting the environment, it also takes positive measures to encourage wildlife. "Farming with nature" means using nature's own systems. Natural habitats for wildlife, such as hedgerows, ancient woodland, trees and peat bogs are therefore left in place. This enriches the countryside for everyone, as we have discovered at Lake House. It is extraordinary how readily nature returns to its primitive state, and extremely satisfying to witness the transformation.

IF ANYONE NEEDS ORGANIC FOOD, CHILDREN DO

Conventional farming has taken its toll on the environment but recently a new science has arisen that is causing considerable concern. Genetic modification transplants genes from one species to another and from animals to plants, creating GMOs (genetically modified organisms). The aim is to transfer desirable qualities from one organism to another, for instance making a crop resistant to a herbicide (so that it can be sprayed more often) or perhaps increasing its shelf life. One example that illustrates the extreme combinations of genetic material that have been produced is the introduction of an anti-freeze gene from an arctic fish into tomatoes, strawberries and potatoes, with the intention of producing resistance to frost.

The supporters of genetic modification have argued that it is merely a continuation of the age-old practice of cross-breeding to improve the quality of crops or livestock. But in fact it is far more than that. Cross-breeding of plants is a natural process, whereas genetic modification cross-breeds organisms that could never normally breed in nature. Scientists are manipulating the life process itself and we simply do not know what the full consequences for the environment will be. Originally it was claimed that GMOs would lead to a reduction in the use of pesticides; instead there has been an increase in their use because certain GM crops are designed to be resistant to them. There is a risk that "superbreeds" of plants and animals might develop, leading to the extinction of natural species. And there is also the likelihood that GM plants will cross-pollinate with ordinary ones, releasing GMOs into the general food supply. Once the genie is out of the bottle, it may well prove impossible to return it.

We cannot predict the effect of GMOs on human health. At the time of writing, controversial research has come to light showing that rats fed on GM potatoes suffered a weakened immune system and damage to their vital organs. More rigorous testing is obviously needed, yet calls for a moratorium on genetically modified food while this is carried out have so far been ignored by the UK government.

The position of organic regulatory bodies is quite clear: they have all imposed a complete ban on the use of GMOs in organic farming, so organic food is at present the only food to be guaranteed GMO free. However, if, as is feared, genetically modified crops eventually cross-pollinate with normal crops, including organic ones, the new seeds will no longer be guaranteed free from the "alien" gene, thus compromising the integrity of future harvests. Unfortunately the legislation to regulate such practices has not kept pace with scientific developments, so no control measures are in place.

Biotechnology companies responsible for genetically engineered seeds have argued that this new technology could spell an end to food shortages. They cite the development of disease-resistant crops as an example of how the techniques have helped Third World farmers. However, what they don't make so public is that they have also developed seeds that only reproduce once. The farmers cannot collect their own seeds for the following year's crop from their own harvest. They must go back to the seed companies to buy more. This is a situation that can only perpetuate Third World poverty.

ANIMAL WELFARE

Animal welfare is paramount in an organic farming system. Intensive farming is banned, which means that animals are either raised outdoors or have outdoor access. Animal feed is provided by the farm as much as possible rather than bought in and the diet, which is mainly organic, is appropriate to the animal.

To me, the beauty of raising animals on an organic farm is that it balances the system so perfectly. Vegetable waste goes to feed the animals and their manure in turn nourishes the land. The pigs are fed with excess milk from the cows. The animals complete the cycle, giving us a self-sufficient, sustainable farming system.

Routine use of antibiotics and other drugs such as growth promoters is not permitted where animals are raised organically, although conventional medicines must be used when necessary to prevent illness or suffering. Good living conditions appropriate to the animals' needs actually prevent many of the health problems associated with intensive farming practices. Animals and poultry on a conventional farm usually receive regular antibiotics to stave off infection. However, these infections are often caused by cramped living conditions, lack of space to graze freely, or animals standing in their own excrement.

By contrast, the animals at Lake House have a good life. Some would even say they are mollycoddled. The pig-house is thatched and the new goat shed is spacious and scrupulously clean. Newborn calves are left to suckle with their mothers for much longer than on a conventional farm, which – just as with human babies – helps build up their immune

OUR HEALTH IS IN OUR HANDS.
OUR HEALTH IS IN THE FOOD WE EAT

system. And the chickens are free to roam at will, while the Aylesbury ducks have access to water. This is a world away from the miserable conditions of intensive farming but it is the norm for an organic smallholding.

If we look after the health of our farm animals the chances are we are protecting our own health too. Not only does organic meat taste considerably better but it carries none of the health risks that have come to be associated with our mainstream meat supply. The two most notorious examples are salmonella poisoning and BSE (bovine spongiform encephalopathy). Salmonella flourishes in intensively farmed chickens and eggs (these are the commonest sources of food poisoning in the U.K.). Although salmonella is endemic in chickens, organically reared birds are far less likely to contain the bug because they are slaughtered later in life when their immune systems are more established; they are also less likely to have caught it from their companions because they have more space.

Besides being a tragedy for the animals slaughtered en masse in an attempt to eradicate the virus (to date, over one million cattle have been destroyed), BSE has had terrifying repercussions for the human race in the form of CJD (Creutzfeld Jakob disease), which is linked with eating diseased meat. BSE was caused by feeding diseased animal protein to cattle. Tampering with the cows' natural diet in this way was intended to raise the protein levels of their feed, thereby increasing milk yields. Despite the disastrous consequences of this unnatural practice, it seems that the food industry refuses to learn from its mistakes. Research has gone into further manipulations of dairy cows' diet in order to produce lower-fat milk and butter that spreads more easily.

Traces of the antibiotics routinely administered to intensively farmed animals can be found in meat, eggs and fish, with far-reaching implications for animal and human health.

Bacteria are growing increasingly resistant to antibiotics, evolving into "superbacteria" that are immune to existing medicines. The problem is that no new antibiotics are available to deal with these bacteria – very soon it may no longer be possible for us to keep one step ahead of infections. Not only are animals suffering as a result of their weakened immune systems but human resistance to antibiotics because of the medication residues in food is now recognized as a potential health problem.

There have been so many reasons for us to go organic and more seem to emerge with each passing year. For us, of course, it was a relatively easy decision to make. We were able to set up our system from scratch and, as we were seeking only to feed ourselves, we did not have to give too much consideration to economic losses while we converted the land. For farmers the decision is not always so straightforward, and government incentives in the U.K. compare poorly with those in other European countries.

The vast majority of people have neither the means nor the space to produce their own organic food. But it is now widely available from supermarkets, specialist shops and through home-delivery box schemes direct from farmers. This gives almost everyone the chance to benefit from eating natural, healthy food. Although organic produce can be more expensive than conventional food, prices are falling as availability improves. With food more than almost anything else you get what you pay for, and if you choose organic food you are getting the best possible diet for yourself and your family.

The more I have researched the issues involved, the more I am convinced we should demand to be kept informed of what we are eating, so that we all have a real choice. Let us not leave our health in the hands of big corporations or politicians. Our health is in our own hands. Our health is in the food we eat.

Growing
our Own

One of our first jobs at Lake House was to tackle the kitchen garden, which had fallen into sad decline. But while a lot of work was necessary to restore it to its former glory we were actually very glad of its condition. Hardly any chemicals had been put into the soil in previous years and that was great news for us if we were to grow our own organic produce.

Over the first couple of years we employed organic gardening and farming experts to help us convert the land and set in action our first planting. We also consulted the Soil Association, the major regulatory organization for organic growers in the U.K. It has set very stringent standards to which its members must adhere in order to be awarded its certificate, and thus its seal of approval. Any food carrying the Soil Association logo is guaranteed to be organic, so it is an invaluable aid for consumers. Although we had no intention of setting ourselves up as a commercial concern it was important to us to know that we were doing things right.

Although our land was relatively free of chemical residues the soil structure was poor, as little or no natural fertilizer had been put back in. Our first major task therefore was to build up the soil's fertility. First the ground was cleared of all the nettles, long grasses and thistles. Without chemical weed killers, this meant digging them out by hand and then turning the ground over. The soil samples then showed that it was good enough to grow crops such as lettuces, but that it was lacking in some trace elements, which meant that green leafy vegetables such as cabbages would not be so successful. There was plenty of leaf mold in the woods, which was dug into the ground, and we added twelve tons of manure, plus organic chicken manure in pellet form, calcified seaweed and fish blood and bone. We now rely on manure from our animals, our own compost made from household waste, and organic chicken manure that we purchase.

ONE OF OUR FIRST JOBS AT LAKE HOUSE WAS TO TACKLE THE KITCHEN GARDEN, WHICH HAD FALLEN INTO SAD DECLINE

Gordon Maskery, our organic gardener for seven years, had twenty years' experience with the Worldwide Fund for Nature before coming to Lake House as Head Gardener. He believes that the condition of the soil is the single most important factor when growing organically:

"I've found that if you continuously put on artificial fertilizers you can get very good crops but your soil structure starts to break down. Once the soil structure goes, then your crop starts to fail. Then it doesn't matter how much artificial fertilizer you put on because the soil surface pans over, forming a seal, and the air supply to the roots is cut off.

"The condition of the soil is the most important element of successful organic farming. We use plenty of manure to fertilize the soil and there are also other methods for building up soil fertility. Crop rotation, for example, and 'green manures' – which means sowing buckwheat, rye or mustard, letting it come up a few inches, then digging it in.

"A vegetable will grow quickly and be healthy if it is in a healthy environment – which means the soil must be healthy. It's like a person. If you're healthy, you're less likely to pick up diseases. But if you're a bit under the weather – like a vegetable struggling to grow – you're more prone to disease."

Within three years the hard work put in by the gardeners paid off. Not only were we the proud holders of the Soil Association Standards Certificate but the soil was good enough to grow almost anything in. We now produce a fine crop of some fifty fruits and vegetables and forty herbs, including cauliflower, cabbage, cavolo nero, Brussels sprouts, kale and curly kale, celery root, squash, zucchini, leeks, onions, garlic, bok choi, kohlrabi, turnips, carrots, Swiss chard, rhubarb chard, runner beans, fava beans, spinach, peas, peppers, eggplants, chives, basil, apples, apricots, grapes and soft fruits.

During the time taken to transform the vegetable garden, the greenhouses were renovated. Now not only do we grow vegetables in them we also cultivate flowers and container plants for the house. Taking pride of place, though, are the tomatoes, cucumbers, melons, peppers, chillies and eggplants. The beds for these are made up of well-rotted organic manure plus soil

that comes from old turf that has been stacked for one year, then chopped down and used in layers – a traditional method we have adopted.

We like to take advantage of the wild foods that can be found growing on the estate. There are plenty of mushrooms, including morels, milk caps (only the *Lactarius deliciosus* variety is edible), blewits and boletus, which Joe loves to cook with. He also makes use of coltsfoot, sowthistle and comfrey for soups and fritters. We quite often find unusual things in the salad – dandelions, wild rose petals, hedge garlic, ivy-leaved toadflax, chickweed, fat hen and bitter cress, among other weeds!

If we have problems with pests on the crops, there is a variety of ways in which we can deal with them. First of all

THE CONDITION OF THE SOIL IS THE MOST IMPORTANT
ELEMENT OF SUCCESSFUL ORGANIC FARMING

there is the good old finger and thumb. Where appropriate, we also use two soap sprays approved by the Soil Association, Savona and Thuricide HP. Pests can be more of a problem at certain times of the year than others so we try to time our planting strategically – for instance, we avoid producing a crop of sprouting broccoli in September when there are a lot of caterpillars. Companion planting is another tried and trusted method of keeping pests down. You can plant marigolds in amongst brassicas, for instance, to keep away certain pests, while chives and garlic next to the black currant bushes is also a useful pairing. Snails and slugs can be combated with soot from log-burning fires and very sharp sand. The team of five gardeners keeps up daily hoeing, which kills off a lot of the tiny black slugs that live just beneath the surface of the soil.

We have introduced natural predators to control pests. The tiny parasitic wasp, *encarsia formosa*, keeps the whitefly down on the tomatoes and cucumbers in the greenhouses. Practices such as this are very rarely used in conventional farming because they are time consuming and therefore costly. This kind of involved management pushes up the prices of organically grown vegetables, but the end result is more nourishing and flavorsome food.

WITHIN THREE YEARS THE

HARD WORK PUT IN BY THE GARDENERS PAID OFF

The surrounding wildlife is a useful ally. We allow some nettles to grow because they attract butterflies, which eat many of the pests we don't want. Encouraging local wildlife by maintaining their natural habitats and introducing more varieties of wildflowers, as well as eliminating any chemical use, has meant that we have been rewarded with even more wildlife coming on to the estate. Gordon Maskery remembers how little bird life there was in our first year or two at Lake House:

the nettles in the paddock where the sheep graze, since we were running out of pasture for the animals. Although the paddock is nowhere near the vegetable garden it was still a regrettable action, especially as it meant that we lost our organic status temporarily for the livestock. We hope to avoid ever taking such drastic measures again.

We are lucky at Lake House to be sheltered from the surrounding farms so there isn't much of a problem with spray drift from other farmers. Also in our favor is a westerly wind, which keeps any spray drift away. Fortunately our vegetable growing areas are right in the middle of the estate, so they are protected.

"When we first came here a lot of the estate was overgrown and there was a fair amount of wildlife at ground level. But there were very few birds. We've encouraged them by growing a wider range of plants and flowers, which gives them a more varied diet, especially the seed-eating birds. There are no nasty sprays used here. No slug pellets thrown about, or rat poison, which is one of the worst wildlife killers."

Where conventional farmers would use chemicals to aid growth and control pests, we rely on various tricks. Cabbages, for instance, have a very waxy cuticle, which means that the moisture needed by the plant tends to run straight off. In industrial agriculture a wetting agent may be applied to the leaves to hold the water on. Instead we put a few drops of soft soap solution on the leaves, which breaks the surface tension of the water so that it doesn't run off in droplets.

Weeding is all done by hand and hoe, except on one occasion when we made the difficult decision to spot-spray

The Soil Association makes annual inspections of the estate, just as it does for commercial farms. It checks our records of crop rotations, plus all the fertilizers we use and the amount of compost and manure we have added to the land. It inspects the vegetables and the soil and can take a sample from anywhere for testing. If any of the results were unsatisfactory we would lose our certificate.

While we are pretty much self-sufficient for about six months of the year, we top up our supplies with fresh produce and dried goods from Sunnyfields Organic Farm in Hampshire, which is run by Ian and Louise Nelson. The quality of their produce is excellent and, as well as making home deliveries and running a box scheme, they also have a farm shop and supply several well-known London restaurants, including the River Cafe. Ian Nelson has stimulating

views on many issues related to organic farming and is in the front line of supplying directly to the consumer. As such, he has an acute sense of responsibility to his customers:

"There's a lot of trust put into suppliers. My customers are very conscious of this. I've got a sprayer for instance, and I spray crops with comfrey and seaweed. But I only spray late at night because anyone watching could think I was spraying anything!"

The issue of trust in what we are feeding our families is, I believe, the major reason people are opting for organic food in such large numbers now. Supermarket chains that have taken up this market opportunity have made organic food accessible to many more people by keeping the prices of most of the produce competitive with non-organic food. While this is good for all of us in the short term, Ian is thinking ahead to the longer-term implications:

"A lot of box schemes and organic shops are taking a lot of money out of the supermarket system. But why buy something from an organic shop for $1.13 when the supermarket is selling it for .57¢? The supermarkets are often selling it for less than they pay for it. This undervalues the value of organic produce, but it brings the higher-spend shopper into the store, and he'll probably go and buy some nice wines at the same time. And in supermarkets the food is often overpackaged, covered in plastic – it might have traveled from the farm next door

door halfway across the country for packaging, then all the way back to the supermarket next to the farm. So there are food mile links involved, the question of freshness, whether the vitamins are still present after five days of traveling. They are threatening a very delicate balance. Soon they could put the smaller suppliers out of business, and then they'll be free to charge what they like. Then it will be the customers who will suffer."

Whether or not Ian is right, we can only live in hope that the food industry will look beyond the next five or ten years' profit projections toward a different kind of future, where health issues are not sidelined in the quest for a quick buck, and sustainable farming systems that respect the environment and its inhabitants (of all species) are the standard by which all food producers will be judged. The key is to be able to run a viable farming concern, which at the same time respects the high value of its produce. Ian hits the nail on the head:

"I worry about people coming on board for purely monetary reasons. Already they're trying to lower standards rather than increase them. One of my sayings is that organic farmers produce food; nonorganic farmers produce a product, which just happens to be food that people put in their mouths."

THE BABY HEART TOMATO

About four or five years ago we spotted a tomato plant that seemed different from the others. We couldn't identify it as an existing breed and at first we were going to throw it out but, having always dabbled in hybridization, Gordon Maskery was quite interested to see how it would turn out. So we left it. It looked as though it was diseased, and we needed to try to find out what the problem was so we could stop the others being affected. But then we realized that it wasn't a disease that had caused it to look different; it was different genetically.

After a lot of research into its parentage we decided to hybridize it. At first it was a cross, which means that the

seed you take from it will not come true. So we had to try to introduce a gene which would make the plant come true every year. This took a few attempts at cross-fertilization with other breeds of tomato, but eventually we managed it. It is important to cross-fertilize with the right varieties. Most modern tomatoes are totally unsuitable because they are hybrids but fortunately at Lake House we grow eight or nine very old varieties, so we chose one of these.

Breeding has spanned five years. Each year a selection has had to be made in order to improve the quality, retain the shape and flavor and strengthen the plant. We are reselecting all the time to try and achieve more commercial results – even-sized fruits that are closer together on the truss. It's coming on quite well.

There are three unusual things about the Baby Heart tomato. The first is the shape: It is small, like a cherry tomato, and heart-shaped, hence the name. The second is the flavor: It has little or no acid. We have given it to arthritis sufferers who can't usually eat tomatoes and they all found they could manage this one with no problem. Of course some people prefer a certain sharpness in a tomato and would find ours a bit bland. But they certainly like it in the house. Joe Sponzo loves it – in fact it's difficult to stop him picking them all.

The third unusual feature of the Baby Heart is that it has very few seeds. Last year we opened fifty fruits and had only three seeds from them. That's good for whoever's eating it but it gives us quite a problem! However, from two plants that we had in 1998, one seeded and germinated and we propagated another half a dozen from cuttings.

Whatever the future of the Baby Heart tomato, we will continue to grow it and enjoy it here at Lake House.

The Animals

The organically run smallholding at Lake House produces milk, butter, cheese, eggs, fish, honey and meat for our own use. We have four Guernsey cows, two Aberdeen Angus and their offspring, nineteen ewes (Scotch half-breeds and Jacobs), seven Anglo-Nubian goats, chickens and laying hens, Aylesbury ducks, turkeys for Christmas, four Tamworth pigs, eleven working beehives, and trout in the lake.

Unlike our experience with the vegetable garden, we did not have to do a lot of preparation work to allow us to keep animals organically, although of course until the land they grazed on had been passed by the Soil Association the meat was not organic. Our first task was to build a large barn to house the cows and goats. We were able to keep sheep from the beginning, as they spend most of the year outdoors anyway. These were followed closely by the goats and hens, then we acquired the bees.

Originally bought as part of a now defunct scheme to breed Anglo-Nubian goats and send them out as aid to Ethiopia, the goats have become indispensable to us. Since my son, Giacomo, was a year old he has been drinking pasteurized goat's milk rather than cow's milk, and we are currently staggering the matings so that we can maintain a steady supply of milk all year round. Depending on how many goats are milking at any one time, we get about five liters of milk a day, two of which are used in the house while the remainder is frozen until there is enough to make a batch of cheese. We follow the same cheesemaking process for some of the excess cow's milk, and both cheeses are delicious.

Goats are extremely clever animals. They have very distinct personalities and moods, so if they decide they like you it is very rewarding. We have recently had a new goat shed built to our farmer's own design, where they spend the nights and the winter evenings. As with the sheep and cows, the only medication they receive is an annual treatment for liver fluke, which is easily picked up from grazing in the water meadows. Any kids that are born are either kept as part of the group or we advertise to find them good homes.

OUR FIRST TASK WAS TO BUILD A LARGE BARN TO HOUSE THE COWS AND GOATS

We keep two breeds of sheep and at mating time we bring in a Suffolk ram, which improves the texture and flavor of the meat. The sheep spend most of the year outside, except when they are lambing in spring. The lambs go outside with their mothers until the end of August, when they are sent to a local butcher for slaughter, and the ewes have a three-month break before the ram visits once more. Sheep take care of themselves to a large extent but their feet must be pared regularly to prevent lameness. Although they are kept very clean in order to keep maggot fly away, they need to be sprayed twice a year with a solution approved by the Soil Association.

Before coming to Lake House our farmer, John Stammers, was in charge of 3,000 ewes, so he had plenty of experience of conventional farming methods. He used to be responsible for dipping the whole flock of sheep, and has given us an insight into the everyday use of chemicals in animal farming and the widespread ignorance of their dangers:

"All the sheep were dipped at least twice a year with OP [organophosphate] dips. I've been in the dip many times. Some animals panic when they get in and you've got to do something to get them out before they drown. You just have to jump in and save them. We didn't know it was dangerous. There was a dip used years ago called dieldrin. They banned that. Then they brought out a new dip and said that was completely safe. That is until a few years ago. OP poisoning is well known. I've been lucky myself, and now of course at Lake House we don't use anything like that, which is much much better."

An early project at Lake House was beekeeping, initiated by one of the first experts we brought in to help us set up the farm, Paul Fairclough. We have always preferred honey to sugar. In the summer of 1998 we had a 200-pound yield, all of which we used ourselves. This quantity sees us through until the first harvest of the following year, in early summer. In 1996 the hives were struck by a parasite known as the Varroa mite and we had to replace most of them. Since then we treat the hives annually – once we have

BEFORE COMING TO LAKE HOUSE OUR FARMER WAS IN CHARGE OF 3000
PLENTY OF EXPERIENCE OF CONVENTIONAL FARMING METHODS

stopped taking the honey in the autumn – to protect the bees from the mite. John Stammers used to look after the bees but on one occasion he was badly stung and had to be rushed to the hospital, so now someone comes in weekly to maintain the hives and collect the honey. Although the bees probably gather most of their pollen from the oilseed rape of the neighboring farms (and therefore our honey is not organic), we have planted a wildflower meadow and what we loosely call The Monet Garden, which gives them more variety. It is difficult to produce truly organic honey because you cannot control where the bees will gather pollen.

The dairy cows are an essential part of the farm – somehow it would not seem complete without the early-morning milking, the soft clang of cow bells as they come back for milking in the afternoon, and the regular calving, which the children particularly enjoy. Newborn calves are left to suckle from their mothers for three to four days, which is twice as long as on a conventional dairy farm. Then they must be taken away if we want the milk, otherwise the cow will withhold its milk and keep it all for the calf. It will still be fed its mother's milk – from a bucket rather than the teat – for another eight or nine weeks, which again is about twice as long as the conventional way. We always hope for females because then we don't have to make the difficult decision of what to do with a bull calf. Bull dairy calves are not used for meat and generally they are sent to the abattoir before they are two weeks old. At Lake we have been known to keep the bull calves as "passengers," just so that they can have a life. At the time of writing, we have recently acquired another 100 acres of land which has gone into conversion, so that will give us more options.

With four Guernsey cows, each producing at their peak of lactation four gallons of milk a day, we often have much more than we can use. It is all pasteurized and skimmed, then used in the house for drinking and cooking or to make cream, ice cream, butter and cheese. We give any excess to a local children's home and any remaining after that goes to the pigs. It is, of course, completely organic, since the cows'

diet consists of grazing on our land and bought-in organic hay and concentrated feed.

The Angus cows have a similar diet except the calves suckle from their mother for around nine months before being taken away. They stay on the farm until they're around two years old but any Angus cow we use for beef must be slaughtered before its two broad teeth at the front come up – at around 30 months. This regulation was brought in to tackle the BSE crisis and applies to organic farms as well as conventional ones, despite the fact that BSE has never been a problem on organic smallholdings.

John Stammers also makes butter every week from the cows' milk (right). The milk is skimmed, and the cream is churned. Then this butter is rinsed four to five times, the last time with iced water, to get all the buttermilk out, or it will taste cheesy. Then follows the time-consuming job of patting the butter into shape with wooden spatulas (scotch hands), adding salt if required.

The way we keep chickens demonstrates the biggest differences between an organic farm and a conventional one. In industrial farming, chickens reared for eating have very little space to move around once they are more than about three weeks old. Their food contains antibiotics until the last five days of life, when they are supposed to be withdrawn so that they are not still in the birds' systems. Our chickens are fed an organic diet, including a little skimmed milk every day. They stay in a warm shed for the first four weeks of life, then they move to another shed where they have free access to outside.

The laying hens are bought in at fourteen weeks old and are fed on layers' pellets and wheat. We have tried different breeds of hen – Morans and Light Sussex – but the problem with both of these is that they lay well for a month or so, then they become broody and we don't get any eggs. So now we have Isa Browns, a hybrid type that lays very well. We also have some Araucana Lavender hens – a gift from Joe – and they produce slightly smaller eggs with a very light blue shell. Needless to say, they are all free to roam pretty much where they like.

The other poultry we keep are Aylesbury ducks, who have a spacious area where they can swim and graze freely, and turkeys, which we bring in to fatten for Christmas. All the chickens, ducks and turkeys are killed, plucked and gutted on site.

Ironically, keeping our own livestock has made us all less likely to eat meat than before, even though we know it is healthy, organic and extremely fresh. Many people eat meat without giving much thought to the fact that it came from a living creature – the packaged product on the supermarket shelf conspires to make us forget this. But because we live alongside these animals and see them living, breathing and running about every day, we are much more aware of what we are eating. I hate to see meat wasted and so I am very strict about the amount that is prepared for meals.

The two most recent additions to the farm are the trout, kept in the lake formed out of the old water meadow, and the pigs, which we keep primarily to make use of household waste and excess milk. The trout provide us with a delicious and healthy alternative source of protein to meat. The pigs are Tamworth Reds, which are a beautiful warm russet color, and we are happy to contribute to building up stocks of this rare breed. They come to us at about eight to ten weeks old and then at around six months the gilts (young females) are sold for breeding. The pig manure is used on the vegetable garden and the two paddocks. As with all the other animals, the pigs' diet is organic and their accommodation warm and spacious.

WATCHING THE PIGS WALLOW IN THE MUD THEN BASKING
IN THE AFTERNOON SUN IS A REAL TREAT. IT'S A HARD LIFE!

Every year at the end of August we put Varroa strips into the beehives, a treatment against the disease varroasis, which is spread by mites. Britain saw its first outbreak in 1992 and by 1998 a quarter of all native species of bee were classified as threatened. Having lost most of our hives to the mite in 1996 we take great care to avoid a recurrence. After six weeks the strips are removed and we check how much honey the bees have left to nourish them through the win-

IN 1996 WE LOST MOST OF OUR HIVES TO THE VARROA MITE

ter. It is unlikely to be enough, so for a two-week period we give them as much sugar and water as possible. When the water evaporates the bees are left with sugar in the combs to keep them going until spring.

With the coming of spring, the weather is mild enough for the bees to fly again. As soon as they bring pollen back to the hives, the queen bee starts to lay eggs by the thousand. From this point until about June or July the hives need monitoring every week or so to remove any new queen cells that have formed, otherwise the queen will take half of the bees away in a swarm.

If the present queen does take off with half the bees, we hope that a new queen cell will hatch. A new queen will stay in the hive for about ten days, then go out for a fly around and mate just once. She will live for four years and produce something like 20,000 eggs a year. When the weather cools down the queen stops laying eggs and many of the bees die off, leaving a small nucleus that stays in the hive throughout the winter.

We harvest the honey from about mid-May to mid-August. The honeycombs are put into an extractor which spins the honey out of them. This is then poured into a bucket and left to settle so that any little bits of wax rise to the surface. After these have been scraped off, the honey, which is very hard, is warmed to 113°F to make it runny. It then goes into a steel tub and is mixed twice a day for two days until the temperature has gone down to 77°F. Then it is left to settle once more. To stop it solidifying again, some of last season's honey, known as the "seed," is mixed in.

GOAT'S CHEESE

Joe came up with the idea of making cheese from our surplus goat's milk several years ago, and after visiting a couple of farms to see how it was done he was able to set up a system at Lake. It has become an enjoyable part of the farm routine for John, our farmer, and the cheese is excellent – soft and creamy but with a good flavor.

The production process is quite time consuming. First the milk is heated to 73 to 75°F, then a starter culture is added, followed by the vegetable rennet, which contains an enzyme that curdles the milk. Twenty-four hours later the resulting curd is thinly cut with a spoon to help the whey drain out, then put into molds. After being left to drain for a few hours, the molds are topped up with more curd. They are left to drain for 18 to 24 hours before the cheese is turned out. Now they must be turned and salted every six hours for one day before going into the drying cabinet, where they are turned every twelve hours for the next three days. The next stage is curing, so the cheeses are stored in the curing room for about three weeks and turned daily until they are ripe.

In the middle of summer when the goats are producing the most milk and the quality is at its best, we can make more than thirty cheeses a week.

JOE CAME UP WITH THE IDEA OF MAKING CHEESE FROM
GOATS' MILK SEVERAL YEARS AGO

Cooking
at Lake
House

Joe Sponzo's
Kitchen

My inspiration to become a chef came from my family. My roots are Italian, and even though my family had emigrated to the United States our home life was full of traditional Italian ways, particularly in the kitchen. Our meals were always freshly prepared with good ingredients and this gave me a taste for real, wholesome food.

Even when I was at university studying hotel and catering management I wanted to buy organic foods. Searching out pure, wholesome food seemed a natural part of the alternative lifestyle I was leading at the time, yet when I went to work in the hotel industry I was appalled by the extent to which the food was processed – and by the fact that none of it tasted any good. Perhaps it was my rural Italian ancestry asserting itself but I craved fresh ingredients and fuller flavors in order to create wholesome, delicious food.

Living in America, you become accustomed to being able to buy almost any fresh ingredient you want all year round. But most of them are four to six days' old by the time they reach the kitchen, and they lack the quality of food that has been produced in harmony with the environment and the seasons. Working at Lake House is ideal for me because the majority of ingredients come straight from the farm and garden, all of them rich with flavor and nutrients.

More exciting than a restaurant, more spontaneous than party catering, Lake House is a chef's playground. The food I produce here is a distillation of all my culinary interests, experiences and inspirations, a wonderful opportunity to combine the family's and my insistence on fresh organic ingredients with a passion for fine dining and concern for good nutrition.

The seasonal nature of cooking at Lake House is something I've had to adapt to but I enjoy the challenge. Each year I adjust the way we work in the kitchen so that we can live off the land even more and enjoy the food at its freshest. This involves liaising closely with the gardeners to ensure we have variety. Next season, for example, I have asked them to increase the range of winter lettuces and herbs. But there is only so much the clever use of polytunnels can achieve. The

desire for variety is tempered by the natural seasonality of plants and animals, so the pressure is constantly on me, as chef, to come up with interesting ways of preparing the raw materials. I'm forced to be creative, to play with texture and color, and that is something I find very exciting.

Fortunately, the foods that inspire me most have always been vegetables, mushrooms, herbs, grains and fish. Unlike most other chefs I tend to have signature ingredients rather than signature dishes. When produce is at its peak of ripeness, the gardeners come into the kitchen with whatever is ready that day and their wheelbarrows and baskets full of vegetables and fruit form the basic palette from which I create.

The people I cook for are as much my inspiration as the food. As chef to a family I have to be sensitive to their needs – it's not like the daily repetition of cooking to a printed menu in a restaurant. If they look as if they could do with something hearty, I'll think about meat, grains and vegetables; if they are not feeling well, it's chicken soup. Sometimes there are two different meals to cook in one evening: one for the children, one for Sting and Trudie. We have a lot of visitors and do a great deal of entertaining, both formal and casual, frequently with little warning. I like to create dishes specially for the guests but the main reason people look forward to meals here is the freshness and quality of the produce.

When the family travels I go with them and it's a great opportunity to take a piece of the country to the city. The cooking I do in New York, for example, is essentially the same as at Lake House but dressed up a little. It's not more complex but more refined: the vegetables are cut uniformly, the sauces carefully strained, the dishes presented with artful precision. Sometimes I'll swap a rustic ingredient for a more sophisticated one, but ultimately the difference between rural Wiltshire and uptown Manhattan is the manner of plating. And that is an important aspect of my choice of dishes for this book. Good food is not about being trendy or stylish, it's about balance and composition. I want to encourage you to shop organically and use fresh produce but

I also want to give you a collection of useful recipes that can be broken down and mixed and matched to create something new every time you cook. That's the way I work at Lake House. I hope you will find it as inspiring as I do.

HOW TO USE THE RECIPES IN THIS BOOK

A recipe is not a destination; it's a point of departure. Try to use this book as a guide rather than a manual. I really believe that the secret of being a good cook is simply to love food – technical skills can be acquired and perfected along the way. As I have found while working on this book, the mere act of writing down a recipe can limit its potential for creative growth. Many of the dishes featured here were originally developed on the spur of the moment, using whatever ingredients we happened to have in the kitchen that day, but because we are passing them on to you we have subsequently tested and retested them many times to ensure that they work. All the recipes have been created using organic ingredients almost exclusively; please also note that all butter used is unsalted, all eggs used are large, and all flour is general all-purpose unless otherwise specified. Also, if grapeseed oil is not readily available, you may substitute Canola oil.

Read each recipe through thoroughly before you start cooking and look at what can be prepared in advance, particularly for the longer recipes. The Basics chapter (see page 203) gives instructions for preparing many staple items. They are things you will find useful to have around the kitchen regularly, to think of as part of your larder, even if they are stored in the refrigerator or freezer. Put them together in your own way and use them to add layers of flavor, color and texture.

Flexibility is an important feature of my cooking and of this book. Do not feel locked into a recipe unless it involves a specific classic technique. You will find that many of the longer recipes comprise several small ones: if you like, break them down into components, then mix them around and add your own ideas – trust your instincts.

At Lake House I have an industrial oven and tend to use restaurant-standard equipment because my philosophy is that you only have to buy it once and it will last forever. Large pots and pans certainly come in handy on the occasions I cook for twenty-five to thirty people, but this is still a family home, not a restaurant. I have done parties for twelve to fifteen people with just two or three saucepans and a four-burner stove and the results were similar to those in any other kitchen, professional or otherwise. So you do not need professional equipment to cook the recipes in this book, or even a large kitchen.

Make sure the main components of the dish – the vegetables, fruit, fish, meat and poultry – are extremely fresh, and shop organically where possible. I taste most of the ingredients raw because I know that if they taste good raw they will taste good cooked. Throughout the cooking process, taste and retaste the dish to make sure you are achieving the right flavors and textures. This is also part of the secret of successful improvisation in the kitchen. It is not experience so much as a creative force and a passion for food that makes a good cook.

Seasonal Cooking

SPRING AND SUMMER

After the dead of winter, a new cycle of birth and growth begins. Spring is perhaps the most eagerly anticipated season in the kitchen. Suddenly there are tomatoes – yellow and red, green zebras, heirlooms – fava beans, fresh peas, Easter radishes and new potatoes. The vegetables are tender yet vibrant, delicately flavored but with sharp overtones. From the farm come spring lamb, ducks, chickens and blue eggs from the Araucana Lavender hens. Winter is chased away once and for all with vividly fresh soups, salads and spring vegetable stews that have just a hint of the heartiness of cold-weather meals. A fish stew enriched with herb oils celebrates garden and sea. We add mint to just about anything, and enjoy chervil, thyme, sorrel, dandelion greens, nasturtiums and violets, too.

Summer is about scent and color, the time I feel I really excel in the kitchen. The children are always running about and there is plenty of laughter. Guided by simple stimuli such as perfectly ripe tomatoes, a fresh bunch of fragrant basil, scented berries or our own apricots, I try to create dishes that reflect the natural environment of Lake House. I think of fresh, crisp salads rich in tastes and textures, incorporating juices and purées for intensity. Sunny yellow zucchini blossoms inspire risottos, frittatas and tempura.

Early-morning and afternoon milkings result in creamy goat's cheese for salads and grilling. There are rocket flowers, fresh eggs, and thick cream for fruit cobblers, and some sauces. Fruits, herbs and flowers are used in drinks, and family meals are taken outdoors.

As summer draws to an end and harvesting begins, inevitably my mind turns to winter food, and in preparation we try to preserve summer's wonderful aromas and flavors to enjoy during the cold months.

AUTUMN AND WINTER

Autumn is the season for satisfying lamb stews, wild game and roast dinners. From the garden we enjoy the last of the figs, and welcome pumpkins, squashes, apples, pears and quince. Any produce we can't consume straight away goes into preserves, and in September we start preparing the Christmas baskets, making cider, sloe gin and herb vinegars, plus chutneys, boxes of shortbread and Lake House honey. There are parties to organize: for Halloween we make chocolate cookies in the shape of black cats, carved pumpkins and spooky ice hands floating in vivid fruit punch. Thanksgiving is celebrated in traditional American style, with turkeys wrapped in wine-soaked muslin before cooking and then served with parsnip cakes alongside cranberries and walnuts.

Winter brings with it an appetite for warm, comforting food. The gardens continue to provide – Brussels sprouts and cabbages, celeriac, horseradish, leeks and winter lettuces. Warm garden beds extend the pumpkin season a little. Big hearty soups are a mainstay of the kitchen, plus root vegetable purées, chicken stew and spit-roasts by the fire. There is more turkey at Christmas – then turkey curry! Winter is the season in which I fully indulge my love of grains – their color palette of black, brown and tan enhances each meal. Desserts rely on apples, pears and wholesome nuts ground into frangipane and praline. Summer's preserves are opened – all that work was worth it, and they give us a promise of spring, which will soon be upon us again.

1

Soups &
Starters

Pea Soup

3¹/₂ pounds peas in the pod, shelled and pods reserved
1 large russet potato, peeled and left whole
1 tablespoon unsalted butter
1 pound (1¹/₂ cups) leeks, white and light-green parts only,
washed and roughly chopped
1 medium onion, peeled and roughly chopped
¹/₂ cup chervil leaves, plus extra for garnish
¹/₂ cup spinach leaves, washed and shredded
1¹/₂ teaspoons salt
Freshly ground black pepper
6 tablespoons crème fraîche, at room temperature
6 edible flowers, such as pansies or nasturtiums, petals torn
SERVES 6

In a large stockpot, combine the reserved pea pods, potato and 14 cups of cold water. Bring to a boil, then reduce the heat and simmer for 1 hour. Strain the stock, reserving the potato but discarding the pea pods. Return the pea stock to the same pot and boil over a high heat for about 30 minutes or until the volume of liquid has reduced to about half.

Meanwhile, crush the potato in a potato ricer and set aside. To a small stockpot or saucepan, over a medium-low heat add the butter, leeks and onion. Cook until the onions are softened but not browned. Increase the heat to medium-high, add the pea stock and riced potato. Bring to a boil then add the peas. Cook for 3 minutes or until the peas are tender.

Immediately transfer the mixture to a food processor or blender and purée in batches, alternately adding the chervil and spinach, until smooth. Skim any foam from the surface and add the salt and pepper.

Remove and serve in warmed soup bowls. Garnish each bowl with 1 tablespoon of crème fraîche, extra chervil leaves and flower petals scattered over the top.

NOTES

• It is important to work fast so the peas retain their vibrant green color, though the spinach helps ensure that.
• The soup can be made two hours ahead. After puréeing the soup, place in the soup pot in an ice bath, stirring to cool down, then refrigerate. Heat through, then serve.

• Chervil is a member of the parsley family; it looks like carrot-top greens but has a subtle anise flavor.
• You could also garnish this soup with Game Crumbs (see page 116) or some reserved fresh peas.
• The stock can be made up to two days in advance.

Tomato Garlic
bread soup

The bread soaks up the flavours of the broth yet retains a toothsome crunch.

FOR THE CROUTONS
1 loaf (8 ounces) country bread, cut into 1-inch cubes
¹/₂ cup olive oil
1¹/₂ tablespoons unsalted butter, melted
¹/₄ teaspoon salt
3 cloves garlic, finely chopped
A pinch of dried red pepper flakes
FOR THE SOUP
3 tablespoons olive oil
3 medium onions, thinly sliced
6 cloves garlic, finely chopped
2 28-ounce cans whole, peeled San Marzano tomatoes
8 cups Light Chicken Stock (see page 209)
1 bunch basil, tied with string, plus 12 basil leaves, torn
14-ounce piece Parmigiano Reggiano cheese rind
¹/₄ cup grated Parmigiano Reggiano, plus extra, shaved, to garnish
Salt and freshly ground black pepper
SERVES 6 TO 8

First bake the croutons. Preheat the oven to 350°F. In a medium bowl, combine the bread, olive oil, butter and salt and toss. Transfer to the oven and bake for 15 minutes, stirring frequently. Add the garlic and red pepper flakes and bake for 5 minutes longer. Remove from the oven and set aside to cool.

To make the soup, in a stockpot, heat 2 tablespoons of the oil over medium heat. Add the onions and cook for 25 to 30 minutes, without browning, until the onions are tender.

Meanwhile, reserve 1 cup of juice from the tomatoes then seed and chop them. Add the garlic to the onions and cook for 1 minute, then add the tomatoes, tomato juice, chicken stock, tied bunch of basil, cheese rind, and some salt and pepper. Raise the heat a little and simmer gently for 45 minutes, stirring occasionally. Remove the cheese rind and adjust the seasoning to taste.

Just before serving, top the soup with the croutons, stir and cook for 1 minute. Transfer the soup to a tureen or individual bowls and garnish with the grated Parmigiano Reggiano and the extra basil leaves. Drizzle with the remaining tablespoon of olive oil and serve the soup immediately.

NOTE

• Variations to this recipe can be the addition of any vegetable, thinly sliced, blanched and added near the end. Peas, potatoes, zucchini, kale, cabbage, carrots and celery are just a few thoughts.

Spiced squash soup

As Sting's favorite soup, this has become a staple at Lake House.

1 small butternut squash
1 small hokkaido, buttercup or red kuri squash
4 sprigs thyme
2 tablespoons unsalted butter
1/2 large sweet potato or 1 medium sweet potato
1 carrot, peeled
Olive oil, for rubbing
1 medium onion, roughly chopped
3 large leeks, white and light green parts only, roughly chopped
3 stalks celery, sliced 1/2 inch thick
1 bay leaf
6 cups Corn Stock, Vegetable Stock or water (see pages 210 and 211)
1/4 cup freshly grated Parmigiano Reggiano, plus 1 piece rind
2 tablespoons heavy cream
1/2 teaspoon cayenne
1/4 teaspoon ground cinnamon
1/4 teaspoon ground cumin
A little freshly grated nutmeg
Salt and freshly ground black pepper
Fresh marjoram or oregano sprigs, torn, to garnish
SERVES 6 TO 8

Preheat the oven to 350°F. Halve the butternut and red kuri squash and remove the seeds. Place them in a large roasting pan and rub the inside cavities with 1 tablespoon of the butter. Place a sprig of thyme in each, season with salt and pepper then turn them skin-side up in the pan. Rub the sweet potato and carrot with olive oil, salt and pepper then add them to the roasting pan with 1 cup of water. Place in the oven for about 40 minutes or until soft.

Remove the roast vegetables from the oven and leave to cool slightly in the cooking juices.

In a small stockpot, heat the remaining 1 tablespoon of butter over a medium heat. Add the onion, leeks and celery and cook until softened and translucent, about 15 minutes.

Scoop the flesh from the roast squashes into the onion mixture. Chop the carrot and add it to the pot. Peel the sweet potato and add it to the pot along with the juices from the roasting pan plus the bay leaf and stock. Bring the mixture to a boil, then reduce the heat, add the cheese rind and simmer for 20 minutes.

Remove the cheese rind and bay leaf from the soup then, using a hand-held blender, purée until smooth and well combined. Add the cream, cayenne, cinnamon, cumin and nutmeg plus some salt and pepper and blend again until combined. If the mixture is too thick, add a little more stock or some water. If the mixture is too thin, return it the the heat and allow it to reduce to the desired consistency.

Stir the grated Parmigiano Reggiano into the soup and serve garnished with the marjoram sprigs. The soup may be refrigerated for up to 3 days in a covered container.

NOTES

• Any squash you choose – hokkaido, buttercup or red kuri – will be fine. They are all tender and sweet with plenty of richness.
• Break some dried spaghetti into 3-inch pieces, boil in salted water for about 5 minutes so that it is still crunchy, then drain and add to the puréed soup, allowing it to simmer for 5 minutes. Serve with a salad and you have a complete meal.
• Instead of soup, make a side dish from the roasted squashes, sweet potato and carrot. Drain the juices from the roasting pan into a small saucepan, add some tomato water and a pinch of saffron and warm through over a low heat. Meanwhile, cut the vegetables into strips, leaving the skins of the squashes on. Place them on a serving dish and pour the sauce over.

Swiss Chard
and pearl barley soup

A light but hearty soup. The toasted barley adds crunch while the shiitakes have a meaty effect. This is Trudie's favorite.

2/3 cup pearl barley
1 pound red Swiss chard
2 canned anchovy fillets, rinsed and drained
3 garlic cloves, roughly chopped
1 tablespoon rosemary leaves
2 tablespoons olive oil
2 medium leeks, washed, white and light green part only, sliced 1/4 inch thick
1 medium onion, finely chopped
3 slices bacon, optional
8 cups Vegetable Stock (see page 211) or water
2 bay leaves
2 pieces Parmigiano Reggiano rind, about 3 inches wide
6 ounces shiitake mushrooms, stemmed and torn in half
2 tablespoons freshly grated Parmigiano Reggiano, to garnish
2 tablespoons extra-virgin olive oil, to garnish
Salt and freshly ground black pepper
FOR THE PISTOU
2 tablespoons parsley leaves
1 tablespoon rosemary leaves
2 cloves garlic peeled
SERVES 6

Preheat the oven to 350°F. Place the pearl barley on a small baking pan and toast in the oven for 10 minutes.

In a medium saucepan, place the toasted barley and 5 cups of water. Bring to a boil then simmer over moderately low heat for 30 to 35 minutes, until just tender. Drain, reserving the cooking water, and set aside.

Meanwhile, remove the Swiss chard leaves from their stalks and discard any that are bruised or discolored. Roughly tear the leaves into 2- to 3-inch pieces, wash in several changes of water then set aside. Trim the Swiss chard stalks and cut them into 1/4-inch pieces. Measure out 2 cups of stalks, wash and set aside.
Finely chop the anchovy fillets, garlic, rosemary leaves and 2 teaspoons of salt together to make a paste. Set aside.

Heat the oil in a medium-sized saucepan and add the leeks, onion and bacon, if using. Sweat over medium-low heat for 4 to 5 minutes, stirring frequently with a wooden spoon. Stir the anchovy paste into the saucepan and cook for another 5 minutes.

Add the stock, reserved barley cooking water, the bay leaves and cheese rind to the pan and cook over a moderate heat for 15 minutes until the flavors combine. Add the cooked pearl barley, chard leaves and stems and shiitake mushrooms and cook for another 15 minutes.

Meanwhile, make the pistou by finely chopping the parsley, rosemary and garlic together. When the soup has finished cooking, remove the cheese rind and bacon. Turn the heat off under the pan and stir in the pistou. Season with salt and freshly ground pepper. Leave to stand for about 3 minutes then serve garnished with the grated Parmigiano Reggiano and extra virgin olive oil.

NOTES

• The bacon is optional, but to make the soup vegetarian you will need to eliminate the anchovies as well.
• For a smokey flavor add one or two whole chipotle chillies and remove before serving.

Children's Veggie Canapés

These fun canapés entice children to eat their vegetables. Use Japanese vegetable cutters, available from good cookshops and Asian food specialists – their deep, sharp cutting edge makes them perfect for firm vegetables. Use only the large ends of the carrots for this recipe as the vegetable slices need to be larger than the cutters (remove the thin tips and reserve them for another use).

2 large russett potatoes (about 1 1/2 pounds)
4 large carrots (about 1 pound), peeled and thin ends removed
1 large English cucumber (about 1 1/4 pounds)
1 cup Sweet Potato Purée (see page 151)
1/2 small raw red beet, peeled and finely grated
3/4 cup Pea Purée (see page 141)
2 radishes, thinly sliced on a mandoline
1 1/4 cups Hummous (see page 136)
20 small sprigs flat-leaf parsley
MAKES ABOUT 75

Peel and rinse the potatoes. Cut them lengthwise into slices ¹/₄ inch thick. Lay the potatoes flat on a clean work surface and stamp out 25 shapes using the Japanese cutters.

Bring a large saucepan of salted water to the boil, add the potato shapes and cook for 5 to 7 minutes until the potatoes are only just tender but still hold their shape well. Drain the potatoes under cold running water and pat dry on a kitchen towel.

Cut the carrots diagonally into slices ¹/₄ inch thick and stamp out 30 shapes using the Japanese cutters. Bring a pan of salted water to the boil and blanch the carrots for 3 to 5 minutes until just tender. Drain under cold running water and pat dry with a kitchen towel.

Roughly peel the cucumber, trim and cut it into slices ¹/₂ inch thick. Leave them to stand on paper towels for 5 minutes to drain. Using the Japanese cutters, stamp out 20 to 25 shapes.

To assemble, place the canapé bases on a clean work surface. Top each cooked potato shape with 1 heaping teaspoon of the Sweet Potato Purée and garnish each with a pinch of grated beet. Top each carrot shape with 1 heaping teaspoon of Pea Purée and garnish with 2 to 3 slices of radish. Top each cucumber piece with 1¹/₂ teaspoons of Hummous and garnish with the small sprigs of parsley.

NOTE

• All components of this recipe can be prepared a day in advance and stored overnight in the refrigerator, covered in separate plastic

containers. Top the canapés with the purées up to 2 hours before required, lightly cover with plastic wrap and keep chilled. Garnish 30 minutes before serving, leaving the canapés to return to room temperature.

Stuffed Red and
Yellow Cherry Tomatoes

1 tablespoon blanched slivered almonds
A pinch of salt
2¹/₂ teaspoons finely chopped radish
¹/₂ cup cream cheese, softened
¹/₄ cup crème fraîche
15 to 20 yellow cherry tomatoes
15 to 20 red cherry tomatoes with stems
MAKES 30 TO 40

Preheat oven to 350°F. On a small baking tray scatter the almonds and place in the oven for 4 to 5 minutes or until browned. Remove and set aside to cool. Grind the almonds using a mortar and pestle, or finely chop.

In a medium bowl, place the ground almonds, salt, radish, cream cheese and crème fraîche and stir with a wooden spoon until thoroughly combined and smooth.

Halve the yellow tomatoes lengthwise. Horizontally slice the top third from the red tomatoes and set the tops aside. Using a small spoon or your finger, carefully hollow out all the tomatoes, discarding the seeds.

Fill one half of each yellow tomato and all of the red tomatoes with 1 teaspoon of filling each.

Top the yellow tomatoes with the remaining halves and the red tomatoes with their reserved tops. Arrange on a platter and serve.

Potato Salmon Fritters

Salmon and potatoes make a wonderful backdrop to caviar.

2 russet potatoes (about 1 pound), peeled and cut into 1-inch cubes
1 teaspoon salt
6 tablespoons milk, warmed
3 tablespoons potato flour
3 large eggs, plus 1 egg white
3 tablespoons heavy cream, plus extra for thinning
salt and freshly ground black pepper
3/4 cup Clarified Butter (see page 215)
12 ounces salmon fillet, skinned and cut into 1 1/2- to 2-inch pieces, 1/4 inch thick
3/4 cup crème fraîche
3 to 4 ounces Ossetra caviar, to garnish
SERVES 6 TO 8

Place the potatoes in a large saucepan with the salt and water to cover. Simmer until tender.

Drain the potatoes and pass them through a food mill into a medium-sized bowl. Using a wooden spoon, stir in the warm milk to combine. Add the potato flour a tablespoon at a time, stirring. Add the eggs one at a time, stirring to incorporate, then add the egg white, and cream, mixing until the potato mixture has the consistency of thick cream. If the mixture is too thick, add some more cream to thin it out. Set aside for 20 to 30 minutes. Season with salt and pepper.

Preheat the oven to the lowest setting and line a baking sheet with greaseproof paper. In a 12-inch well-seasoned cast-iron skillet, heat 2 tablespoons of clarified butter over medium-high heat until very hot but not smoking. Using a large metal spoon or ladle, drop spoonfuls of the potato mixture into the butter, making 4 or 5 fritters at a time. Lightly press 1 piece of salmon into the center of each fritter and cook until the edges are golden brown.

Turn over the fritters and cook for another 30 seconds, then remove them from the pan, place on the paper-lined baking sheet and keep warm in the oven. Repeat, adding more butter to the pan as necessary.

Serve 2 to 3 fritters per person, topped with a dollop of crème fraîche and garnished with caviar.

Chicken Wishbones
"Frogs' Legs" Style

When chicken breasts are portioned into fillets, a significant amount of meat is left attached to the wishbone. It's a shame to let it go to waste, so I cook the wishbones in the traditional style of frogs' legs, with plenty of garlic and butter. Ask your butcher to save the meaty wishbones for you – he'll be grateful for an opportunity to sell them. Adding some fresh breadcrumbs to the pan after the persillade is optional: they soak up the butter and give more body to the dish.

10 large whole garlic cloves, peeled
10 chicken wishbones
1/2 cup flour
1/2 cup unsalted butter
2 heaped tablespoons fresh bread crumbs, optional
2 tablespoons lemon juice
Salt and freshly ground black pepper
FOR THE PARSLEY SAUCE
2 cups curly parsley, stems removed
2 tablespoons olive oil
1 tablespoon Roasted Garlic, mashed to a paste (see page 217)
1 teaspoon lemon juice
FOR THE PERSILLADE
1 large shallot, finely chopped
3 cloves garlic, finely chopped
1/4 cup parsley, finely chopped
SERVES 5

To make the parsley sauce, bring a medium saucepan of salted water to a boil and add the parsley. Cook for 1 minute, then drain, reserving 1 cup of the cooking liquid, and refresh under cold running water. Drain thoroughly then chop the parsley and squeeze it dry. Place it in a blender or food processor with the reserved cooking liquid, olive oil, Roasted Garlic, lemon juice and a little salt and pepper, and purée until smooth. Strain the sauce through a medium sieve, discarding the solids, and set aside in a warm place until needed.

In a bowl, mix the persillade ingredients and set aside.

Bring a small saucepan of salted water to the boil, then lower the heat and add the whole garlic cloves. Poach them for 10 minutes then drain and keep warm.

Meanwhile, season the chicken wishbones with salt and pepper then dredge them in the flour. Transfer to a sieve and toss to remove any excess flour.

In a medium frying pan over moderate heat, melt 2 tablespoons of the butter and, when it starts to foam, add half the chicken. Cook for 1 1/2 minutes, then turn and add another tablespoon of butter to the pan. Continue cooking for another 1 1/2 minutes, gently tossing, until the chicken is lightly colored and crispy, being careful not to burn the

butter. Add another tablespoon of butter to the pan along with half the persillade and stir to coat evenly, cooking for 10 to 15 seconds to release the flavor. At this point you can add 1 heaped tablespoon of bread crumbs to the pan, if desired.

Remove the chicken and place on a baking tray and wipe the pan clean. Drizzle the chicken with 1 tablespoon of lemon juice and keep warm while you repeat the cooking procedure with the remaining chicken, persillade and bread crumbs, if desired.

Coat a warm serving platter with the parsley sauce. Stack the wishbones in the centre and surround them with the poached garlic cloves.

Grilled Scallops with Roasted Red and Yellow Cherry Tomatoes, Crispy Shallots and Herb Sauce

Scallops and herb sauce are a perfect, timeless combination. The flavors are sweet and tangy, and are enhanced here by the pop of tomato water left in the oven-dried tomatoes. Strands of crispy shallots stand on top adding crunch. To serve this dish you will need 6 large scallop shells, warmed.

FOR THE ROASTED CHERRY TOMATOES
3 yellow and 3 red cherry tomatoes, halved lengthwise
1 clove garlic, thinly sliced
4 sprigs thyme, plus 2 teaspoons thyme flowers, to garnish
1/2 teaspoon olive oil
1/8 teaspoon salt
Freshly ground black pepper
FOR THE SCALLOPS
18 medium fresh Sea scallops (about 1 pound), coral attached if desired
1 teaspoon salt
Freshly ground black pepper, to taste
1 1/2 tablespoons olive oil
Crispy Shallot Rings, to garnish (see page 216)
12 thin slices Preserved Lemons, cleaned, to garnish (see page 205)
FOR THE HERB SAUCE
4 tablespoons (1/4 cup) champagne vinegar
1 cup dry white wine, preferably Burgundy
3 ounces white button mushrooms, thinly sliced
3 tablespoons finely chopped shallots
4 peppercorns
1 dried bay leaf
1/4 cup heavy cream
3/4 cup unsalted butter, chilled and diced
1 teaspoon red wine vinegar
1/4 teaspoon salt
1 1/2 tablespoons olive oil
1 small clove garlic, smashed and finely chopped
2 teaspoons finely chopped basil
2 teaspoons finely chopped chives
2 teaspoons finely chopped parsley
1 teaspoon finely chopped tarragon
SERVES 6

To prepare the roast cherry tomatoes, preheat the oven to 400°F. Place the tomatoes, cut side up, on a rack set over a small baking sheet. Top with the garlic and thyme sprigs, drizzle with olive oil and season with the salt and pepper.

Transfer the tomatoes to the oven and roast for 20 to 25 minutes. Remove from oven and let cool slightly. Place in a small bowl, sprinkle with the thyme flowers and set aside.

Meanwhile, prepare the scallops. Remove and reserve the small side muscle from each scallop for use in the herb sauce. Refrigerate the scallops until needed.

To make the herb sauce, combine the champagne vinegar, wine, mushrooms, shallots, peppercorns and bay leaf with the scallop side muscles in a small saucepan. Bring to the boil over a high heat and simmer until the mixture has reduced to a volume of 2 tablespoons, about 15 to 20 minutes.

Stir in the cream and boil for 5 to 8 minutes, or until the sauce has reduced by half. Over low heat, whisk in the butter, one piece at a time, until the sauce emulsifies. Stir in the red wine vinegar then strain the sauce through a sieve into a small saucepan, discarding the solids. Stir in the remaining sauce ingredients and adjust the seasoning as necessary with more lemon juice, salt and pepper. Set the sauce aside in a warm place while you cook the scallops.

Heat a griddle over medium-high heat. Brush the scallops with oil and season both sides with salt and pepper.

Place the scallops on the griddle. Cook for 1 minute then rotate the scallops 90 degrees to form hatch marks and cook for another 1 to 2 minutes. Turn the scallops over and cook on the other side for 1 to 1 1/2 minutes or until medium-rare.

Meanwhile, spoon about 1 1/2 tablespoons of herb sauce into each of the 6 warmed scallop shells. Remove the scallops from the griddle and place hatch-side up on top of the sauce. Garnish with the crispy shallots, preserved lemons and roasted tomatoes.

NOTES

• Shrimp may be substituted for the scallops.

Stuffed Zucchini
blossoms

This dish definitely indicates that summer is here! Everything about it is redolent of the garden. It's a mixture of flavors with the crunch of almost-invisible tempura batter.

Grapeseed oil, for frying
1 small eggplant, finely diced
1/2 teaspoon saffron threads
1 small onion, finely chopped
2 cloves garlic, finely chopped
1 1/2 tablespoons olive oil
4 plum tomatoes, peeled, seeded and diced
1 zucchini (about 8 ounces), cut into 1/4-inch dice
1 yellow squash (about 8 ounces), cut into 1/4-inch dice
2 tablespoons finely diced roasted yellow pepper
2 tablespoons finely diced roasted red pepper
1 tablespoon finely chopped basil leaves
1 tablespoon finely chopped parsley
1/2 teaspoon salt
Freshly ground black pepper
16 to 18 zucchini blossoms, pistils removed
Flour for dusting
FOR THE TEMPURA BATTER
1 cup ice cubes
2 egg yolks
1 1/4 cups + 3 tablespoons flour
Cayenne pepper
Salt
MAKES 16 TO 18

To make the batter, place the ice cubes in a large measuring cup and fill with cold water to make a volume of 1 2/3 cups. Using chopsticks, combine the ice, cold water and egg yolks thoroughly in a mixing bowl, then stir in the flour. Some lumps will remain. Season with salt and cayenne pepper, stir and set aside.

To make the stuffing, heat 1 cup of grapeseed oil to 350 to 375°F in a large, heavy saucepan and fry the diced eggplant in two batches until brown and crispy. Remove to a plate lined with paper towels to drain. Set aside.

In a small frying pan, toast the saffron threads until fragrant then remove from the pan and set aside. In a medium saucepan over low heat, add the onion, garlic, olive oil and 2 tablespoons of water and cook for 5 minutes or until the onions are soft. Add the tomatoes and toasted saffron to the pan and cook for 10 minutes, stirring occasionally.

Meanwhile, in a pan of boiling salted water, blanch the zucchini and yellow squash for 30 to 45 seconds, then drain thoroughly under cold running water. Stir them into the tomato mixture and cook for 3 to 4 minutes. Remove the pan from the heat and add the fried eggplant, bell peppers, basil and parsley, stirring to combine. Season to taste with salt and pepper and set aside to cool.

Be sure the zucchini blossoms are thoroughly clean, then fill each one with 1 to 2 tablespoons of the cooled vegetable mixture. Close each blossom gently but tightly around the filling.

Fill a large, heavy saucepan with grapeseed oil to a depth of 4 inches and slowly heat to 350°F. Meanwhile, place some flour for dusting on a large plate. Working with 2 or 3 blossoms at a time, roll each in the flour to lightly coat, shaking off the excess, then dip them in the batter, lightly coating and letting the excess drip off. Place the blossoms bottom-first into the hot oil and fry for 3 to 5 minutes or until crisp and lightly colored, turning once. Drain on paper towels and repeat with the remaining flowers. Serve immediately.

NOTE

• Zucchini blossoms, a favorite of Italian cooks, are delicate and need to be used quickly after harvesting. Pick only the male blossoms, which have thin stems, and leave the female ones on the plant so their stems can develop into zucchini. Check the blossoms carefully for any tiny bugs before filling them.
• The zucchini blossom is shown here with Shrimp with Shrimp Sauce and Pesto (see page 95).

2
Main Courses
& Small Dishes

Baby Pumpkins filled
with Black Spaghetti
and Meatballs

12 baby pumpkins (about 10 ounces each)
12 sprigs fresh thyme
1 pound dried black squid-ink spaghetti
2 tablespoons unsalted butter
Salt and freshly ground black pepper
Julie's Meatballs in Tomato Sauce (see page 115)
Freshly grated Parmigiano Reggiano, to garnish
SERVES 12

Preheat the oven to 375°F. Using a large, firm-bladed serrated knife, carefully cut off the top section of each pumpkin to a depth of about ¹/4 inch using a sawing motion. Reserve the tops then scoop out the seeds and membrane of each pumpkin and discard.

Place 1 sprig of thyme plus a little salt and pepper inside each pumpkin and replace the tops. Transfer the pumpkins to a baking sheet and cover with aluminum foil. Bake for 30 to 35 minutes or until the pumpkins are just soft inside, being sure not to lose their shape.

Bring a large pot of salted water to the boil. Add the black spaghetti and cook until al dente, stirring occasionally. Drain, toss with the butter and season to taste with salt. Meanwhile, warm through the meatballs in tomato sauce.

Remove the pumpkins from the oven, discard the thyme and fill each one with the hot black spaghetti. Top each pumpkin with some of the sauce and 2 meatballs, then garnish with Parmigiano Reggiano. Rest the pumpkin tops alongside the pumpkins and serve immediately.

NOTES

• Make sure the spaghetti, tomato sauce, meatballs and pumpkins are all ready at the same time.
• Serve with Black Thai Rice Witch Hats (see page 95).

Gnocchi with Pesto Sauce

Why does gnocchi have ridges? To hold the sauce near to it.

3 large russet potatoes (about 2 pounds), unpeeled
2 cups flour, plus extra for rolling and shaping
2 large eggs, lightly beaten
1 teaspoon salt
2 tablespoons freshly grated Parmigiano Reggiano, plus extra to garnish
FOR THE PESTO SAUCE
4$^{1}/_{2}$ cups packed basil leaves, stems removed
1 cup packed parsley leaves
3 tablespoons pine nuts, toasted
3 cloves of garlic, crushed
$^{1}/_{2}$ teaspoon salt
$^{1}/_{2}$ cup olive oil, plus extra for storing
3 tablespoons freshly grated Parmigiano Reggiano
3 tablespoons freshly grated Pecorino Romano
SERVES 6

Preheat the oven to 300°F. Place the whole potatoes and salt in a medium saucepan and add water to cover. Bring to a boil and simmer until fork tender, 25 to 30 minutes.

Drain the potatoes, spread them out on a baking sheet and place in the oven for 10 minutes. Using a tea towel (so that you can handle them), peel the potatoes and cut them lengthwise into quarters.

Fit a ricer with a small-holed disc and rice the potatoes directly into a large bowl. Leave to cool for 20 minutes.

To make the pesto, in a food processor fitted with the steel blade, purée the basil, parsley, pine nuts, garlic and salt until thoroughly combined. With the machine running, add the olive oil in a steady stream and process until the mixture emulsifies.

Remove the mixture to a small bowl and fold in the cheeses using a rubber spatula. Use immediately or transfer to an airtight jar and cover the surface of the pesto with a thin film of olive oil to prevent it from spoiling. Store in the refrigerator for up to a week, stirring the excess oil into the sauce before use.

In the bowl, sprinkle the flour over the riced potatoes and gently work them together using a fork just until combined. Form a well in the center of the potato mixture, crack the eggs into a small mixing bowl, whisk briefly and pour the eggs into the well. Add 1 teaspoon of salt. Using a fork, work the eggs into the potato mixture.

Lightly flour a work surface and gently knead the potato mixture, adding more flour if necessary, until a soft, sticky dough forms.

Sprinkle some more flour over the work surface and roll the dough with your hands into a 12-inch cylinder. Cut the dough crosswise into six 2-inch pieces. Take one piece of dough and roll it into a 20-inch rope. Cut the rope into $^{1}/_{2}$-inch pieces, using more flour as necessary.

Working with one piece of gnocchi at a time, press it with your thumb against the back of the tines of a fork to create ridges. As you complete each piece of gnocchi, transfer it to a large kitchen towel dusted with flour, keeping the gnocchi in a single layer. Repeat until you have used all the dough.

Bring a large pot of salted water to a boil. Working in batches if necessary, carefully add the gnocchi to the pot, stirring gently and being careful not to overcrowd the pot. When the gnocchi rise to the surface of the water, let them cook for an additional 1 minute.

Meanwhile, in a large bowl, combine the pesto with $^{1}/_{2}$ cup of the gnocchi's cooking water. Using a slotted spoon, remove the gnocchi from the pot and stir them into the pesto. Lightly mix in the grated cheese and serve, accompanied by extra grated cheese, if desired.

Spaghetti al Aglio
et Olio

The correct balance of salted water, garlic, oil and red pepper flakes enables this simple dish to reach perfection.

1 pound spaghetti
Salt
3/4 cup to 1 cup extra-virgin olive oil
6 to 8 cloves garlic, chopped
1 1/2 teaspoons dried red pepper flakes
SERVES 4 TO 6

Cook the pasta in a large pot of boiling salted water until barely tender but firm to the bite. Drain and reserve 1/4 cup of the cooking water.

While the pasta is cooking, begin the sauce. In a large saucepan over medium heat, place the extra-virgin olive oil and warm for 2 to 3 minutes. Add the garlic and red pepper flakes.

Lower the heat and immediately add the drained hot pasta and the reserved cooking water to the oil. Toss and stir so that the oil and water emulsify. Serve immediately.

NOTE

• Pasta cooking water is the secret ingredient of this dish. It has unique flavor, a combination of the salt and high starch content. Restaurants in Italy use it like the French would use a fine stock. Throughout the day, they use the same water to cook all the pasta, topping the pot with fresh water only every so often so that the flavor is retained.

Tagliatelle
with Tomato Sauce

3 tablespoons olive oil
1 small onion, diced
2 cloves garlic, finely chopped
4 sprigs basil, plus 10 basil leaves, torn, plus extra to garnish
2 28-ounce cans of plum tomatoes
3 tablespoons heavy cream
2 tablespoons unsalted butter
1/8 teaspoon dried red pepper flakes
1 teaspoon salt, plus extra for cooking pasta
1 pound dried egg tagliatelle
3 1/2 tablespoons freshly grated Parmigiano Reggiano, plus extra to garnish
SERVES 4 TO 6

In a medium-sized, heavy saucepan, place the olive oil, onion, garlic and the sprigs of basil. Cook, stirring frequently, over medium-low heat for about 5 minutes or until the onions are translucent.

Meanwhile, pass the tomatoes and their juices through a food mill to purée them. Add them to the onion mixture and cook for 40 to 45 minutes, stirring occasionally, until the mixture thickens. Remove the basil sprigs then add the cream, butter, red pepper flakes and salt, stir and cook for another 10 minutes. Remove from the heat and set aside.

In a large pot of boiling salted water, cook the pasta until al dente, about 7 to 8 minutes. Drain, reserving 1/2 cup of the cooking water.

Stir the reserved water into the tomato sauce. Add the cooked pasta, Parmigiano Reggiano and the torn basil leaves and toss to combine. Serve garnished with the extra cheese and basil leaves.

NOTE

• When fresh tomatoes are out of season I use canned tomatoes. The best are whole peeled plum tomatoes with juice and basil leaves. They should always be the San Marzano variety grown near Naples.

Lake House Crab Cakes
with Almond Aïoli

4 tablespoons unsalted butter

1 pound (1¼ cups) onions, finely chopped

3 stalks (1 cup) celery, finely chopped

1½ tablespoons English mustard powder

½ teaspoon cayenne pepper

2 to 2½ pounds fresh or frozen crab meat

½ cup Mayonnaise (see page 213)

2 large eggs, lightly beaten

¾ cup fresh bread crumbs

¼ cup cilantro, roughly chopped

3 tablespoons mint, torn

1½ tablespoons lemon juice, plus 1 teaspoon grated lemon zest

1½ tablespoons lime juice, plus 1 teaspoon grated lime zest

½ cup grapeseed oil

¾ cup Almond Aïoli (recipe follows), to serve

FOR THE CRUMB COATING

¾ cup dried bread crumbs

¾ cup whole blanched almonds, ground

FOR THE ALMOND AÏOLI

2 to 3 cloves garlic, crushed

A large pinch of coarse salt

1 large egg yolk

1½ tablespoons freshly squeezed lemon juice

1¼ cups olive oil

5 tablespoons slivered almonds, toasted and finely chopped

¼ cup Roasted Pepper Purée (see page 218)

¼ teaspoon cayenne pepper, or to taste

1 tablespoon red wine vinegar

Freshly ground black pepper

MAKES 1⅓ CUPS

SERVES 6 TO 8

To make the aïoli, pound the garlic and salt to a smooth paste. In a food processor fitted with a steel blade, combine the egg yolk, lemon juice and garlic paste until blended. With the machine still running, gradually add the olive oil in a steady stream until the mixture thickens and emulsifies. Add the remaining ingredients, processing until combined. Season to taste then transfer the mixture to the refrigerator.

In a medium saucepan, melt the butter over medium heat then add the onions and celery and cook for 5 to 7 minutes or until translucent. Stir in the mustard and cayenne pepper and cook for another 3 to 4 minutes then remove from the heat and leave to cool completely.

Meanwhile, pick over the crabmeat to remove any cartilage and shell, trying not to break up the pieces of meat. Drain the crabmeat thoroughly.

When the onion mixture has cooled, place it in a mixing bowl with the crab, mayonnaise, eggs, fresh bread crumbs, cilantro leaves, mint and the juice and zest of the lemon and lime. Stir to combine. Shape the mixture into 12 patties about ¾ inch thick.

For the crumb coating, line a baking sheet with baking parchment. In a medium bowl, combine the dried bread crumbs and ground almonds for the coating and season the mixture with salt and pepper. Transfer to a small baking sheet. Press both sides of each crab cake into the bread crumb mixture and place them on the baking sheet as each one is coated. Place in the refrigerator to chill for at least 30 minutes and up to 8 hours.

To cook the crab cakes, coat the base of a large, heavy frying pan with grapeseed oil to a depth of ⅛ inch and place over medium-high heat. Heat the oven to 300°F and line another baking sheet with parchment paper. Working in batches, add the crab cakes to the pan, making sure they do not touch each other, and cook for 1½ minutes or until golden brown. Carefully turn and cook the other side for 1½ minutes before removing to the prepared baking sheet. Repeat with the remaining crab cakes.

Transfer the baking tray of browned crab cakes to the hot oven and heat through for 5 to 8 minutes. Serve 2 crab cakes and 2 tablespoons of almond aïoli per person.

NOTES

• For great al fresco eating, this makes a delightful lunch served with dandelion salad and grilled polenta bread.

• Alternatively, form the mixture into tiny cakes and serve at a cocktail party.

• You can use cooked cod or salmon instead of crab.

• Try the bread crumb mixture on other fish.

• Almond aïoli goes well with many other dishes, including burgers, cold roast meats, fish and boiled vegetables.

Cape Cod
Fish Stew

This is perhaps the most complex recipe in the book, but it's not difficult. Once you have done all the preparations it takes just 5 to 10 minutes to serve and a lifetime to enjoy. It's worth the effort because the flavors are fresh and uplifting, like eating Cape Cod. The clam juice and tomato water set the base; the addition of celery plays with your tastebuds.

3 stalks celery, plus 1/2 cup chopped celery

1 head garlic, 1 small onion from Roasted Garlic and Roasted Onion (see page 217)

3/4 to 1 cup Tomato Water (see page 211)

12-ounce center-cut salmon fillet, trimmed, cut crosswise into 6 pieces

3 tablespoons shredded unsweetened coconut

1 to 2 ounces kadaifi (see notes page 87)

6 large shrimp, peeled and deveined with tail left intact

1/2 cup flour

4 tablespoons olive oil

3 baby squid, cleaned, halved lengthways, tentacles separated and reserved

6 medium scallops, roe attached

3 whole small red mullet or red snapper, filleted, skin left on

2 sprigs lemon thyme

6 razor clams (optional), washed thoroughly

1 tablespoon unsalted butter

6 raw cherrystone clams, shucked, meat and juices reserved together

3 tablespoons Parsley Oil (see page 214)

3 tablespoons Dill Oil (see page 214)

3 tablespoons Chive Oil (see page 214)

2 tablespoons freshly squeezed lemon juice

Fresh chives to garnish

Salt and freshly ground black pepper

SERVES 6

Process the stalks of celery in a juice extractor to give about 8 tablespoons (1/2 cup) of juice and set aside.

Bring a small saucepan of salted water to a boil, add the chopped celery and cook for about 5 minutes or until soft. Drain, reserving 1/4 cup of the blanching water, then purée the celery and reserved water in a blender. Remove from the blender, set aside.

Squeeze the cloves from the head of roasted garlic and purée them in a blender with 2 to 3 tablespoons of tomato water. Remove and set aside. Then purée the roasted onion with 2 to 3 tablespoons of tomato water. Remove and set aside.

Gently fold the strips of salmon in half with the former skin side on the inside and secure the ends with a toothpick.

Heat the oven to 350°F. Toast the shredded coconut in a single layer on a baking sheet for 5 to 8 minutes or until light brown. Remove from the oven and set aside until cool.

Meanwhile, on a small baking sheet lined with baking parchment, divide the kadaifi into 6 portions measuring approximately 4 x 1/2 inch. Working quickly, curl each portion of pastry around to mimic the curve of the shrimp. If the pastry begins to dry up while you are working with it, lightly mist it with some water. Sprinkle 3/4 teaspoon of the toasted coconut over the 6 portions of kadaifi, then press the shrimp gently on top. Top each shrimp with another 3/4 teaspoon of toasted coconut, then press the remaining kadaifi on top of each shrimp, molding it to the shape. Cover with a damp kitchen towel and refrigerate.

Place the flour in a large dish and season with salt and pepper. In a large frying pan over medium heat, place 1 tablespoon of olive oil. Add the squid and tentacles to the frying pan, season with salt and pepper, and cook for a total of 1 1/2 to 2 minutes. As soon as they start to curl, flip them over and press down with a metal spatula to flatten them. Remove the squid from the frying pan and set aside on a baking tray. Wipe the frying pan out with a paper towel.

Lightly press both sides of the salmon and scallops in the seasoned flour, shaking off any excess. Add 1 tablespoon of oil to the frying pan and place over a medium high heat. Cook the scallops for 1 minute then turn over and cook for another minute more before setting them aside with the squid. Add the salmon to the pan and sear it for 20 seconds on each side. Remove from pan and set aside with the other cooked seafood. Wipe the frying pan clean with a paper towel.

In the same frying pan, over medium-high heat, place 1 tablespoon of olive oil. Add the mullet, skin side down. After 30 seconds turn and cook for 15 seconds, lightly pressing with a metal spatula. Remove from the frying pan and set aside with the other cooked fish. Wipe the frying pan clean.

Meanwhile, prepare the razor clams, if using. In a large saucepan, combine 1 cup of water and the lemon thyme. Bring to a simmer, add the razor clams, cover and cook for 2 to 3 minutes or until they just open. Remove the clams to a plate, cover and set aside in a warm place.

Add 1 tablespoon of olive oil and the butter to the frying pan and set over a medium heat. Cook the kadaifi-coated shrimp for 1 1/2 minutes per side, or until golden brown, then remove to the baking tray with the other fish and place them all in a very low oven to keep warm and just finish cooking, for about 5 minutes.

In a shallow, medium-sized saucepan over medium-low heat, place the cherrystone clam meat and juices. Add remaining tomato water and cook for about 2 minutes or until they just come to a simmer. Add the celery juice, garlic purée and 3 tablespoons of onion purée, combine, then return to warm through. Add the celery purée, stirring.

Remove the pan from the heat, add all the herb oils, stirring, and process the mixture with a hand blender for 15 to 20 seconds, just until the sauce has emulsified. Taste and adjust the seasoning.

To serve, spoon about 1/2 cup of sauce over each plate and place 1 of each variety of fish on each. Drizzle with 1 teaspoon of freshly squeezed lemon juice and garnish with the chives.

NOTES

- The ingredients can all be prepared 1 day in advance. The kadaifi shrimp can be made the previous day if kept covered and refrigerated.
- Once the fish is in the oven, start the sauce and have the plates and garnish ready.
- Prepare all your sauce ingredients one hour before serving.
- The razor clams are optional. If using them take particular care to soak them thoroughly and wash them in copious amounts of fresh water.
- When using the hand blender be sure not to rough up the clams.
- The sauce for this stew can be used for any fish dish.

Nori Rolls

The nutty flavor of the short-grain rice accentuates the pungent wasabi and pickled plum paste.

1 cup short-grain brown rice, rinsed and soaked overnight

3 tablespoons rice wine vinegar

2 teaspoons sugar

3/4 teaspoon salt

1 1/2 tablespoons lemon juice

A piece of peeled English cucumber, 8 inches long

A piece of peeled carrot, 5 1/2 inches long

A piece of peeled diakon, 2 inches long

1/4 cup wasabi powder

1 1/2 teaspoons finely chopped dill

3/4 cup crabmeat

5 sheets toasted nori, cut into 5 inch x 7 inch rectangles

1 1/4 teaspoons pickled plum paste

2 scallions, finely chopped

1/2 cup radish sprouts

1/2 avocado, cut into 10 thin slices

Juice of 1/2 lime

Pickled ginger, for serving

Soy sauce, for serving

Wasabi, for serving

SERVES 4

Drain the soaked rice in a small-holed colander or large sieve for 1 hour. Put the drained rice in a medium saucepan with 2 cups of water. Bring to a boil over high heat, then lower the heat to medium-low, cover and cook for 20 minutes. Then turn the heat to low and cook for another 10 minutes.

Remove the pan from the heat, take off the lid and cover the pan with a kitchen towel. Replace the lid and leave to stand for 15 minutes. Then turn the hot cooked rice out into a non-metal bowl, preferably wooden.

In a small saucepan over low heat place the rice wine vinegar, sugar, salt and lemon juice. Warm to dissolve the sugar and salt. Using a wooden spoon fold the vinegar mixture into the rice, folding gently for 3 to 4 minutes. Cover with a kitchen towel and set aside to cool completely.

Meanwhile, prepare the vegetables by using a mandoline. Cut the pieces of cucumber, daikon and carrot into fine strands.

Combine the wasabi power with 3 1/2 tablespoons of water to form a paste. Mix the dill into the crabmeat. Set both aside.

Position a bamboo sushi mat horizontally on a work surface. Place a nori sheet, shiny side down, on the bamboo mat. Using wet hands, pat 1/3 cup of cooked rice into the nori in an even layer, leaving a 1/2 inch uncovered border on the side nearest you and the two shorter sides, and a 1 inch border on the far side.

Use your fingers to make a horizontal groove along the rice, slightly less than halfway up the nori. Take about 1/2 teaspoon of the wasabi paste and spread it with your forefinger along the groove. Then spread about 1/4 teaspoon of the plum paste in a line above the wasabi.

Cover the rice with 2 tablespoons of the crabmeat. Place a row of the cucumber, daikon and carrot along the center of the sushi. Then sprinkle with the chopped scallion and arrange a row of radish sprouts, then a row of sliced avocado on top. Drizzle with about 1/4 teaspoon of the lime juice.

Starting at the edge closest to you, lift the mat and gently roll it over, lifting the nori so that the end closest to you is directly above the far side. Press down gently along the mat to compact the rice and form a slight square. Lift up the top end of the mat then use the mat to lightly roll the sushi toward you, squeezing it all around to hold it together in a tight roll. Unroll the mat and set the roll aside. Repeat this process for another 4 rolls.

Cut the rolls with a sharp knife, first slicing carefully at the halfway point of the sushi roll without using a lot of pressure. Then cut each half into three equal pieces so that each roll makes 6 rings. Serve with pickled ginger, soy sauce and wasabi.

Kadaifi Shrimps with a Lemongrass Dipping Sauce

Spiky yet sumptuous, these shrimps are an intensely over-the-top experience.

16 jumbo shrimp (about 1 pound), peeled leaving tail section intact, and deveined
3 large eggs plus 1 egg yolk
1/4 cup soy sauce
5 tablespoons freshly squeezed lemon juice
1/4 teaspoon chilli oil
2 teaspoons white sesame seeds, toasted
2 teaspoons black sesame seeds
FOR THE SAUCE
1/4 cup Clam Juice (see page 210), or freshly bottled clam juice
A pinch of cayenne
1 cup Lemongrass Oil (see page 215)
4 to 5 cups grapeseed oil
8 ounces kadaifi pastry
2 lemons, cut into wedges
Salt
MAKES 16

Place the shrimp in a shallow baking dish. In a small bowl, lightly beat 2 of the eggs then mix in the soy sauce, 4 tablespoons of the lemon juice, the chilli oil, both types of sesame seeds and 3 tablespoons of water. Pour the mixture over the shrimp and toss to coat. Set aside to marinate for 10 to 15 minutes while you make the sauce.

In a small saucepan, warm the clam juice. Place the remaining egg and yolk in a food processor fitted with the steel blade and, with the machine running, slowly pour in the warm clam juice in order to cook the egg. Then, with the machine still running, slowly pour in the Lemongrass Oil until the mixture emulsifies. Add the remaining 1 tablespoon of lemon juice, the cayenne and some salt, mixing to combine. Remove and set the dipping sauce aside.

Heat the grapeseed oil in a deep-sided, heavy saucepan over a medium-high heat until it reaches 375°F. Meanwhile, remove the kadaifi from the refrigerator and, keeping it in its plastic bag and covered with a damp towel to prevent it drying out, remove a small section of the pastry, keeping the long strands intact. Lift a shrimp from the marinade, and wrap the kadaifi along the center section of the body, leaving about 1/2 inch of shrimp exposed at either end.

Transfer the wrapped shrimp to a parchment-lined baking pan and cover with a barely damp kitchen towel. Repeat with the remaining shrimp. If the kadaifi-wrapped shrimp begin to dry out, finely mist them with water.

Heat the oven to a very low setting. Place 4 to 5 shrimp in the hot oil at a time and fry for 1 1/2 to 2 minutes or until golden brown and crispy, turning once. Repeat with remaining shrimps. Remove the shrimp to a baking sheet lined with baking parchment and keep warm in the oven. Remove from oven and place on a serving plate. Squeeze the juice from half a lemon over the shrimps. Serve with additional lemon wedges and lemongrass dipping sauce.

Notes

• Kadaifi is a Greek, Turkish and Middle Eastern dough that cooks up like Shredded Wheat. In Greece it is made by a kadaifi baker who spins out threadlike batter onto a hot copper plate, from which it is immediately removed before it has a chance to brown. Packaged like phyllo, it can usually be purchased at Greek stores or in the frozen section of large supermarkets.
• The lemongrass dipping sauce can also be served with salmon.
• Add the shrimp to a salad and serve as a main course.
• The kadaifi shrimp can be made up to 2 hours before frying. Cover with a damp kitchen towel and store in a refrigerator until ready for use.

Paella

Paella has a comfort-food quality and this particular version is redolent of the sea. It has wonderfully complex textures and traditional flavors, with the lobster, shrimp and scallops forming a strong base. The mussels and clams are embedded in the tender rice and are discovered only when "dug for." It's a dish that will surely please, and although it may seem overwhelming, its components can be broken down and made several days in advance.

FOR THE PAELLA
2 tablespoons saffron threads
5 live lobsters (1¹/₂ pounds each), freshly killed (see Note)
45 to 50 Manila clams or 20 littleneck clams
30 small mussels
12 sea scallops (about 1 pound)
16 large shrimp, shells on
10 tablespoons olive oil, plus extra for rubbing
4 sprigs thyme
12 baby artichokes, peeled, trimmed and rubbed thoroughly with lemon juice or olive oil
1¹/₂ to 2 pounds tomatoes
¹/₂ red bell pepper, cored and seeded
¹/₂ green bell pepper, cored and seeded
1 fresh poblano chilli pepper
1 cup fresh peas
1¹/₂ large onions, thinly sliced
3 canned anchovy fillets
8 garlic cloves
1 teaspoon dried red pepper flakes
4 cups paella or short-grain white rice
Salt and freshly ground black pepper
FOR THE MARINADE
2¹/₂ pounds ripe tomatoes (about 12 medium) or 42 ounces canned tomatoes, chopped, juices reserved
6 cloves garlic, thinly sliced
4 tablespoons olive oil
1 cup white wine
1 teaspoon cayenne
6 sprigs cilantro
6 sprigs parsley
2 bay leaves
FOR THE LOBSTER STOCK
2 tablespoons unsalted butter
1 pound leeks (white and light green part only), washed and thinly sliced

4 stalks celery, cut into ¹/₂-inch pieces
4 carrots, peeled and cut into ¹/₂-inch pieces
1 medium onion, peeled and cut into ¹/₂-inch pieces
1 pound tomatoes, roughly chopped
8 ounces fennel (including fronds), chopped into ¹/₂-inch pieces
Pared zest of ¹/₂ orange, in 1-inch pieces
1¹/₂ tablespoons tomato paste
¹/₄ cup brandy
1¹/₂ cups white wine
15 peppercorns
6 coriander seeds
2 bay leaves
A bouquet garni made from 8 sprigs cilantro and 8 sprigs tarragon tied together with string
1 head garlic, halved crosswise
TO GARNISH
2¹/₂ tablespoons cilantro leaves
1¹/₂ tablespoons chervil leaves
1 tablespoon tarragon leaves
6 sage leaves, torn in half if large
SERVES 8 TO 10

In a dry frying pan over medium-low heat, toast the saffron until fragrant then remove from the heat and set aside.

Prepare the shellfish. From each lobster body, detach the tail and two claws. Remove the shell from the body, clean and remove the poisonous grainy sac from behind the eyes. Reserve the body for making the lobster stock. Halve the tails lengthwise, cutting through from the underside. With the back of a heavy chef's knife, crack the claws once. Wash the clams and mussels in several changes of cold salted water, scrubbing the shells clean. Remove the beards from the mussels. Place the clams, mussels, lobster tails and claws, scallops and shrimp in a large non-reactive dish and set aside.

To make the marinade, combine a third of the toasted saffron with all the marinade ingredients including the reserved juices and pour over the shellfish. Gently mix to coat then marinate in the refrigerator overnight.

To make the stock, melt the butter in a stockpot over medium-low heat then add the leeks, celery, carrot, onion, tomatoes, fennel, orange zest, tomato paste and half the remaining saffron. Sweat for 10 minutes, stirring occasionally.

When the vegetables are soft, stir in the brandy, bring to the boil and simmer for 2 minutes to reduce. Add the lobster bodies, stir to combine, smashing the bodies with a heavy wooden spoon. Add the white wine and simmer for 2 to 3 minutes, then stir in the peppercorns, coriander seeds and bay leaves. Cook, stirring, for 1 minute.

Stir 14 cups of water into the stockpot then add the bouquet garni and garlic. Bring to a boil, reduce the heat to low and simmer for 1 hour, skimming as necessary. Strain, pressing hard on the solids to extract as much flavor as possible. Discard the solids. Return the lobster stock to the pot and boil over a high heat, skimming as necessary, until the stock has reduced to 10 cups in volume.

Meanwhile, in a large saucepan of salted cold water, whisk in 1 tablespoon of olive oil and add the thyme. Bring to the boil then lower the heat to a simmer. Add the artichokes and cook for 12 to 15 minutes or until just soft. Remove the artichokes from the saucepan and set aside. When cool enough to handle, cut the artichokes in half lengthwise and set aside.

Preheat the grill. Place the tomatoes, bell peppers and poblano chilli under a grill or on a grill pan and cook until the skins are blistered and blackened, turning the tomatoes frequently and removing each vegetable from the heat as it is done. Alternatively, put them directly onto a gas flame. Peel and seed the tomatoes then chop the flesh. Peel the bell peppers and slice them 1/4 inch thick. Peel and seed the chilli and slice it 1/4 inch thick. Set the tomatoes, peppers and chilli aside.

Bring a small saucepan of salted water to the boil, add the peas and simmer for 1 minute. Drain under cold running water and set aside.

Remove the shellfish from the marinade and set each variety aside separately on trays, leaving as much of the marinade on as possible and discarding the rest. Bring the lobster stock to a simmer and add the lobster claws. Simmer them for 4 to 5 minutes then remove them from the stock using a slotted spoon and set aside. Remove the stock from the heat and set aside in a warm place.

Heat the oven to 375°F. Set a heavy 18-inch seasoned paella pan over moderate heat and add 2 tablespoons of olive oil, swirling it round to cover the pan. When hot, add the artichokes, cut side down, and fry for 4 minutes until golden brown and crispy. Turn and cook for another minute. Remove the artichokes and set aside.

Lower the heat slightly and add another 2 tablespoons of olive oil. Cook the lobster tails flesh-side down for 2 1/2 minutes, then turn and cook for another 1 1/2 minutes on the other side. Remove from the pan and set aside.

Increase the heat to medium and add 1 tablespoon of olive oil. Add the shrimp and some salt and pepper to the pan and sear them for 30 seconds on each side. Remove and set aside.

Add 1 cup of lobster stock to the paella pan and deglaze. Using a wooden spoon, stir vigorously to incorporate the caramelized cooking juices. Strain the liquid back into the stockpot.

Wipe the paella pan clean and place over a medium heat, adding 2 tablespoons of olive oil and the onions. Cook for 4 to 5 minutes, stirring occasionally, until soft. Meanwhile, mash the anchovies and garlic cloves together with 1 teaspoon of salt to make a paste. Season the onions with 1 teaspoon of salt, the red pepper flakes and the remaining toasted saffron, then add the garlic-anchovy paste and cook for 1 minute.

Stir the rice into the onion mixture until the grains are well coated and cook for about 5 minutes. Add 1 1/2 cups of the stock, stirring to combine. Raise the heat slightly and add the mussels and clams. Cook, stirring, until the liquid evaporates. When dry, add another 2 cups of stock and continue stirring (if the mixture begins to stick to the bottom of the pan, lower the heat slightly). Scatter half the peppers, half the tomatoes and half the artichokes over the rice, reserving the rest to use as a garnish. Add another 2 cups of stock to the pan, gently stir, then place the pan at the bottom of the oven for 5 to 8 minutes. Remove and add another 2 cups of stock and return to the bottom of the oven for 18 minutes.

Shell and devein the shrimp, leaving the tails on, and set aside. Remove all the meat from the lobster claws and 5 of the lobster-tail halves and chop it into thirds. With the remaining 5 lobster-tail halves, pull the meat only half out, leaving it attached at the tail end. Set aside.

Remove the paella from the oven. Evenly distribute the chopped lobster meat, 8 of the shrimp, 6 scallops and 1 1/2 cups of stock, stir and return to the oven for another 5 minutes.

Remove the paella. Over the rice, add the remaining peppers, artichokes, lobster tails, scallops, and shrimp. Sprinkle with the peas and tomatoes. Do not stir. Return the paella to the oven for 5 minutes or until everything has heated through. Remove from the oven, sprinkle with the cilantro, chervil, tarragon and sage leaves and drizzle with the remaining 2 tablespoons of olive oil before serving.

NOTES

NOTES

• When killing lobsters, I prefer to freeze them for 15 to 20 minutes to render them unconscious, and then place a knife in the back of their heads an inch behind the eyes.
• The marinating can be done overnight, while the stock can be made 2 days in advance.
• I like to add the shells from the lobster and shrimp to the stockpot.

Basmati Rice
with Shrimp and Exotic Fruit

2¹/₂ cups Light Chicken Stock or water (see page 209)
1 tablespoon unsalted butter
1 small onion, cut into ¹/₄-inch pieces
1 cup brown basmati rice
1¹/₂ tablespoons currants
4 teaspoons sliced almonds
1¹/₂ teaspoons Madras curry powder
¹/₂ teaspoon saffron threads
1 teaspoon salt
1 heaped tablespoon finely diced pineapple
1 heaped tablespoon finely diced peeled Granny Smith apple
1 heaped tablespoon finely diced mango
1 heaped tablespoon finely diced banana
1 ounce (¹/₄ cup) cooked baby shrimp
10 cilantro leaves, torn
SERVES 4

Preheat the oven to 400°F. In a small saucepan, heat the stock to a low simmer. In a flameproof casserole over a moderate heat, combine the butter and onion and cook, stirring occasionally, for 1¹/₂ minutes, until soft but not colored. Add the rice, currants, almonds, curry powder, saffron and salt and stir until the rice is toasted and well coated with the other ingredients.

Add the hot stock, stir, cover and transfer the casserole to the oven for 45 to 50 minutes. Remove from the oven and let stand for 10 minutes without lifting the lid.

Uncover and fluff the rice up with a fork. Gently fold in the pineapple, apple, mango, banana, shrimp, and cilantro leaves and serve.

Red Snapper
with Basmati Rice and Spiced Saffron Curry Sauce

The crisp skin and moist flesh of the snapper allow it to be paired with fruits and a curry sauce, providing a perfectly balanced contrast of texture and flavor.

2 tablespoons unsalted butter, plus extra for greasing

1 small onion, cut into 1/4-inch pieces

1/2 cup finely chopped fennel bulb

1/2 cup peeled, cored, finely chopped Granny Smith apple

1 clove garlic, crushed

1 teaspoon Thai red curry paste

1 teaspoon saffron, plus extra 4 pinches

4 teaspoons Madras curry powder

1 teaspoon turmeric powder

11/2-inch piece fresh lemongrass, flattened

2 cups Light Chicken Stock, Lobster Fumet, or water (see pages 209 and 210)

6 sprigs cilantro

1 kaffir lime leaf

1/2 cup heavy cream

1/2 cup canned coconut milk

1/2 teaspoon fenugreek

1/2 teaspoon fennel seeds

1/2 teaspoon yellow mustard seeds

1/2 star anise

1 green cardamom pod, shell removed

2 red snappers (about 11/2 pounds each), scaled and filleted

3 to 4 tablespoons olive oil

Salt and freshly ground black pepper

Basmati Rice with Shrimp and Exotic Fruit, to serve (see page 91)

1 Preserved Lemon, finely julienned, to garnish (see page 205)

2 tablespoons Chive Oil, to garnish (see page 214)

SERVES 4

In a medium saucepan, heat 1 tablespoon of the butter with the onion, fennel, apple, garlic, Thai red curry paste and 3 tablespoons of water over moderate heat. Cook until softened but not browned. Stir in 1 teaspoon of saffron, the curry powder, turmeric and lemongrass, then the stock, 2 sprigs of cilantro and the kaffir lime leaf.

Bring the mixture to a boil over a high heat, then reduce the heat to medium-high and briskly simmer for 10 minutes or until the mixture is reduced by half. Strain the mixture, discarding the solids, then return the sauce to the pan and add the cream and coconut milk. Simmer until the volume of liquid has reduced to about 1 cup. Set aside in a warm place.

In a dry frying pan over moderate heat, combine the fenugreek, fennel seeds, mustard seeds, star anise and cardamom and toast until fragrant. Transfer to a spice mill and grind coarsely, or grind using a mortar and pestle. Set aside.

Preheat the oven to 400°F. Use a knife to make a cross in the skin of each fish fillet to prevent curling. Season both sides of the fillets with salt and pepper, smearing a pinch of saffron over the skin side of each, then dust with the ground spices.

In a large ovenproof skillet, heat the oil over medium-high heat. When it is very hot, fry the fish skin-side down for 3 to 4 minutes or until the skin is brown and crisp, lightly pressing with a metal spatula to ensure a crisp skin. Turn the fish over and place the pan in the oven to finish cooking for about 2 minutes or until the flesh is firm.

Meanwhile, over medium-low heat, use a hand blender to whisk 1 tablespoon of butter into the sauce and blend until frothy. Remove the fish from the oven. Serve the fillets, skin-side up, on a bed of Basmati Rice with Shrimp and Exotic Fruit. Drizzle the sauce around the rice and garnish each plate with a sprig of fresh cilantro, a few strips of Preserved Lemon and dots of Chive Oil.

NOTES

• You can use swordfish, tuna or salmon instead of the red snapper.

• Cook a mixture of vegetables such as peppers, onions, eggplant and potatoes in the sauce. Place them on a bed of jasmine rice or noodles and pour the sauce over the vegetables and rice. Add some grilled shrimp brochettes if you like.

• Try the sauce with steamed lobster meat and potato gnocchi.

John Dory with Calamari, Morels and New Potatoes

Ramps, or wild leeks, resemble green onions with broad leaves, have an assertive, garlicky flavor and at Lake House are in season from March until June.

4 cups Lobster Fumet (see page 210)
12 ounces small fingerling potatoes or new potoates, washed
3 tablespoons olive oil
1 medium onion, peeled and finely chopped
3 cloves garlic, roughly chopped
4 small calamari, cleaned and rinsed, sliced into 1/2-inch rings
1 cup white burgundy wine
1 14-ounce can whole peeled plum tomatoes, or equal amount of fresh tomatoes
20 ramps, trimmed and leaves reserved for another use, or 15 baby leeks, trimmed and washed
3 tablespoons unsalted butter
8 ounces small fresh morels, thoroughly rinsed and dried
2 John Dory (2 pounds each), head, tail, fins and skin removed, trimmed but left on the bone
8 sprigs tarragon
12 Tomato Petals (see page 217)
4 teaspoons chopped flat-leaf parsley, to garnish
2 teaspoons white truffle oil, to garnish
1 teaspoon coarse sea salt, to garnish
Salt and freshly ground black pepper
SERVES 4

In a small saucepan over medium-high heat, place the fumet and boil until reduced to 2 cups. Meanwhile, in a pan of salted water, boil the potatoes until fork-tender. Set both aside.

In a heavy-bottomed casserole over medium heat, place 1 tablespoon of olive oil. Cook the onion and garlic for 4 to 5 minutes, stirring occasionally, until lightly colored. Add the calamari and cook, stirring, for 2 to 3 minutes.

Add the wine and simmer until it has reduced by a little more than half its volume. Meanwhile, put the tomatoes through a food mill to give 1 cup of puréed tomatoes, and reserve the remaining for another

use. Add it to the casserole and simmer for 2 minutes, then add the reduced fumet and simmer gently for 15 minutes, skimming as necessary. Add the cooked potatoes, season and set aside.

Meanwhile, in a saucepan of boiling salted water, blanch the ramps or baby leeks. Refresh under cold running water and set aside. In a skillet over medium heat, add 1 tablespoon of the butter and, when foaming, add the mushrooms and sauté briefly until lightly cooked. Set aside.

Heat the oven to 450°F. Season the fish on both sides with salt and pepper. In a large skillet over medium-high heat, place 1 tablespoon of olive oil and 1/2 tablespoon of butter. When the butter begins to foam, add one of the John Dory and 4 sprigs of tarragon. Cook for 1 1/2 to 2 minutes on each side, until golden, then remove from the pan. Wipe out the pan and repeat with the remaining John Dory.

In the casserole arrange the cooked morels and ramps or leeks over the potatoes, then top with the fish. Place the Tomato Petals around the fish and dot each fish with 1/2 tablespoon of butter. Transfer the casserole to the oven for 8 minutes, then turn the fish over and cook for another 8 minutes, or until just cooked.

Remove the fish to a cutting board. Using a knife, detach the fillets from the bones. To serve, divide the vegetables and broth among 4 shallow bowls and top each with a fish fillet. Garnish each bowl with 1 teaspoon of parsley, drizzle with 1/2 teaspoon of truffle oil and sprinkle with 1/4 teaspoon of sea salt.

Black Thai Rice
Witch Hats

To make the witch hats, you will need a piece of acetate or plastic lid measuring about 5 1/2 inches in diameter.

1 1/2 cups black Thai rice
1/2 teaspoon salt, plus extra for seasoning
Unsalted butter, to grease
6 pounds swordfish, cut into 12 pieces measuring at least 4 x 5 inches wide and 3/4 inch thick
2 tablespoons freshly squeezed lemon juice
MAKES 12

Rinse the rice under cold running water. In a medium pot, combine the rice with 3 cups water and the salt. Bring the water to a boil, reduce the heat to low, cover, and simmer for 25 to 30 minutes. Remove the rice from the heat and set aside for about 1 1/2 hours or until completely cool.

Meanwhile, using a permanent marker, draw a witch's hat measuring approximately 4 inches wide by 5 inches high on a piece of acetate or a plastic lid. Cut out the hat with scissors for use as a template.

Preheat the oven to 325°F. Line 2 baking sheets with lightly buttered greaseproof paper. Using the template, cut out 1 witch hat from each piece of swordfish and transfer the fish to the prepared baking sheets. Brush each hat with some lemon juice and season with a pinch of salt.

Place 1/4 cup of the cooled rice onto each piece of fish and pat out to completely cover the top surface, reshaping the edges if necessary to resemble a hat. Transfer to oven and bake for 8 to 10 minutes or until the fish is opaque.

N O T E S

• Short-grained black Thai rice is either dark black or deep red in color, sticky when cooked, and has a rich nutty taste.
• Use the scraps of swordfish to make brochettes by alternating them on skewers with Fire-Roasted Onions (see page 148) then marinating them in some Herb Oil (see page 215). Grill the brochettes and then brush them with BBQ Sauce (see page 212).

Shrimp with Shrimp Sauce and Pesto

Sweet shrimp combined with pesto and zucchini encapsulate a perfect summer beach day.

1 cup Mediterranean Shrimp Sauce (see page 96)
20 large shrimp, peeled, leaving tail section of shell intact, and deveined
1/3 cup Basil and Parsley Pesto (see page 96)
3 small zucchini, thinly sliced lengthwise, leaving the core, into 40 slices using a mandoline
2 tablespoons unsalted butter
1/4 cup Roasted Red Pepper Purée, to garnish (see page 218)
Salt and freshly ground black pepper
SERVES 4

Make the Mediterranean Shrimp Sauce according to the recipe and keep it warm until ready to serve (see page 96).

In a medium bowl, combine the shrimp and pesto, stirring to coat the shrimp. Wrap 2 slices of zucchini around the center section of each shrimp and fasten with a toothpick. Set aside on a baking tin lined with greaseproof paper. Season with salt and pepper.

Heat 1 tablespoon of butter in a 12-inch non-stick frying pan over medium heat. When the foam in the pan has subsided, add half the shrimp and cook for 1 1/2 minutes per side. Remove the shrimp from the pan and set aside in a warm place. Wipe the pan clean with a paper towel, then heat the remaining butter and cook the remaining shrimp.

Pour 1/4 cup of the Mediterranean Shrimp Sauce onto a serving plate or into a shallow bowl, tilting it to cover the base. Remove the toothpicks from the cooked shrimp and stand the shrimp in the sauce. Garnish the perimeter with 1 tablespoon of Roasted Red Pepper Purée, dotting it around the plate. Repeat for a total of 4 servings.

N O T E S

• In springtime, you can use the tender blanched green leaves of ramp instead of the zucchini in this recipe.
• Skewer the pesto-coated shrimp and grill or barbecue, then serve with the Mediterranean sauce on the side.
• Alternatively, serve the pesto shrimp on toasted country bread as a sandwich.

• Accompany with goat cheese rolled in bread crumbs lightly sautéed in butter, warmed in the oven, placed on top of mixed spring greens.

MEDITERRANEAN SHRIMP SAUCE

1 tablespoon olive oil

1 cup small shrimp with shells, roughly chopped, or 8 ounces shrimp shells

1 small yellow onion, thinly sliced lengthwise

10 cloves garlic, peeled and smashed

1/2 fennel bulb with fronds attached, thinly sliced lengthwise

2 teaspoons grated orange zest

1 teaspoon fennel seeds

1 teaspoon saffron threads

1/2 teaspoon harissa sauce

1 1/2 tablespoons tomato paste

1 cup freshly squeezed orange juice

1 cup white wine

2 cups Clam Juice (see page 210)

A bouquet garni made from 10 basil leaves with stems and 2 bay leaves, tied with string

2 tablespoons unsalted butter, chilled and diced, or 2 tablespoons extra-virgin olive oil (optional)

MAKES 1 CUP

In a medium saucepan, heat the olive oil over medium heat. Add the shrimp or shrimp shells, onion, garlic, fennel bulb, orange zest, fennel seeds, saffron and harissa sauce and sauté for 5 minutes, or until softened, using a wooden spoon to mash the shrimp mixture.

Raise the heat to medium-high and add the tomato paste and orange juice. Simmer the mixture until slightly syrupy, for about 1 to 2 minutes. Add the white wine, return to the boil and simmer for 8 minutes or until the volume of liquid has reduced by half.

Add the clam juice, 1 cup of water and the bouquet garni and simmer for 20 minutes. Remove the bouquet garni and transfer the mixture to a food processor fitted with a steel blade. Pulse a few times, just until combined. Strain through a fine sieve, pressing hard on the solids. You should have about 2 cups.

Return the mixture to the saucepan, bring to the boil and simmer over high heat for 15 to 20 minutes or until it has reduced by half. Remove from the heat. Using a hand-held blender, add the butter or extra-virgin oil a little at a time until fully incorporated. Serve the sauce immediately.

NOTES

• Before the butter or extra-virgin oil is added, the sauce can be set aside in a warm place for up to 30 minutes until ready to assemble the dish. Once the butter or extra-virgin oil has been added, however, the sauce must be served immediately.
• This version of shrimp sauce is reminiscent of bouillabaisse. The harissa sauce perks it up but doesn't take it too far from its Mediterranean roots.
• The sauce can be served with most fish dishes.

FOR THE BASIL AND PARSLEY PESTO

2 tablespoons pine nuts

3 tablespoons fresh bread crumbs

2 cloves garlic, finely chopped

4 lightly packed cups basil, washed and dried

1 lightly packed cup flat-leaf parsley, washed and dried

1/4 teaspoon salt

A pinch of dried red pepper flakes

1/2 cup extra-virgin olive oil

MAKES 1 CUP

To make the pesto, heat the oven to 350°F. Take two small baking sheets, and place the pine nuts on one and the bread crumbs on the other. Transfer them to the oven and toast until lightly browned all over, removing the pine nuts after 5 minutes and the bread crumbs after 8 to 10 minutes. Set them aside separately to cool.

In a food processor fitted with a steel blade, combine the garlic, basil, parsley, pine nuts, salt and red pepper flakes and chop briefly. With the machine running, add the olive oil until the mixture emulsifies. Once the oil has been incorporated, remove and fold in the bread crumbs.

The pesto may be refrigerated up to 3 days and frozen for up to 1 month in a covered container.

NOTES

• Cook some pasta; in a bowl place some pesto and mashed fresh goat cheese; then add the hot cooked pasta and toss.
• Take 6 thick slices of crusty country-style bread and toast or grill; rub with a raw garlic clove then top with sliced ripe tomato, buffalo mozzarella and a dab of pesto.

Dover Sole with Sun-dried Tomatoes and Capers

Serve with broccoli rabe and smashed potato cakes.

1 teaspoon plus 2 tablespoons olive oil

11 tablespoons plus 1 teaspoon unsalted butter, chilled, plus extra for greasing

2 cloves garlic

3/4 cup tiny bread cubes cut from a baguette, crusts removed

1/2 cup flour

2 whole Dover lemon or gray soles (1 to 1 1/4 pounds each), fins removed, gray skin removed and white skin descaled

6 sprigs thyme

1 tablespoon capers in brine, drained, plus 2 teaspoons brine from the jar

3 sage leaves

1 tablespoon freshly squeezed lemon juice

1 tablespoon finely chopped sun-dried tomatoes (not packed in oil)

1 small lemon, peeled, sectioned, and sections halved

4 sprigs Fried Parsley (see page 216)

Salt and freshly ground black pepper

FOR THE BROCCOLI RABE

1 tablespoon olive oil

1 clove garlic, roughly chopped

1 bunch broccoli rabe, stems trimmed to 6 inches

Salt and a pinch of dried red pepper flakes

FOR THE SMASHED POTATO CAKES

1 1/2 to 2 pounds (25 to 30) new potatoes, unpeeled and halved

4 tablespoons extra-virgin olive oil

1 tablespoon chopped rosemary leaves

2 teaspoons finely chopped garlic

8 whole black olives, pitted and halved

Salt and freshly ground black pepper

SERVES 4

In a medium frying pan, gently heat 1 teaspoon of olive oil and 1 teaspoon of butter with 1 whole clove of garlic over medium heat. When the foam subsides, add the bread cubes and cook, stirring frequently, until toasted. Remove the bread cubes from the pan, discard the garlic and set aside.

On a medium-sized baking sheet, place the flour and set aside.

Dice 2 tablespoons butter and set aside ready to add to the fish.

Preheat the oven to 400°F and lightly butter a baking tin. In a large skillet over medium-high heat, place 1 tablespoon of olive oil. Season 1 Dover sole with salt and pepper, dredge it in the flour, and shake off any excess. When the skillet is hot, carefully add 3 sprigs of thyme and place the first fish flesh-side down on the top of the thyme. Cook for 30 seconds, then add half the diced butter to the pan, dotting it around the fish. Cook for another 1 to 1 1/2 minutes, spooning some of the butter over the fish and lowering the heat if needed, then turn and cook for 1 minute so both sides are brown and crisp. Transfer the fish to the prepared baking sheet, pouring the butter and thyme over the fish.

Wipe out the skillet, let it cool, then repeat the cooking procedure with the remaining fish. Place them in the oven for 6 to 7 minutes to finish cooking. At this point start to prepare the sauce. In a medium frying pan over medium-low heat, melt 8 tablespoons of butter and, when just melted, add 1 whole clove of garlic, then the capers, and cook for 2 minutes or until the capers begin to fry and the butter browns. Add the caper brine, sage leaves and lemon juice, then remove the pan from the heat and whisk in 1 tablespoon of cold butter until it emulsifies. Remove the garlic clove and sage leaves. Stir in the sun-dried tomatoes, lemon sections and bread cubes. Set aside.

When the fish are just finished, remove them from the oven and let rest for 2 to 3 minutes or until you can handle them. Using a fish knife and a fork, remove the fillets from both sides of each fish. Set the fillets back onto the baking sheet and keep warm.

To make the broccoli rabe, heat the olive oil with the garlic over medium heat in a large skillet until the garlic begins to soften. Add the red pepper flakes, some salt and the broccoli rabe, stirring to combine. Add 1/2 cup of water and cook, stirring occasionally, until tender, 8 to 10 minutes.

To make the smashed potato cakes, combine the potatoes with 2 teaspoons of salt and plenty of water to cover, in a pot over a high heat. Bring to a boil and boil for 10 to 12 minutes or until tender. Strain through a colander then return the potatoes to the pan and mash them coarsely with a fork or potato masher. Stir in the remaining ingredients adding salt and pepper to taste.

To assemble the dish, place a metal ring mold, about 2 1/2 to 3 inches wide, in the center of a serving plate and place a quarter of the potato mixture in the ring, pressing down lightly to make a cake. Remove the ring carefully and repeat with the remaining potato mixture.
Place the broccoli rabe around the potato cakes, dividing it equally among the serving plates. Place two fish fillets on top of each potato cake, pour over the sauce and garnish with fried parsley.

NOTES

• You will be busy making the sauce while the fish is in the oven, so cook the broccoli rabe and the potato mixture in advance and keep them warm at the side of the stove until ready to serve.
• Try using the brine from the Pickled Chillies (see page 204) in this recipe instead of caper brine.

Sautéed Cod with Baby Leeks and Jerusalem Artichokes

Nutty, sweet Jerusalem artichokes, soft and savory leeks and delicate cod make an elegant combination. Here, the sturdy sauce of mussel juice and herb oil is given a bright note with the addition of fresh cucumber juice.

6 medium Jerusalem artichokes (sunchokes), washed and well scrubbed
2 tablespoons plus 2 teaspoons olive oil
9 sprigs thyme
3 pounds cod fillets, trimmed and cut into 6 portions about 6 ounces each
12 baby leeks (white and light green parts only), trimmed and well cleaned
4 tablespoons unsalted butter, plus extra for greasing
12 baby carrots, peeled and trimmed, leaving 1 inch of stem
1/2 cup flour
1/2 English cucumber, trimmed
3/4 cup Mussel or Clam Juice (see page 210)
1/4 cup Herb Oil (see page 215)
1 tablespoon freshly squeezed lemon juice
4 teaspoons Red Wine Reduction (see page 213)
Salt and freshly ground black pepper
SERVES 6

Preheat the oven to 400°F. Place the Jerusalem artichokes in a small baking dish. Drizzle them with 2 teaspoons of the olive oil, top with 3 thyme sprigs and season with salt and pepper. Cover the dish with foil and roast for 1 3/4 hours, turning the vegetables halfway through cooking. Remove the foil during the last 20 minutes to ensure proper browning, then remove from the oven, set aside and keep warm. Leave the oven on.

On a baking tray lined with greaseproof paper, place the 6 pieces of cod and lightly salt them. Refrigerate until needed.

In a small saucepan, place the leeks with 2 tablespoons of the butter, 1 cup of water and a little salt and pepper. Bring to a boil and cook for 5 minutes or until fork-tender. Drain, reserving 1/4 cup of the cooking liquid, then set aside and keep warm.

Cook the carrots in a small pan of boiling salted water for about 2 1/2 minutes or until tender but still a little crunchy. Drain and keep warm.

Lightly butter a baking dish large enough to hold the 6 portions of cod and set aside. Place the flour in a shallow dish and set aside. Remove the cod from the refrigerator. Using a kitchen towel, pat the fish dry and set aside.

In a large, well-seasoned frying pan, heat 1 tablespoon of the olive oil and 1 tablespoon of butter over a medium-high heat. When the butter begins to foam, season three of the cod fillets with pepper then lightly press the flesh side in the flour, shaking off any excess. Place them in the frying pan, flesh-side down, and add 3 sprigs of thyme. Cook the fish for about 2 to 3 minutes or until golden. Transfer the fillets to the buttered baking dish, cooked side up. Place the thyme from the frying pan on the cod fillets and drizzle with the cooking juices.

Wipe out the pan with a paper towel and repeat the cooking procedure with the remaining oil, butter, cod fillets and thyme. Place the baking dish in the oven for about 10 minutes, depending on the thickness of the fish, or until the cod is just cooked through.

Meanwhile, juice the cucumber in a juice extractor and set the liquid aside. In a small saucepan, combine the Mussel Juice and reserved leek cooking liquid over medium heat and bring to a simmer. Remove the saucepan from the heat and whisk in the Herb Oil. Stir in the cucumber juice and lemon juice, then season the sauce with salt and pepper to taste.

To serve, cover each plate with 4 tablespoons of herb sauce. Cut the Jerusalem artichokes into 1/4-inch slices on the bias. Place sliced Jerusalem artichoke in the center of each plate with 2 leeks. Arrange the cod over the vegetables and sprinkle with the remaining tablespoon of lemon juice. Lean 2 baby carrots upright against each piece of fish. Garnish each plate with 1 teaspoon of the Red Wine Reduction dotted around the sauce and serve immediately.

• Cod has a delicate flesh that becomes meltingly tender when sautéed. After filleting, salt the cod lightly, which will extract the excess moisture and concentrate the flavors.

• At Lake House I don't usually use flour when sautéeing fish, because we have a commercial stove with large burners and access to high heat. Black steel heavy gauge pans also work well with fish. However, flour does help brown and give a crust.

• Tuna, salmon, halibut and lobster can be substituted for the cod.

Spiced Potato
Pancakes

4 baking potatoes, unpeeled
4 ounces tender fennel bulb and fronds, optional
$2^1/2$ tablespoons curry powder
4 teaspoons salt
10 tablespoons unsalted butter, softened
$1/2$ cup flour
$1/4$ cup currants
$1/2$ teaspoon anise seeds
2 tablespoons olive oil, plus extra if necessary
MAKES 12

In a large saucepan, place the potatoes, fennel (if using), 2 tablespoons of curry powder and 1 tablespoon of salt. Cover with water to a depth of 2 inches and bring to a boil over a high heat.

Lower the heat to a simmer and cook until tender, about 30 minutes. Meanwhile, heat the oven to 350°F. Drain the potatoes and discard any fennel. Transfer the potatoes to a small roasting pan and place in the oven for 10 minutes.

Remove the potatoes from the oven and, using a kitchen towel to protect your hands, immediately peel the hot potatoes. Cut into 1-inch cubes and, while still warm, pass the potatoes through a ricer fitted with a fine-holed disc, or through a food mill, into a medium bowl.
Add $1/2$ cup softened butter, the flour, currants, 1 teaspoon of salt and the remaining 1 teaspoon of curry powder to the potatoes and stir gently to combine.

On a lightly floured work surface, roll the mixture into a log about 12 inches long and $2^3/4$ inches in diameter. Slice the log into 12 rounds 1 inch thick. Place the rounds on a parchment-lined baking sheet and chill in the refrigerator for at least 1 hour, and up to 24 hours.

In a small saucepan, melt the remaining 2 tablespoons of butter. Remove the pancakes from the refrigerator and brush them on both sides with the melted butter. Sprinkle both sides with the anise seeds and remaining $1/2$ teaspoon of curry powder.

Heat the oven to 325°F. In a 12-inch nonstick frying pan over medium heat, place 1 tablespoon of olive oil. Working in batches, brown the pancakes for 2 minutes on each side, adding another tablespoon of oil to the pan as necessary. As the pancakes cook, transfer them back to the parchment-lined baking sheet. When ready to serve, transfer to the oven and finish the cooking for 5 to 8 minutes.

NOTE

• Serve these pancakes as a main course on a vegetarian menu.

Sea Bass with
Sautéed Wild Mushrooms and Roast Carrot Confit

2¹/₂ tablespoons unsalted butter

2 teaspoons grapeseed oil, plus extra for brushing

2 teaspoons finely chopped shallots

8 ounces fresh chanterelle mushrooms (see note)

2 ounces fresh black trumpet mushrooms (see note)

Roast Carrot Confit (see page 148)

2 sea bass (about 1 pound each), filleted

6 sprigs tarragon

¹/₂ lemon, thinly sliced

1 cup fresh peas

2 sprigs mint

Salt and freshly ground black pepper

SERVES 4

In a medium frying pan over medium-high heat, heat 1 tablespoon of the butter and 1 teaspoon of the oil. When the butter starts to foam, add half the shallots and cook for 30 seconds before adding the chanterelles. Cook for 1¹/₂ to 2¹/₂ minutes, stirring frequently. Add a pinch of salt and pepper. Remove from the heat, transfer to a baking dish and set aside. Wipe the frying pan with a paper towel. Add another tablespoon of butter and 1 teaspoon of oil and repeat the cooking process with the remaining shallots and the black trumpets. Transfer them to the baking dish.

Heat the oven to a very low setting. Leaving the Roast Carrot Confit in its baking dish, place it in the oven with the mushrooms to keep warm until ready to assemble.

Fill with water a large pot in which a bamboo steamer will fit, add the tarragon and lemon and bring to a boil. Season the sea bass on both sides with salt and pepper. Brush the bottom of the steamer with oil. Just before serving, place the steamer over the boiling water, sit the bass in the steamer skin-side up, cover and steam for 4 to 5 minutes depending on the thickness of the fish.

Meanwhile, in a small saucepan, place the peas, 4 tablespoons of water, ¹/₂ tablespoon of butter, the mint and some salt and pepper. Heat gently until just warm then discard the mint.

To serve, divide the carrots among 4 serving plates, reserving 8 tablespoons of the liquid from the confit. Top with the sea bass, placing it skin-side up. Arrange a quarter of the chanterelles on each plate to one side of the carrots and scatter the black trumpets on the other. Place a pile of peas next to each type of mushroom. Stir the reserved juice from the carrot confit then drizzle it over the bass and serve.

NOTE

• Sea bass has a wonderful clean flavor that is light and delicate but holds up to the assertive elements in this dish.
• Cod, halibut or trout could be substituted for the sea bass.
• The chanterelles should be carefully wiped clean of debris with a kitchen towel. However, black trumpets really need to be soaked to rid them of all dirt, then removed to a kitchen towel and patted dry. Snip off the woody and dry tips of the stems before use.

Trout Duxelles with
Fingerling Potatoes, Corn and Fava Beans

Lake House has a lake which is stocked with baby brown trout. Brown trout can live in lakes and streams or migrate to the sea. Hence brown trout will then turn into sea trout or salmon trout. Brown trout can grow up to 40 pounds, but most weigh between 1 to 2 pounds. At Lake House they range between 4 to 6 pounds which is a versatile size.

FOR THE MUSHROOM DUXELLES

1 pound wild mushrooms, rinsed, stemmed and dried

1 shallot, finely chopped

1 clove garlic, finely chopped

2 teaspoons olive oil

1 tablespoon unsalted butter

1 tablespoon heavy cream

1¹/₂ teaspoons finely chopped dill

Salt and freshly ground black pepper

FOR THE PEA SAUCE

2 teaspoons grapeseed oil

1 medium leek (white part only), finely chopped

³/₄ cup Clam Juice (see page 210)

¹/₂ cup Tomato Water (see page 211)

¹/₄ cup diced peeled potato

2 sprigs chervil

2 sprigs tarragon

1 cup fresh peas

1/4 cup spinach leaves, finely shredded

2 tablespoons heavy cream

1 tablespoon lemon juice

1/2 tablespoon extra-virgin olive oil

Freshly ground black pepper

FOR THE TROUT

1 trout (about 5 pounds), gutted, trimmed, head, tail and fins removed

1 teaspoon salt

1/4 teaspoon sugar

2 tablespoons agar-agar

1 1/2 tablespoons mixed chopped herb leaves such as chervil, chives, dill, flat-leafed parsley and tarragon

Milk, for poaching

2 bay leaves

2 lovage leaves

5 black peppercorns

FOR THE POTATOES

6 small fingerling potatoes

1 tablespoon unsalted butter

FOR THE SWEET CORN AND FAVA BEANS

1 1/2 cups fresh corn kernels

1 1/2 cups (9 ounces) fava beans

1 tablespoon unsalted butter

1 1/2 tablespoons tarragon leaves

2 teaspoons olive oil

FOR THE CARROT PURÉE

8 ounces carrots (2 to 3), peeled and thinly sliced on the diagonal

1/3 cup heavy cream

TO SERVE

Blood Orange Reduction (see page 136)

Crab-Stuffed Zucchini Blossoms (see page 104)

SERVES 6

To make the mushroom duxelles, place the mushrooms in a food processor and pulse to form a rough purée. In a small saucepan over medium heat, sweat the shallot and garlic in the olive oil and butter until soft and translucent. Add the mushroom purée and cook, stirring frequently, for 18 to 20 minutes, until the mixture is dry. Set aside to cool to room temperature, then stir in the cream and dill and season with salt and pepper.

To make the Pea Sauce, heat the oil in a medium saucepan over medium heat. Add the leek and sweat for 4 to 5 minutes until soft. Add the clam juice, tomato water, potato, chervil and tarragon and

bring to a boil. Simmer for 2 to 3 minutes, then add the peas, spinach leaves and some pepper and boil for another minute.

Pour the mixture into a blender and purée. Add the cream, lemon juice and extra-virgin olive oil and continue to blend for 2 to 3 minutes. If the sauce is too thick, add 1 or 2 tablespoons of water. Transfer the sauce to a small bowl and set over a bowl of iced water to cool. When cool, transfer the sauce back to a medium saucepan and rewarm as necessary.

Meanwhile, using a sharp knife, continue the stomach slit of the fish on one side of the backbone as far as the tail, then cut down the other side of the backbone to open the fish fully. Place the trout on its back, tail toward you, and spread it open. Carefully holding a boning knife blade-side up, slide the point of the blade up the right side of the trout's ribcage, keeping the knife flush to the bone, working from the tail to the head. Keep cutting behind the ribcage to expose all the backbone, being careful not to cut into the flesh or through the skin.

Repeat on the other side of the trout, then, starting from the head end, slide the knife under the ribcage until the backbone is loose and the ribcage exposed. Cut behind the ribcage and down, releasing the bones from the fillets but keeping the fish in one piece. Use scissors to cut the backbone away from where it joins the underside of the skin, then carefully pull the backbone away. Trim out the white central cartilage running the length of the fish.

With the knife, remove the thin membrane from over the flesh of the flaps. Slice off any extra fins and bones without cutting into the flesh. Using kitchen tweezers, remove any small bones. At this point, weigh the trout and record the weight.

On a clean work surface lay the trout open on its back, season the flesh with the salt, sugar and a few grindings of pepper. Leave to stand for 15 minutes then dry with a kitchen towel to remove any liquid.

Sprinkle the agar-agar on top of the trout flesh and cover with the mixed herbs. Carefully place the mushroom duxelles on one fillet and fold the connecting fillet over to form a slight roll.

Cut two sheets of plastic wrap 4 inches longer than the trout and lay them slightly overlapping lengthwise. Place the trout in the center of the plastic, then tightly roll it up to give a round shape, tuck in ends.

Dampen a kitchen towel and roll the trout in it the same way as with the plastic, then tie with butcher's twine at 1 inch intervals along the fish to help maintain its cylindrical shape.

Fill a large broad pot three-quarters of the way up the side with a mixture of half water and half milk. Add the bay leaves, lovage and peppercorns, bring to a boil then reduce the heat to 158°F. Place the trout in the pot, maintaining the temperature at 158°F, and cook for 2½ minutes per pound. Halfway through the cooking time, rotate the trout to ensure even cooking. Turn off the heat and let the trout stand in the pot for 1 hour.

Meanwhile, cook the potatoes in plenty of boiling salted water until fork-tender, then drain.

For the sweet corn and fava beans, in a saucepan of boiling water, blanch the corn kernels for 3 minutes, drain and set aside. Then blanch the fava beans for 30 seconds, drain and peel away the

skins before setting the beans aside.

To make the carrot purée, in a small saucepan, place the carrots, cream and ¼ cup of water and bring to a boil. Lower the heat to a simmer and cook for 20 minutes or until soft. Remove from the heat and transfer the mixture to the bowl of a food processor fitted with a steel blade. Purée, adding 2 or 3 tablespoons of water if needed. Return the mixture to the saucepan and place over low heat. Cook until the carrot purée dries out and has a slightly stiff consistency. Season to taste with salt and pepper.

Remove the fish from the pot, leave it to stand for 10 to 15 minutes. In a small pan over medium heat, melt the 1 tablespoon butter and, when it starts to foam, add the cooked potatoes. Sauté them for about

2 minutes, turning frequently, until browned. Season with salt and pepper and set aside in a small baking dish.

In a separate pan, melt another tablespoon of butter with the 2 teaspoons olive oil, then add the corn, fava beans and 1½ tablespoons tarragon and heat through gently for 3 to 4 minutes. Season to taste and set aside in another small baking dish.

Carefully remove the string, cloth and plastic wrap from the fish. Cut the trout into 6 equal portions and set aside in a baking dish, covered.

To assemble the dish, preheat the oven to 200°F and place the baking dishes containing the potatoes, corn and fava beans and the trout in the oven to warm through. Place the pea sauce, carrot purée and Blood Orange Reduction in separate saucepans over a low heat to warm them through. Place the zucchini blossoms in a bamboo steamer over boiling water and heat through for 2 to 3 minutes.

On a clean work surface, place 6 large serving plates. Remove the baking dishes from the oven. Spoon a mound of corn and fava beans in the center of each plate. Ladle some of the pea sauce around the corn mixture. Place some potatoes and a quenelle of carrot purée on either side of the corn and fava beans. Arrange a piece of trout standing upright on the corn and fava beans. Drizzle the Blood Orange Reduction over the trout and around the plate. Top each fish with one stuffed zucchini blossom, place another on the side and serve immediately.

NOTES

• Trout caught from lakes are generally larger and coarser in flavor than river trout.

• Agar-agar is made from seaweed and is a healthy substitute for gelatin.

• As a change from this preparation, serve the trout with corn and fava beans tossed in vinaigrette and a side dish of Crispy Grains with Portabella Mushrooms (see page 126).

• Alternatively, serve the stuffed trout cold with mayonnaise, dill oil and Millet and Aduki Bean Salad (see page 139).

• Salmon can be used instead of trout.

• The pea sauce can be served with any fish and works well with lobster. For example, serve some poached lobster with Basmati Rice with Prawns and Exotic Fruit (page 91) and surround the plates with pea sauce and blood orange reduction, or serve just the pea sauce, exotic fruits (mixed with vanilla seeds), lobster and blood orange reduction.

• You can also replace the clam juice with chicken stock, vegetable stock or corn stock and serve it with poached or sautéed chicken breasts or fish.

Crab-stuffed
Zucchini Blossoms

Shiso leaf is a jagged-edged leaf that is part of the mint and basil family. You can find it in Asian markets. Use mint leaves if unavailable.

12 zucchini blossoms
8 ounces crabmeat, picked and drained
2 tablespoons lemon juice
2 tablespoons lime juice
1 tablespoon finely sliced basil
1 tablespoon finely sliced purple basil
1 tablespoon finely chopped chives
1 shiso leaf or 2 mint leaves, shredded
2 teaspoons olive oil
½ teaspoon grated lemon zest
½ teaspoon grated lime zest
½ teaspoon sherry vinegar
Salt and freshly ground black pepper
MAKES 12

Rinse the zucchini blossoms with cold water and remove the pistils. Pat dry with paper towels and set aside.

Combine the crab, lemon and lime juices, herbs, oil, grated zests and vinegar in a bowl. Add some salt and pepper. Stir until just mixed. Carefully stuff each of the zucchini blossoms with a heaped tablespoon of the mixture.

In a bamboo steamer set over boiling water, steam the flowers for 2 to 3 minutes just before serving.

NOTES

• The zucchini blossoms can be made 2 to 3 hours ahead and kept refrigerated.

• Infuse some tomato water with lemon verbena, then add some blanched ramps and asparagus tips. Divide the mixture between bowls, place a steamed stuffed zucchini blossom in each and serve garnished with dots of dill oil.

• Alternatively, fill the zucchini blossoms as above but coat them in Tempura Batter as on page 76 and serve with some Carrot Purée and a swirl of Lemongrass Sauce (page 87).

Burgundian Beef Stew

Slow, even cooking makes this classic stew highly deserving of its reputation.

5 pounds prime chuck steak, trimmed and cut into 1/2-inch pieces

3 bottles red wine (750 ml each), preferably Burgundy

2 medium red onions, cut into 1 1/4-inch pieces

3 stalks celery, cut into 1 1/4-inch pieces

1 large carrot, peeled, cut into 1-inch pieces

6 cloves garlic, peeled and smashed

11 tablespoons olive oil

5 sprigs thyme, plus 2 tablespoons fresh thyme leaves

2 bay leaves, crushed

3 sprigs parsley

1 tablespoon juniper berries, crushed

1 tablespoon black peppercorns, crushed

1 cup brandy

2 teaspoons salt

6 cups Brown Chicken Stock (see page 209)

A bouquet garni made with 2 bay leaves, 3 sprigs parsley and 3 sprigs thyme, tied together with string

1 teaspoon tomato paste

8 ounces pancetta, sliced 1/2-inch thick and cut into 1 1/2 × 1-inch lardons

3 tablespoons unsalted butter

1 pound small button mushrooms

SERVES 6 TO 8

In a large nonreactive bowl, combine the beef, 2 bottles of the red wine, the onions, celery, carrot, garlic, 6 tablespoons of the olive oil, 3 sprigs of thyme, the bay leaves, parsley, juniper berries and the peppercorns. Cover and marinate overnight in the refrigerator.

Line 2 baking sheets with kitchen towels. Strain the marinated meat through a medium sieve, reserving the liquid. Place the meat and vegetables separately on the prepared baking sheets. Add the reserved liquid and the remaining bottle of red wine to a large saucepan and bring to a boil over a medium-high heat. Simmer, skimming occasionally, until reduced to 1 to 1 1/2 cups in volume, about 1 hour. Set aside.

Meanwhile, in a wide, deep skillet large enough to hold one-third of the meat in one layer, heat 1 tablespoon of the olive oil over medium-high heat. Add 2 sprigs of the thyme and one-third of the meat. Cook for about 6 minutes, turning occasionally, until the meat is well

browned on all sides. Using a slotted spoon, transfer the meat to a large flameproof casserole. Drain the excess fat from the pan and discard.

Repeat the cooking procedure with the remaining meat, adding 1 tablespoon of oil for each batch. Drain any excess fat from the skillet and return it to the stove over medium-high heat. Add the brandy to the pan to deglaze it, stirring vigorously with a wooden spoon to incorporate the caramelized cooking juices in the base of the pan. Allow the brandy to reduce slightly, being careful if it ignites.

Strain the brandy and the reduced red wine mixture over the meat in the casserole and sprinkle in 1 teaspoon of salt.

Preheat the oven to 250°F. Wipe out the skillet with a paper towel, then add 2 teaspoons of olive oil and heat over medium-low heat. Pat the marinated vegetables dry and add them to the pan in two batches, cooking until well browned, about 10 minutes per batch. Transfer the cooked vegetables to the casserole.

Add the chicken stock and bouquet garni to the casserole. Place it over medium-high heat and bring to a boil, stirring occasionally and skimming as necessary. Cover and transfer the casserole to the oven. Cook for 3 to 3 1/2 hours, until the meat is meltingly tender.

Remove the casserole from the oven and use a slotted spoon to transfer the meat to a baking dish, cover and keep warm. Using a fine sieve, strain the sauce into a medium saucepan and discard the vegetables. Use a spoon to skim the fat from the surface. Stir in the tomato paste. Bring to a boil over medium-high heat then reduce to a brisk simmer and cook until the sauce has reduced to a volume of 1 1/2 cups, about 1 hour. Return the meat and reduced sauce to the casserole, cover and set aside. (The dish can be prepared up to this point one day in advance and refrigerated.)

Bring a small saucepan of water to a boil and blanch the pancetta for 30 to 45 seconds. Remove from the heat and drain.

In a large frying pan over medium heat, place 2 teaspoons of olive oil and the pancetta and cook for about 5 minutes or until crisp. Remove and drain on a paper towel, reserving the fat in the frying pan. Add the pancetta to the casserole.

Return the skillet to medium-high heat and add 2 tablespoons of butter to the reserved fat. Add the mushrooms and sauté for 5 to 6 minutes until golden brown, stirring frequently. Add the mushrooms to the casserole and stir gently to combine.

Using a slotted spoon, divide the beef, mushrooms and pancetta among 6 serving plates. Return the pan of sauce to the stove over medium heat. When slightly simmering, add 1 tablespoon of diced butter and whisk until the sauce is slightly thickened. Taste and adjust the seasoning if necessary, then divide the sauce among the plates. Sprinkle with thyme leaves before serving.

NOTES

• The sauce is very rich, so use it sparingly.
• Serve with Spiced Potato Pancakes (see page 99).
• Venison stewing meat can be substituted for the beef.

Buttermilk Fried
Chicken

2 chickens (about 2¹/₂ pounds each), cut into 8 pieces each
2 cups buttermilk
4 to 5 cups solid vegetable shortening
4 cups flour
Salt and freshly ground black pepper
SERVES 8

Combine the chicken, buttermilk, salt and pepper in a large bowl. Cover and marinate in the refrigerator for 1 hour.

Place the shortening in a large, deep heavy skillet, preferably cast-iron. Using a deep-fat thermometer, heat the shortening over medium heat until it reaches 350°F.

Spread 2 cups of flour in a shallow baking dish and season with salt and pepper. Remove half the chicken from the buttermilk and drain.

Add the chicken to the seasoned flour, tossing to coat, then lift out, shaking off any excess flour. Discard the flour. Preheat the oven to the lowest setting.

Fry 5 to 6 pieces of chicken at a time in the hot fat for 5 to 6 minutes, turning frequently.

When the chicken is golden brown, remove it to a baking sheet lined with parchment paper to drain, and keep warm. Repeat with the remaining flour and chicken.

NOTES

• The buttermilk draws out the sweetness and tenderness of the chicken.
• Serve with Sweet Chilli Sauce and Coco's Curls (see pages 213 and 147) and you have Chicken and Curls.

Grilled Chicken Sticks
with Fire-roasted Onions

For this recipe you will need 12 metal or bamboo skewers.

Fire-Roasted Onions (see page 148)
4 boneless, skinless chicken breast halves (about 1¹/₂ pounds total)
1¹/₂ cups BBQ Sauce (see page 212)
12 bay leaves
Salt and freshly ground black pepper
MAKES 12

Bake the Fire-Roasted Onions according to the recipe. Meanwhile, lightly pound the chicken breasts between 2 sheets of plastic wrap then cut each breast fillet into 3 pieces about 6 inches long by 1 to 1¹/₂ inches wide. Line a baking sheet with greaseproof paper and place the chicken on it. Season with salt and pepper.

If using bamboo skewers, soak them in cold water for 20 minutes to prevent burning while cooking.

Prepare a grill for a medium-high setting or preheat the broiler. Thread one piece of chicken onto each skewer. Open the parcels of Fire-Roasted Onions and drizzle the cooking juices over each piece of chicken. Add a cooked onion to each skewer, threading it on crosswise, then add a piece of bacon from each parcel, and finally a bay leaf. Season with salt and pepper.

Place the chicken sticks on the grill or broiler pan and brush each with about 1 tablespoon of the BBQ Sauce. Grill for 8 to 10 minutes, turning halfway through and basting a few times during cooking. Brush each chicken stick with another tablespoon of BBQ Sauce after grilling, then serve.

Chicken Stew
with Matzo Ball Dumplings

This is not gastronomical voodoo but it will capture the heart and soul of any mother.

1 lemon, halved
1 chicken (about 4 pounds), cut into 8 pieces
2 cups dry white wine
3 cloves garlic, thinly sliced
1 1/2 tablespoons fresh thyme leaves
1 1/2 tablespoons fresh rosemary
1 teaspoon dried red pepper flakes
Salt and freshly ground black pepper
1/4 cup olive oil
1/2 cup red onion, chopped
4 cups Brown Chicken Stock (see page 209)
A bouquet garni made from 6 sprigs parsley, 2 sprigs rosemary, and 2 bay leaves, tied together
1/2 cup large pitted green olives
FOR THE DUMPLINGS
3 ounces day-old white bread, crusts removed, cut into 1/2-inch cubes, plus 1/2 cup fresh bread crumbs
1/2 cup milk
3 teaspoons unsalted butter
3 teaspoons olive oil
1/4 cup finely chopped onion
2 ounces prosciutto, roughly chopped
2 eggs
2 tablespoons grated Parmigiano Reggiano
1 tablespoon finely chopped parsley
6 tablespoons matzo meal
Salt and freshly ground black pepper
Flour, for dusting
FOR THE TOMATO SAUCE
1 tablespoon olive oil
2 tablespoons finely chopped onion
1/2 stalk celery, finely chopped
1 clove garlic, finely chopped
1 pound plum tomatoes, peeled, seeded and chopped, juices reserved
1 teaspoon tomato paste
FOR THE GREMOLATA
1/4 cup finely chopped parsley
1 teaspoon finely chopped lemon zest

1 teaspoon finely chopped fresh rosemary
2 cloves garlic, finely chopped
SERVES 6

Squeeze the juice from one half of the lemon and thinly slice the remainder. Place them in a large nonreactive bowl with the chicken pieces, 1 cup of the wine, the garlic, thyme, rosemary, red pepper flakes and 1 teaspoon of salt. Cover and place in the refrigerator to marinate overnight.

Next day, remove the chicken from the marinade and pat dry with paper towels. Discard the marinade. Season the chicken with some salt and pepper. Heat 2 tablespoons of olive oil in a large casserole over medium-high heat. Add the breasts of the chicken and brown on all sides for about 8 to 10 minutes. Remove from the pan and set aside. Heat another 2 tablespoons of olive oil in the pan, reducing the heat to medium-low. Slowly brown the remaining chicken pieces, turning occasionally, for 20 to 25 minutes.

Meanwhile, begin the dumplings. Combine the cubed bread and the milk in a small bowl and leave them to soak for 15 minutes. Heat 1 teaspoon of the butter and 1 teaspoon of the olive oil in a small skillet over medium heat. Add the onion and cook for 3 minutes or until translucent. Transfer the onion to a medium bowl and stir in the prosciutto, eggs, cheese, parsley, 1/4 teaspoon of salt and a large pinch of pepper. When combined, stir in the soaked bread and milk, then the matzo meal and fresh bread crumbs. Set aside to rest for 30 minutes.

Remove the browned chicken pieces and pour off any fat in the casserole but do not wipe it clean. Return the casserole to the heat and add the red onion. Cook over a medium heat until the onion begins to color, being careful not to burn the caramelized cooking juices in the base of the pan.

Add the remaining 1 cup of wine to the casserole, allowing it to reduce to a glazing consistency while you stir vigorously with a wooden spoon to incorporate the caramelized crust. After 2 to 3 minutes, add 1 1/2 cups of the chicken stock and the bouquet garni to the pan, then return all the chicken except the breasts, and simmer, covered, over a medium-low heat for 30 minutes.

Meanwhile, make the tomato sauce. Heat the olive oil in a small saucepan over medium heat. Add the onion, celery, garlic and 2 tablespoons of water. Cook for 5 minutes or until the vegetables are soft. Add the chopped tomatoes with their juices, tomato paste and 1/4 teaspoon of salt and cook for another 15 minutes.

While the casserole and tomato sauce are simmering, use well-floured hands to shape the dumpling mixture into 16 equal balls. In a small nonstick frying pan, heat 2 teaspoons of butter and 2 teaspoons of olive oil over medium-low heat and gently brown the dumplings all over, cooking them for about 4 minutes in total.

Remove the chicken from the casserole and set aside in a warm place. Discard the bouquet garni then raise the heat to medium-high. Bring the sauce to a boil and reduce by three-quarters, about 5 minutes.

Lower the heat to medium and add the tomato sauce along with another 2 cups of chicken stock. Stir, then return the chicken pieces, except the breasts, to the casserole and add the browned dumplings. Cover and cook for 5 to 8 minutes.

Meanwhile, in a small bowl, combine all the ingredients for the gremolata, then add it to the casserole with the olives, 1 teaspoon of salt and $1/2$ teaspoon of freshly ground black pepper. Return the chicken breasts to the casserole, tucking them neatly under the sauce. Add the remaining $1/2$ cup of chicken stock if necessary. Cook uncovered over a low heat for 8 to 10 minutes until the sauce thickens slightly. Adjust the seasoning to taste, remove from the heat and serve.

Duck "ham" Skewers
with Figs and Rosemary

The vanilla, mint and citrus combination in this glaze is wild.

2 duck breasts, excess fat removed
1 tablespoon salt
1 teaspoon freshly ground black pepper, plus extra to season
2 bay leaves, crushed
4 juniper berries, smashed
3 whole cloves
3 cloves garlic
10 small sprigs rosemary
5 fresh figs, halved lengthwise
FOR THE GLAZE
$1/2$ cup freshly squeezed orange juice
$1/4$ cup freshly squeezed lemon juice
$1/4$ cup freshly squeezed grapefruit juice
$1/4$ cup sugar
2 fresh figs, chopped into $1/4$-inch cubes
1 sprig mint
$1/4$ vanilla pod, split lengthwise
MAKES 10

Use a knife to make hatch marks in the skin of each duck breast. Combine the salt, pepper, bay leaves and juniper berries in a small bowl and rub the mixture all over the duck breasts.

Place the duck breasts slightly overlapping lengthwise in a non-reactive dish. Press a clove into each clove of garlic and tuck the garlic between the duck breasts. Leave in the refrigerator to marinate for 24 hours.

To make the glaze, mix the juices and sugar in a saucepan and boil over a high heat for about 10 minutes or until the mixture has reduced to $1/2$ cup. Keep warm until you are almost ready to cook the duck, then add the chopped fig. Add the mint and vanilla pod and leave to infuse for 5 minutes before removing.

When ready to cook, prepare (medium heat) a grill or preheat the broiler. Remove the duck breasts from the dish, thoroughly wipe off the marinade and pat dry. Cut each duck breast lengthwise into 5 strips. Weave each strip onto a metal skewer, about 10 inches long,

then top with a sprig of rosemary. Add a fig half and season with freshly ground pepper.

Grill or broil the skewers for 3 to 4 minutes, carefully turning over halfway through cooking. Remove from the heat and pour the fig glaze over before serving.

NOTES

• This is a classic way of curing duck legs for confit but also works well with duck breasts.
• Make sure the figs are just ripe.
• The glaze can also be used on chicken, pork, even lobster.

Halloween Chicken
with willow sticks

For this recipe you will need 16 to 18 willow sticks, trimmed and soaked in cold water for at least 2 hours to prevent them burning during cooking. The willow sticks can be found on your next foraging expedition.

4 boneless, skinless chicken breast halves (about 1$\frac{1}{2}$ pounds total)
Olive oil, for brushing
FOR THE MARINADE
$\frac{1}{4}$ cup tamari or soy sauce
2$\frac{1}{2}$ teaspoons honey
2 tablespoons mirin
1 teaspoon toasted sesame oil
2 tablespoons rice wine vinegar
FOR THE SAUCE
$\frac{1}{2}$ cup Sweet Chilli Sauce (see recipe page 213)
1$\frac{1}{2}$ tablespoons lime juice
3 tablespoons finely chopped green onions
SERVES 6 TO 8

Lightly brush the chicken breasts with olive oil. Place each chicken breast between 2 sheets of plastic wrap and pound to an even thickness of $\frac{1}{2}$ inch. Cut a total of 16 to 18 pieces, measuring approximately 5 x 1 inch.

Thoroughly combine all the ingredients for the marinade in a small bowl. Place the chicken in a shallow baking dish, pour on the marinade and coat evenly. Marinate the chicken in the refrigerator for 20 minutes.

Preheat the oven to 350°F and heat a cast-iron grill pan over medium heat, lightly brushing the pan with oil. Remove the chicken from the marinade and pat it with paper towels to dry. Thread the chicken pieces onto the willow sticks (or metal skewers) then divide them into 3 or 4 batches for cooking.

To cook the chicken, place one batch on the grill pan and cook for 1$\frac{1}{2}$ minutes, then rotate the chicken 90 degrees and cook for another 1$\frac{1}{2}$ minutes to create cross-hatch marks. Turn the chicken over and grill for a further 1 minute. Transfer to a baking dish and set aside while you cook the remaining chicken. Cover the baking dish

with foil and place in the oven for 5 minutes or until cooked through. Meanwhile, combine the ingredients for the sauce in a bowl. Remove the chicken sticks from the oven and spoon some sauce over each one. Serve warm with the leftover sauce in a bowl for dipping.

Curried Lamb Shanks

Warming winter food, this casserole has great authentic Asian undertones of curry leaves, ginger and sour-tangy tamarind.

6 lamb shanks, trimmed of excess fat

4$^{1}/_{2}$ to 8$^{1}/_{2}$ tablespoons olive oil

1 pound onions, peeled and thinly sliced

10 cloves garlic, peeled and chopped

1 tablespoon minced fresh ginger

2 green apples, peeled, cored and cut into $^{1}/_{4}$-inch cubes

2 cups white wine

5 cups Brown Chicken Stock (see recipe page 209)

A bouquet garni made from 6 sprigs of mint and 15 sprigs of coriander, folded in half and tied with string

10 curry leaves

2 teaspoons salt

2 rounded teaspoons tamarind

3 plum tomatoes, peeled, seeded and chopped

Yellow Dhal, to serve (see recipe page 114)

FOR THE GARAM MASALA

1 tablespoon yellow mustard seeds

2 tablespoons cumin seeds

1 tablespoon coriander seeds

2 sticks cinnamon

$^{1}/_{2}$ teaspoon fennel seeds

1 tablespoon green cardamom pods (remove the shell)

1 tablespoon black peppercorns

4 star anise

6 tablespoons ground turmeric

1 tablespoon salt

$^{1}/_{2}$ teaspoon cayenne pepper

FOR THE MARINADE

1 medium onion, peeled and thinly sliced

1 carrot, peeled and thinly sliced

4 cloves garlic, peeled and crushed

4 sprigs thyme

10 curry leaves

SERVES 6

To make the garam masala, combine the mustard, cumin, coriander, cinnamon, fennel, cardamom seeds, peppercorns and star anise in a dry frying pan over a medium heat. Toast them for 1 to 2 minutes, stirring, until fragrant. Grind the toasted spices to a fine powder using a spice mill or mortar and pestle. Then place the spice mix in a small bowl and stir in the turmeric, salt and cayenne. Set 8 tablespoons of the spice mixture aside.

In a large nonreactive bowl, mix the remaining garam masala with all the marinade ingredients, then add the lamb shanks and stir to thoroughly coat the meat. Leave to marinate in the refrigerator for several hours or up to 2 days, turning often.

Preheat the oven to 325°F. Remove the shanks from the marinade, leaving some of the marinade on the meat but discarding the onions, carrots and herbs.

Heat 3 to 4 tablespoons of olive oil in a large heavy flameproof casserole over a medium heat and brown the shanks in 2 batches, for about 5 minutes per side, adding more oil to the pan for the second batch if necessary. Remove the shanks from the pan and set aside.

Pour out the excess cooking oil from the casserole, then add 1$^{1}/_{2}$ tablespoons of oil to the casserole plus the onions, garlic, ginger and apples and cook over a low heat, stirring often, until soft, for 10 to 15 minutes. Add 7$^{1}/_{2}$ tablespoons of the reserved garam masala, stir and cook for 1 to 2 minutes.

Increase the heat to medium-high and add the white wine to the pan, stirring vigorously to incorporate the caramelized cooking juices. Return the lamb shanks to the pan, stir and add the stock, bouquet garni, curry leaves and salt. Bring to the boil, cover, then place the casserole on the middle shelf of the oven and cook for about 2$^{1}/_{2}$ hours or until the meat is just falling off the bone.

Meanwhile, place the tamarind concentrate in a small bowl with 2 tablespoons of hot water and stir to dissolve. Strain and reserve 2 tablespoons of the tamarind liquid.

Remove the casserole from the oven, lift out the lamb shanks and set them aside in a warm place. Strain the sauce, discarding the solids, and wipe out the casserole. Place the strained sauce in the casserole over a high heat. Bring to the boil and boil vigorously for about 30 minutes or until the sauce has reduced to a volume of about 2 cups. Add the tamarind liquid. Skim as necessary. Stir in the chopped tomatoes and keep warm until ready to serve.

Meanwhile, reheat the lamb shanks in the oven. Arrange the dhal in the center of 6 serving plates, place the lamb shanks on top and divide half the sauce among them. Sprinkle the dishes with the remaining $^{1}/_{2}$ tablespoon of garam masala and a pinch of salt and serve, accompanied by the leftover sauce.

Yellow Dhal

1 cup chana or toovar dhal
1 tablespoon ground turmeric
1 bay leaf
3/4 teaspoon salt
1/4 teaspoon cayenne pepper
3 tablespoons grapeseed oil or ghee
1 teaspoon cumin seeds
1 tablespoon finely sliced fresh red chilli
1 tablespoon finely sliced jalapeño chilli
3 tablespoons finely sliced shallot
1 medium tomato, cored and chopped
1 tablespoon pickled chilli brine (see page 204, optional)
MAKES 2 CUPS

Pick over the dhal and wash it under cold running water. In a large saucepan, place the dhal over high heat and lightly toast it, stirring, for 2 minutes.

Add 3 1/2 cups of cold water to the pan and stir in the turmeric, bay leaf, salt and cayenne pepper. Bring to a boil, lower the heat, partially cover and simmer for about 1 hour – the dhal should be tender and the liquid absorbed but not dry. Add another 1/2 cup of hot water if the dhal seems to be thickening too quickly.

During the final 5 minutes of the dhal's cooking time, heat the oil in a small skillet over medium heat and add the cumin seeds. Cook for 30 seconds until the seeds start to pop. Add the chillies and shallot to the cumin and cook, stirring, for 1 to 2 minutes until the shallot softens. Add the chopped tomatoes, stir and fry until softened.

When the dhal is cooked, remove it from the heat and stir in the pickled chilli brine (if using). Pour the contents of the frying pan into the dhal and stir to combine. Serve.

NOTES

• Serve underneath the Curried Lamb Shanks (see page 113).
• This makes a perfect small dish if served with Pita Bread (see page 219).

Lamb and Herb
sausages

2 pounds minced lamb, 1/4 of the weight in fat
1/2 cup finely grated Pecorino cheese
2 tablespoons finely chopped garlic
3 tablespoons chopped mint
1 1/2 tablespoons chopped parsley
1 1/2 teaspoons sweet paprika
2 teaspoons freshly ground black pepper
1 1/2 teaspoons salt
1/2 teaspoon cayenne pepper
11 feet narrow sausage casing, soaked in cold water
Olive oil, for brushing
MAKES 25

In a large bowl, combine the lamb, cheese, garlic, herbs, paprika, pepper, salt, cayenne and 3 tablespoons of cold water. Mix well with your hands. Form a tiny patty from the mixture and fry it, then taste and adjust the quantities of herbs and spices as necessary.

Thread the casing onto the nozzle of the sink tap and turn on the cold water to rinse away all traces of salt and residue on the casing.

Using the sausage attachment of an electric mixer, attach the open end of the casing to the nozzle and thread the required length toward the end of the nozzle. Add the lamb mixture then turn on the machine. With your hands, guide the casing so that it fills at a regular pace. To create sausage links, twist the casing at 5-inch intervals. Alternatively, you can shape the mixture into small patties.

To cook the sausages, brush them lightly with olive oil and grill or broil for 2 to 3 minutes on each side.

NOTES

• These are fresh sausages, made without nitrates or additives, so cook them within a day or two of making.
• I get the casings from the village butcher and they will keep in the refrigerator for months; alternatively, freeze them in batches for use as needed.
• Serve with Mini Goat Cheese Burgers (right) and Brioche rolls (see page 196)
• Brush the sausages with herb brushes (see pages 200–201) before grilling.

Mini Goat Cheese
Burgers

2¹/₂ pounds minced lean beef
2¹/₂ ounces goat cheese, softened
1 teaspoon finely chopped fresh thyme leaves
A pinch of cayenne
Oil, for brushing
3¹/₂ tablespoons Moroccan Spices (see page 216)
Salt and freshly ground black pepper
MAKES 10

Place the meat in a large bowl and season it generously with salt and pepper. Mix to combine the seasoning. In a small bowl, beat together the goat cheese, thyme and cayenne until well combined. Roll the goat cheese into 5 balls of equal size, about 1 inch in diameter.

Divide the meat into 10 equal portions. Place a portion of meat in the palm of your hand and shape it into a burger. Make an indentation with a finger in the center of the burger, place a goat cheese ball in the indentation and wrap the meat mixture around to enclose it completely. Repeat with the remaining goat cheese balls to give a total of 5 goat cheese burgers.

Form the remaining portions of meat into burgers and brush each one with a little olive oil. Pat about 1 teaspoon of Moroccan spices onto each side of each burger so that the spices adhere to the meat.

Heat a cast-iron grill pan over a moderate heat or prepare the grill (medium heat). Season the goat cheese burgers with salt and pepper and grill for about 4 minutes per side to give a medium-rare burger. Cook the unstuffed burgers for about 4 to 5 minutes per side for medium-rare. Serve hot.

NOTE

• Serve with Lamb and Herb Sausages (left) and Brioche rolls (see page 196).

Julie's Meatballs
in tomato sauce

Every Sunday my mother, Julie, would make 10 to 12 large meatballs, fry them and place them in her tomato sauce. But by the time dinner was served, the sauce would be meatless.

FOR THE TOMATO SAUCE
3 14-ounce cans peeled plum tomatoes
1 tablespoon olive oil
1 medium onion, finely chopped
1 clove garlic, finely chopped
6 basil leaves
¹/₂ teaspoon sugar
A pat of butter
Salt and freshly ground black pepper
FOR THE MEATBALLS
3 ounces crustless white bread, torn into small pieces (about 1¹/₂ cups)
¹/₄ cup milk
5¹/₂ ounces minced beef, preferably chuck
5¹/₂ ounces minced pork
1 large egg
2 tablespoons finely chopped onion
2 tablespoons freshly grated Parmigiano Reggiano
2 teaspoons finely chopped parsley
2 tablespoons olive oil
MAKES 24

Pass the tomatoes and juices through a food mill fitted with a medium disc, discarding the solids.

To make the tomato sauce, heat the olive oil in a large saucepan over a moderately high heat and add the onion. Cook for 3 to 4 minutes or until the onion is translucent. Add the garlic, season with salt and pepper, then add the puréed tomatoes and basil and reduce the heat to medium. Cook the sauce for about 50 minutes, stirring occasionally, until the sauce is thick and has reduced to a volume of 2 cups. Stir in the sugar and butter, then adjust the seasoning to taste.

Meanwhile, make the meatballs. Soak the bread in the milk for about 5 minutes. In a medium bowl, combine the meats, egg, onion, cheese, parsley and some salt and pepper. Add the soaked bread and any milk left in the bowl and stir until thoroughly combined. Refrigerate the mixture for 30 minutes, then form it into 24 balls about 1¹/₄ inch in diameter.

Heat 1 tablespoon of the olive oil in a large frying pan over medium heat. Cook half the meatballs gently for 5 to 7 minutes until well browned all over, then transfer them to a baking sheet lined with greaseproof paper. Heat the remaining 1 tablespoon of oil in the skillet and cook the remaining meatballs.

Add all the meatballs to the sauce, stirring gently to coat, and cook through gently over low heat for about 10 minutes. Serve.

NOTE

• You can toss the tomato sauce and meatballs with cooked plain spaghetti, or use the mixture to fill pumpkins at Hallowe'en.

Roast Pork with Prune
and Quince Stuffing

FOR THE BRINE

3/4 cup sugar

6 tablespoons salt

1 teaspoon each of juniper berries, black peppercorns, yellow mustard seeds and fennel seeds

6 cloves garlic, smashed

3 bay leaves, cracked

10 sprigs thyme

1 boneless pork loin (5 to 5 1/2 pounds and 16 inches long; skin and 1/2 inch of fat removed in one piece, reserved for crackling)

FOR THE PRUNE AND QUINCE STUFFING

1/3 cup pitted prunes, sliced thinly lengthwise

1/4 cup Armagnac

4 tablespoons lemon juice

1 small quince, cut into 1/4-inch cubes (about 1 cup)

1 1/2 teaspoons unsalted butter

1 tablespoon olive oil

1/2 cup finely chopped onion

1 1/2 stalks celery, finely chopped (about 1/2 cup)

1 small clove garlic, crushed

2 tablespoons Calvados

1 cup Brown Chicken Stock, Vegetable Stock or water (see recipes on pages 209 and 210)

1 1/2 teaspoons finely chopped thyme

1 1/2 teaspoons finely chopped sage

1 teaspoon finely chopped parsley

Salt and freshly ground black pepper

FOR THE GAME CRUMBS

1 1/2 teaspoons olive oil

1 tablespoon unsalted butter

1 small clove garlic, smashed

1 cup tiny bread cubes, cut from a baguette

1 1/2 teaspoons red wine vinegar

FOR THE PORK

3 tablespoons balsamic vinegar

3 tablespoons red wine vinegar

1 1/2 tablespoons olive oil

6 cloves garlic, unpeeled

10 sprigs thyme

10 sage leaves

SERVES 6 TO 8

Make the brine by dissolving the sugar and salt in 1$^1/_2$ gallons of warm water. Set aside to cool. Combine the bay leaves and spices in a spice grinder and grind them coarsely.

Place the pork in a large nonreactive roasting pan and rub the bay leaf, spices and garlic into the meat. Pour the cooled brine over the pork and add the thyme. Completely submerge the pork in the brine, weighting it down if necessary. Refrigerate for 24 hours, rotating occasionally.

To make the stuffing, soak the prunes in the Armagnac for at least 2 hours. To a small saucepan, add 2 cups of water, 3 tablespoons of the lemon juice and the quince. Place over high heat and bring to a boil. Lower the heat and simmer for 5 to 6 minutes or until the quince is just tender. Strain and set aside.

Meanwhile, in a medium skillet over medium heat, add the butter and olive oil. When hot, add the onion, celery and garlic, stir and cook for 2 minutes. Add 1 tablespoon of water and cook until translucent, about 3 to 4 minutes. Add the cooked quince and Calvados and cook for 1 to 2 minutes, stirring; add the prune mixture and cook another minute.

Increase the heat to medium-high, pour in the stock and simmer for 3 to 4 minutes, stirring gently, until the liquid has reduced by three-quarters and the pan's contents are almost dry but there is still some liquid remaining.

To make the game crumbs, heat the oil and butter in a large frying pan over medium-high heat. When the mixture is hot and foaming, add the garlic and bread cubes. Increase the heat to high and sauté, stirring constantly, until brown and crisp, about 4 minutes. Add the vinegar and continue to sauté until crisp again. Season.

Fold the game crumbs into the prune mixture, then add the herbs and the remaining 1 tablespoon of lemon juice.

Preheat the oven to 400°F. Remove the pork from the brine and pat it dry with paper towels. Butterfly the pork, using a long slicing knife to make an even cut lengthwise down the middle of the pork to a depth of 1 inch from the bottom. Open the cut pork out like a book, pounding it very slightly at the base of the cut.

Season the meat with salt and pepper, then spoon the stuffing down the center in the crevice. Fold one side of meat back over the stuffing to meet the other side and tie the pork up securely at 3-inch intervals with kitchen string.

In a small bowl, mix together the balsamic and red wine vinegars and set aside.

In a large roasting pan over medium-high heat, add the 1$^1/_2$ tablespoons olive oil and brown the pork on all sides. Remove the pork from the pan and set aside on a baking sheet.

Drain the fat from the roasting pan, then add the unpeeled garlic, thyme and sage leaves and place the pork on top of them. Place in the oven or alternatively hang the pork from a hook and chain in front of an open fire with a drip pan underneath. Roast the pork for 50 minutes or until it reaches an internal temperature of 160°F, brushing it every 15 minutes with the mixture of balsamic and red wine vinegars.

When cooked, remove the pork from the roasting pan and set aside to rest for 10 minutes. Strain the cooking juices from the pan through a sieve and let stand for a few minutes before skimming off any excess fat that rises to the surface. Remove the string from the pork and carve the meat. Pour the reserved pan juices over the meat and serve.

NOTES

• Pork and fruit is a classic combination and mixing prunes with the meat is especially popular in the Gascony region of France.
• The brine tenderizes and breaks down the meat tissue, but take care not to marinate it for too long.
• The game crumbs can also be sprinkled over oven-roasted fish, racks of lamb, slow-roasted garlic tomatoes and any duck, pheasant or squab dish.

PORK CRACKLING

Use a sharp knife to remove the skin and $^1/_2$ inch of the fat beneath it from the pork loin. Then score the rind to a depth of $^1/_4$ inch, cutting straight lines across the skin in one direction, then the other, to give a crosshatched effect. The width of the lines will determine the size of the crackling portions.

The crackling needs to be supported during cooking and this can be done simply by scrunching balls of kitchen foil and arranging them on a baking tray. Lay the skin over the top, rub the cut side of a lemon directly on the skin and sprinkle generously with salt and pepper. Place the baking tray in the oven at 350°F and cook the crackling until it is browned and crispy. Alternatively, the crackling can be placed in front of an open fire to cook, adjusting the position of the baking tray as necessary to ensure even cooking.

Roast Chicken with Corn, Fava Beans and Tomatoes

3¼ ounces (½ cup) fava beans

2 to 3 plum tomatoes, cored

2 whole chickens (3 to 3½ pounds each)

5 tablespoons olive oil

3 teaspoons salt

Freshly ground black pepper

8 sprigs marjoram

½ lemon, seeds removed

4 cloves garlic, peeled and halved

4 to 5 corns on the cob to give 4 cups raw kernels

¾ cup Corn Stock, Vegetable Stock (see pages 211 and 210) or water

Red Pepper Juice Oil (see page 140), optional

FOR THE BASIL BUTTER

1 clove garlic, finely chopped

4 tablespoons unsalted butter, softened

8 basil leaves, finely chopped

FOR THE CARAMELIZED ONION AND GARLIC SAUCE (OPTIONAL)

½ pound onions, thinly sliced

3 cloves garlic, sliced into thirds, or smashed

2 tablespoons unsalted butter

1 teaspoon oil

¼ cup Madeira

½ ounce dried porcini, soaked and rinsed clean

3 cups Brown Chicken Stock (see page 209)

2 sprigs tarragon

Salt and freshly ground black pepper

SERVES 4 TO 6

Thoroughly combine all the ingredients for the basil butter in a small bowl and place in the refrigerator to chill.

In a pan of boiling salted water, blanch the fava beans for about 30 seconds then drain under cold running water and peel off the skins. Set the beans aside.

Cut a cross in the base of each tomato. Plunge them into boiling water for about 30 seconds to 1 minute then remove. Place under cold running water. Peel, seed and chop the tomatoes. Set aside.

Meanwhile make the Caramelized Onion and Garlic Sauce (if using). In a medium saucepan over a moderate heat, cook the onions and garlic with 1 tablespoon of butter and the oil, stirring occasionally, for about 20 minutes or until caramelized.

Add the Madeira and porcini, bring to a boil and simmer for 3 to 4 minutes or until the liquid has almost evaporated. Add the chicken stock, return to the boil and briskly simmer over a medium heat for 20 minutes.

Strain the mixture into a smaller pan and reduce over a high heat, skimming as necessary, until the volume of liquid has reduced to ⅔ cup. Remove from the heat, add the tarragon sprigs and set aside to infuse for 10 minutes. Remove the tarragon from the sauce, bring it to a low simmer and whisk in the remaining butter. Season with salt and pepper.

Split the chickens in half and remove the backbones. Leaving the wings attached and the skin on, separate the breasts from the leg and thigh sections. Remove the wing tips. Leaving the thighs and drumsticks attached, remove the thigh bones.

Preheat the oven to 450°F. Place a casserole large enough to hold the 4 chicken breasts over moderate-high heat. Add 3 tablespoons of the olive oil and, when hot, add the 4 chicken breasts, skin-side down. Sprinkle with 1 teaspoon of salt, a few grinds of pepper and half the marjoram. Cook for 3 to 4 minutes or until browned and crisp. Turn, adding another teaspoon of salt and some more pepper and cook until browned, about 2 minutes. With metal tongs, hold the chicken breasts on their sides to ensure they are browned all over, then remove from casserole and set aside in a baking pan.

Reduce the heat to medium. Add 2 tablespoons of olive oil to the casserole and cook the chicken leg-thigh pieces skin-side down for 4 to 5 minutes or until brown. Sprinkle with ½ teaspoon of salt, a little pepper and the remaining marjoram. Turn and cook for 2½ to 3 minutes, adding another ½ teaspoon of salt and a little more pepper. Using metal tongs, turn the chicken thighs onto their sides and brown. Remove from the casserole to the baking pan.

Squeeze the lemon over the chicken and top with the marjoram sprigs. Add the garlic over the chicken and place in the oven for 14 to 16 minutes.

Meanwhile, in a medium saucepan over medium-high heat, add the raw corn kernels and Corn Stock and bring to the boil, stirring. Cook for 2 minutes, or until creamy, then add the fava beans and season with salt and pepper. Using a wooden spoon, stir in the basil butter. When it is fully incorporated into the corn mixture, remove the saucepan from the heat and set it aside in a warm place for up to 5 minutes. Remove the chicken from the oven and place on a cutting board. Cut the remaining carcass bones away from underneath the breasts. Stir the chopped tomato into the corn mixture, then divide it among 4 serving plates with a slotted spoon. Place the chicken pieces on top of the corn mixture and spoon the onion sauce around the corn. Drizzle some red pepper juice oil around each plate and serve.

NOTES

• When removing the corn from the cob, be sure to cut just into the cob to release the milky sweet flavor of the whole corn.
• Use a sharp knife when chopping the basil to avoid bruising it.
• Your butcher can prepare the chicken for you, if asked.

Roast Duck

Lake House ducks are incredible. They have just the right amount of fat to meat and a real gaminess of flavor that is not overpowering.

1 teaspoon cloves
1 teaspoon green peppercorns
2 bay leaves
1 tablespoon salt
1 duckling (5 to 6 pounds) with excess fat removed
FOR THE STUFFING
1 pear, cut into 6 pieces
3 tablespoons chopped fresh ginger
6 sprigs thyme
Salt and freshly ground black pepper
FOR THE SAUCE AND GLAZE
3 cups Brown Chicken Stock (see page 209)
5 slices fresh ginger, $1/4$ inch thick
2 tablespoons honey
2 teaspoons sherry vinegar
SERVES 4

Using a spice grinder or mortar and pestle, coarsely grind the cloves, green peppercorns, and bay leaves then mix with the salt. Sprinkle the spice mixture over the duck and rub until well distributed. Place the duck in a large bowl, cover and refrigerate for several hours or overnight, turning it 1 or 2 times during marinating.

Preheat the oven to 500°F. Bring the duck to room temperature and wipe the marinade from the duck with a paper towel. Place it in a roasting pan on a rack. Stuff the cavity with the pear, ginger and thyme and season with salt and pepper. Place the duck in the oven with the legs facing the back of the oven (or attach to a spit in front of an open fire), and roast for 50 minutes, rotating the bird once during cooking.

Meanwhile, make the sauce and glaze. In a medium saucepan, bring the stock, ginger and honey to a boil, stirring to combine, and simmer for 40 minutes or until the volume of liquid has reduced to $1 1/3$ cups. Strain and stir in the sherry vinegar then measure out $1/3$ cup to use as a glaze, reserving the remaining 1 cup for the sauce.

After the duck has been roasting for 50 minutes, remove it from the oven and pour off the rendered duck fat in the pan, reserving it for another use. Baste the bird with half the reserved glaze and return it to the oven for $2 1/2$ minutes. Baste with the remaining glaze and roast for another $2 1/2$ minutes.

Remove the duck from the oven and let it rest for 15 to 20 minutes. If the legs are too rare, reduce the oven to 400°F and remove the breasts, legs and thighs from the bird. Set the breasts aside and return the legs and thighs to the oven for 15 minutes.

Combine the cooking juices from the duck with the remaining glaze in a small saucepan. Bring to a boil and simmer for 5 to 10 minutes to give about $1/2$ cup of sauce. Serve alongside the duck.

NOTES

• With the duck, serve some blanched baby carrots tossed in brown butter and chopped parsley.
• Use the rendered duck fat to roast some tiny new potatoes and garnish with a little lavender – we have it growing in the front walk at Lake House.

ROASTING OVER AN OPEN FIRE

• The attraction of cooking over an open fire is immense: a mysterious combination of the sight of the naked flame, the warmth of the glowing coals and the scent of the smoke which result in sensational flavoring of the food. Such cooking should not be confined to the summer months, but can be enjoyed any time of year, indoors or out.

• Cooking over an open fire is one of the oldest culinary methods and is simple to do, although you will find it takes some trial and error. Spit roasting can be done in your own fireplace. Any kind of mature hardwood charcoal can be used to fuel the fire, but commercial coal briquettes are not recommended as they are chemically treated and do not generate sufficient heat. At Lake House, we gather old grape vines and other such fruit wood varieties, soak them in water, then add them to the fire. This creates a scented smoke that permeates the food and enhances the flavor.

• For spit roasting chicken, duck, pheasant, squab or quail, a horizontal spit can be set up in front of the fire and the meat threaded evenly along it. To avoid burning, make sure the birds are as uniform in size as possible. Turn the spit manually at regular intervals throughout cooking.

• When roasting beef, lamb or pork, boned joints should be tied then hung vertically in front of the fire, suspended from a metal chain attached to hooks on the mantel of the fireplace. Twist the chain manually to ensure the joint rotates steadily throughout the cooking process. This vertical roasting method can also be used for joints such as a leg of lamb, where the chain needs to be attached to the shank bone, just above the heel.

• Place a drip pan on the hearth below the meat to catch the juices that drip while it cooks. The meat should also be regularly basted to moisten it and enhance the flavor.

• The recipes for roasting duck, lamb and pork in this book stipulate conventional oven temperatures and the cooking times required. If, however, you choose to try spit roasting, the same internal cooking temperatures will apply, though the cooking time will vary according to the fire and the type of wood or charcoal used to fuel it.

Roast rolled Leg of Lamb
with chilli paste

A Moroccan mechoui is a spit-roasted whole baby lamb. This recipe simulates it, adding subtle Mexican overtones. The garlic has a toasty sweetness when it is baked.

1 leg of lamb (5 to 6 pounds), boned and butterflied
6 cloves garlic, thinly sliced into slivers
2 rosemary sprigs
3 sprigs parsley
1 tablespoon olive oil
1 large red onion, roughly chopped
1 carrot, roughly chopped
1 stalk celery, roughly chopped
2 large handfuls thyme sprigs, broken
FOR THE MARINADE
1½ cups red Burgundy wine
¼ cup olive oil
1 medium onion, thinly sliced
Leaves of 2 small sprigs rosemary
1 teaspoon salt
1 teaspoon black peppercorns, crushed
FOR THE BASTE
2 heads garlic, plus extra 3 cloves, trimmed and unpeeled
½ cup freshly squeezed lemon juice
¼ cup white wine
⅓ cup olive oil
1 tablespoon paprika
2 teaspoons salt
FOR THE CHILLI PASTE
2 teaspoons cumin seeds
¼ teaspoon fennel seeds
2 star anise
2 New Mexican chillies
3 tablespoons olive oil
1½ teaspoons paprika
½ teaspoon ground cinnamon
1 teaspoon cocoa powder
½ teaspoon salt
SERVES 8

Trim the lamb to remove any excess fat. Make shallow incisions in the meat and insert a sliver of garlic in each one. Place it in a large,

Trim the lamb to remove any excess fat. Make shallow incisions in the meat and insert a sliver of garlic in each one. Place it in a large, nonreactive dish big enough to lay the meat flat. Evenly distribute all the marinade ingredients. Cover and marinate for 4 hours or overnight in the refrigerator, turning frequently.

Meanwhile, make the baste. Separate the garlic cloves from the whole heads of garlic, leaving the skin on, and place them in a skillet over low heat with the extra 3 garlic cloves. Roast the garlic cloves for 15 to 18 minutes, turning them once or twice during cooking. When soft, set aside 3 of the cloves then remove the skin of the remaining cloves and mash them to a smooth paste using the flat side of a knife. You should have about 1/2 cup of garlic paste. Place the paste in a bowl with the lemon juice, white wine, oil, paprika and salt and whisk until evenly combined. Set aside.

To make the chilli paste, toast the cumin, fennel and star anise in a small skillet until the seeds start to pop. Remove from the heat, place in a spice mill, finely grind and set aside. Toast the New Mexican chillis over an open flame or in the skillet until dry and crackly, then deseed, core and chop the flesh roughly. Grind the chilli flesh and add it to the toasted spice mixture. Set aside.

Peel and mash the reserved 3 roasted garlic cloves and add them to the chilli mixture along with the olive oil, paprika, cinnamon, cocoa powder, and salt. Mix thoroughly to combine and set aside.

Preheat the oven to 350°F. Remove the lamb from the marinade and pat dry, discarding the marinade. Lay the leg of lamb flat across a cutting board, skin-side down, with the long side facing you. Using a spatula, spread the chilli paste over the entire surface, then lay the rosemary and parsley sprigs down the center of the meat. Roll up the meat on a diagonal and tie tightly at regular intervals.

Heat the olive oil in a large frying pan over medium-high heat and brown the rolled lamb on all sides, turning, for a total of 10 to 12 minutes. Meanwhile, place the chopped onion, carrot, celery and thyme leaves in a medium roasting pan. When the lamb is browned, place it on top of the vegetables in the center of the roasting pan.

Transfer to the middle rack of the oven and roast for 1 hour 10 mintues, basting with the garlic mixture three or four times during cooking. Alternatively, hang the lamb from a hook and chain in front of an open fire and place a drip pan directly under the meat. Roast, turning and basting frequently during cooking. The lamb is cooked when a meat thermometer reads an internal temperature of 125°F for rare, 145°F for medium rare, and 160°F for medium.

Leave the meat to rest for about 20 minutes before slicing.

NOTES

• The pan juices from roasting the lamb can be served as a sauce.
• Serve with 5 or 6 heads of roasted garlic, some Roast Carrot Confit (pages 217 and 148) and a bowl of couscous that you have flavored with butter, cinnamon and minced Preserved Lemon (see page 205).
• Alternatively, roughly chop the leftover lamb, mix it with some tomato sauce and cook slowly until tender. Pour over Baked Polenta (see page 124).

Turkey Sticks with
orange cheese sauce

1 pound boneless, skinless turkey breast
1/2 teaspoon salt
1 1/4 cups fresh bread crumbs, toasted
2 teaspoons turmeric
1 teaspoon paprika
1/4 teaspoon freshly grated nutmeg
1/2 cup flour
2 large eggs, lightly beaten
3 tablespoons olive oil
3 tablespoons unsalted butter
FOR THE CHEESE SAUCE
2 cups mild orange cheddar cheese, grated
3/4 cup heavy cream
2 teaspoons prepared English mustard
MAKES 18

To make the cheese sauce, combine the cheese, cream and mustard in a double boiler over barely simmering water. Cook for 15 to 20 minutes, stirring occasionally, until melted and well combined.

Meanwhile, preheat the oven to 350°F. Cut the turkey into 18 pieces measuring approximately 1 1/2 x 2 inches. Using a mallet or the bottom of a heavy skillet, flatten the turkey pieces until they are about 1/2 inch thick. Season on both sides with salt and set aside.

Combine the bread crumbs, turmeric, paprika and nutmeg in a small bowl. Place the flour and eggs in two separate bowls. Dip the turkey first in the flour, shaking off any excess, then dip it in the egg and let any excess drip off, then press it in the crumb mixture on both sides to coat the pieces evenly.

In a large nonstick skillet, heat 1 tablespoon of oil and 1 tablespoon

In a large nonstick skillet, heat 1 tablespoon of oil and 1 tablespoon of butter over medium heat. When hot, add one-third of the breaded turkey and cook for 2 minutes on each side. Transfer the cooked turkey to a parchment-lined baking sheet and wipe out the pan with paper towels. Repeat with the remaining turkey, adding more oil and butter, and wiping out the pan between batches. Transfer the baking sheet to the oven and bake the turkey for 4 to 5 minutes. Serve with the cheese sauce.

NOTES

• You can make the cheese sauce in advance if necessary. Do not worry if it firms up. Rewarm it in a double boiler over simmering water, stirring until smooth.
• We sometimes serve the sauce in a hollowed-out squash.

Butternut Squash
and mango chutney

Finely grated zest and juice of 3 limes
Finely grated zest and juice of 1 lemon
1/2 cup sugar
1/3 cup cider vinegar
2 tablespoons finely chopped shallot
1 tablespoon grated ginger
2 cloves garlic, finely chopped
4 cups butternut squash, peeled, seeded and cut into 1/4-inch cubes
2 mangoes, peeled, seeded and cut into 1/2-inch cubes, about 2 1/2 cups
3 tablespoons cilantro leaves, torn in half
2 teaspoons olive oil
1/4 cup pumpkin seeds
1/4 teaspoon salt
1 teaspoon chilli powder
MAKES 3 1/2 CUPS

In a medium saucepan, combine the citrus zests and juices, sugar, vinegar, shallot, ginger and garlic. Cook for 15 minutes over medium-high heat until just syrupy.

Reduce the heat to medium-low, add the squash and cook for 25 minutes, stirring, until the squash is tender but not mushy. Add the mangoes and continue cooking for another 8 minutes until the mangoes are soft but still hold their shape. Set aside to cool, then stir in the cilantro leaves.

In a small skillet, heat the olive oil over medium-high heat. Add the pumpkin seeds and salt and cook for 3 to 4 minutes, stirring, until the pumpkin seeds are lightly toasted and popping. Sprinkle the seeds with the chilli powder and stir to coat. Remove the frying pan from the heat and let cool. Garnish the chutney with the chilli-flavored pumpkin seeds.

NOTES

• Serve as an accompaniment to chicken, pork or grilled brochettes of fish.
• The spicy pumpkin seeds can be served on their own or as part of a salad.

Baked Polenta with
cream, herbs and garlic

Polenta has no limits, only the imagination of the cook.

3 cups milk
1/2 head garlic, plus 3 cloves extra garlic, smashed
6 sprigs thyme
4 black peppercorns
2 bay leaves
2 1/2 teaspoons salt
1 1/2 cups coarse polenta or yellow cornmeal
1 1/4 cups grated Fontina cheese
3/4 cup heavy cream
3 tablespoons unsalted butter, plus extra for greasing
3 sage leaves
Freshly ground black pepper
SERVES 6

In a large, heavy skillet, combine the milk, 1/2 head garlic, thyme, black peppercorns, bay leaves and 3 cups of water over high heat. Bring to a boil then remove the pan from the heat and leave to infuse for 30 minutes.

Strain the infused liquid, then return it to the pan, add the salt and bring to a boil. Using a wire whisk, add the polenta in a steady stream, letting it fall through your fingers like snow while whisking constantly with the other hand. When all the polenta is incorporated, lower the heat and change the whisk for a wooden spoon. Cook, stirring frequently, for 30 to 40 minutes or until the polenta comes away easily from the sides of the pan.

Meanwhile, lightly butter an 8-inch ceramic ovenproof dish measuring approximately 2 inches deep. In a small saucepan, cook the butter with the 3 cloves of smashed garlic and the sage leaves over medium-low heat until the butter turns nut-brown. Remove from the heat and set aside.

Preheat the oven to 350°F. Pour half the polenta into the dish, smoothing it out so that it dips in the center. Pour in 1/2 cup of the cream and sprinkle with 3/4 cup of the Fontina and some black pepper. Add the remaining polenta to the dish, smoothing it over to encase the cream and cheese, then top with the remaining cream and cheese. Pour on the brown butter topping and bake for 30 minutes. Remove from the oven and serve hot.

N O T E

• Fontina is an Italian cheese, sweeter and more buttery than Gruyère and particularly good for cooking.

Baked Beans

4 cups dried red kidney beans

1/2 medium onion

1 carrot, cut into thirds

1 stalk celery, cut into thirds

1 plum tomato, halved lengthwise

1 canned chipotle chilli in adobo sauce, or 1 dried chipotle chilli

2 bay leaves

1 head garlic, excess paper removed, cut in half horizontally

1 tablespoon salt

2 tablespoons light brown sugar

1/3 cup Balsamic Glaze (see page 211)

3 cups BBQ Sauce (see page 212)

SERVES 8

Soak the beans for several hours or overnight in plenty of cold water, then drain.

In a large casserole, combine the beans, onion, carrot, celery, tomato, chilli, bay leaves, garlic and enough fresh water to cover beans by 1 1/2 inches. Bring the mixture to a boil and boil hard for 10 minutes. Reduce the heat to a simmer, cover and cook for 35 to 40 minutes or until the beans are tender. Remove and discard the vegetables. Set the beans aside to cool in the cooking liquid.

Preheat the oven to 325°F. Strain the beans, reserving 4 cups of the cooking liquid. (If there is less than this amount, make up the deficit with fresh water.) Return the beans and reserved cooking liquid to the casserole. Combine the salt, brown sugar, Balsamic Glaze and BBQ Sauce. Partially cover the casserole and transfer it to the oven. Bake for 4 1/2 to 5 hours, until the beans are tender and most of the cooking liquid has been absorbed. Serve hot, or cool and store in a covered container in the refrigerator for up to 3 days.

N O T E

• Chipotles in adobo are worth looking for. They taste both smoky and spicy.

Crispy Grains
with Portabella Mushrooms

There are so many things you can do with grains: roasting, braising and frying them, as well as boiling. This recipe is a good example.

¹/₃ cup wheatberries
¹/₂ cup wild rice
¹/₂ cup pearl barley
¹/₃ cup millet
1 cup quinoa
¹/₃ cup buckwheat
2 tablespoons olive oil
1 tablespoon tarragon leaves
1 tablespoon parsley leaves
1 tablespoon thyme leaves
1 tablespoon finely chopped chives
4 tablespoons freshly squeezed lemon juice
Salt and freshly ground black pepper
FOR THE MUSHROOMS
3 medium portabella mushrooms
2 cloves garlic, sliced
1 tablespoon olive oil
SERVES 6

Place the wheatberries in a saucepan with 4 cups of salted water. Bring to a boil, then lower the heat and simmer for 40 minutes. Drain and rinse under cold running water and set aside.

Meanwhile, preheat the oven to 400°F. Place the wild rice in a saucepan with 3 cups of salted water. Bring to a boil, reduce the heat and simmer for 20 to 25 minutes. Drain and rinse under cold running water and set aside.

To cook the mushrooms, remove the stems and thoroughly clean the caps. Place them ribbed-side up in a baking dish and scatter the garlic over them. Drizzle with the olive oil, season with salt and pepper and pour in ¹/₂ cup of water. Cover and transfer to the oven for 25 to 30 minutes.

Place the barley in a small saucepan with 3 cups of salted water. Bring to a boil, reduce the heat and simmer for 18 to 20 minutes. Drain and rinse under cold running water. Set aside.

Place the millet in a saucepan with 1 cup of salted water. Bring to a boil, reduce the heat and simmer for 10 minutes. Drain and rinse under cold running water and set aside.

In a small saucepan, toast the quinoa over medium-high heat for 2 minutes. Add 3 cups of salted water. Bring to a boil, reduce the heat and simmer for 5 minutes. Drain and rinse under cold running water and set aside.

In a small saucepan, toast the buckwheat over medium-high heat for about 1¹/₂ minutes until it becomes fragrant. Add 1 cup of salted water and bring to a boil, stirring occasionally. Cook until the buckwheat grains just begin to split, about 2 to 3 minutes. Drain and rinse under cold running water and set aside.

Place all the grains in a large bowl, stir gently until well mixed then transfer the grains to a baking sheet lined with a kitchen towel and leave them to dry completely. (The grains can be prepared 1 day in advance up to this point then covered and refrigerated.)

Remove the mushrooms from the oven and discard the garlic. Cut the mushrooms into triangles. Strain and reserve the cooking juices. Set aside.

Divide the grains into 3 batches. In a large nonstick skillet over high heat, add 2 teaspoons of olive oil. Add one-third of the grain mixture to the pan and spread it out to evenly cover the skillet. Without stirring, cook the grains for 2 minutes or until they form a light brown crust and begin to pop. Then stir the grains, toss and continue cooking for another 2 minutes. Remove the grains to a medium bowl and set aside in a warm place. Repeat the cooking procedure with the remaining two batches of grains.

To the bowl of grains, add the herbs, lemon juice, mushrooms, salt and pepper and stir to combine. Serve with the reserved mushroom cooking juices spooned around.

Garden Risotto

The embodiment of a summer meal: a light, creamy risotto with strong herbal overtones, a bright green color with traces of golden yellow and the scent of a hot garden.

2 cups spinach leaves, thinly sliced
4 1/2 ounces (3/4 cup) fava beans
3/4 cup sugar snap peas, cleaned and cut into 1/4-inch pieces
1/2 cup zucchini or summer squash, washed, halved and sliced thinly on the diagonal
3/4 cup peas
1/3 cup freshly grated Parmigiano Reggiano
1/4 cup cream
1 teaspoon finely chopped basil leaves
1 teaspoon finely chopped chives
1 teaspoon finely chopped mint leaves
1 teaspoon finely chopped summer savory leaves
1 teaspoon finely chopped flat-leafed parsley leaves
1 teaspoon finely chopped thyme
6 cups Corn Stock (see page 211)
3 tablespoons unsalted butter, diced
1 tablespoon olive oil
1/4 cup finely chopped onion
2 cups arborio rice
1/2 cup white wine
1 teaspoon saffron threads
1/2 cup zucchini blossoms, stems and pistils removed, roughly chopped
Salt and freshly ground black pepper
SERVES 4 TO 6

Bring a large saucepan of water to the boil, add the spinach and cook for 2 minutes. Drain, reserving about 1/4 cup of the blanching liquid, then refresh the spinach under cold running water and drain again thoroughly. Squeeze the spinach dry then purée it in a food processor adding just enough of the cooking liquid to give a smooth, thick sauce. Set aside.

Refill the saucepan with salted water, bring to the boil then add the fava beans and cook for 30 seconds. Remove and drain, refresh under cold running water, then peel and discard the shells. Set aside.

In the same saucepan, add the sugar snap peas, zucchini and peas, and blanch them for 1 minute before draining and refreshing them under cold running water.

In a small bowl, combine 2 tablespoons of the grated Parmigiano Reggiano with the cream and all the herbs and set aside.

Place the Corn Stock in a medium-sized saucepan and bring to the boil. Turn off the heat and leave the pan at the back of the stove.

In a large, heavy saucepan, combine 2 tablespoons of the butter, the oil and onion over medium heat and cook until soft. Add the rice and cook, stirring, for 4 to 5 minutes until coated and translucent. Stir in the white wine, saffron and 1 teaspoon of salt and cook for another 2 to 3 minutes.

Using a ladle, add just enough stock to cover the rice mixture and stir over medium heat until the stock is absorbed. Continue adding the stock, a ladleful at a time, stirring until the rice is al dente and the risotto is slightly soupy, about another 12 minutes.

Stir in the spinach purée, fava beans, sugar snap peas, zucchini and peas, then add some more stock and stir for another 2 to 3 minutes. Remove the pan from the heat and stir in the zucchini blossoms, herb cream and the remaining butter, stirring briskly.

Adjust the seasoning to taste with salt and pepper, then spoon the risotto into bowls and garnish with the remaining Parmigiano Reggiano.

Zucchini Blossom
frittata

Cooking the eggs quickly over a high heat ensures that the texture of the frittata will be light and fluffy.

6 to 8 zucchini blossoms, stems and pistils discarded
1 tablespoon fresh bread crumbs
1 large tomato, cut into $1/4$-inch dice
3 tablespoons olive oil
Salt and freshly ground black pepper
5 to 6 large eggs
3 tablespoons freshly grated Parmesan, plus extra for sprinkling
2 tablespoons chopped mint leaves, plus extra, torn, for garnishing
1 tablespoon extra-virgin olive oil
SERVES 4 TO 6

Preheat the grill. Make sure the zucchini blossoms are thoroughly cleaned then cut each one crosswise into three equal pieces. Toast the bread crumbs and set aside. In a small bowl, season the diced tomato with salt and pepper and 1 tablespoon of olive oil.

Crack the eggs into a bowl and beat lightly with a fork, adding the cheese, bread crumbs, chopped mint plus a little salt and pepper and beating until thoroughly combined.

In a large nonstick skillet with an ovenproof handle, heat 2 tablespoons of olive oil over a high heat, spreading the oil around to coat the bottom and sides of the pan. Add the zucchini blossoms and cook for 45 seconds to 1 minute, stirring. Pour in the egg mixture and scramble gently with a wooden spoon for 30 seconds until the mixture forms small curds. Then leave to cook undisturbed for another 45 seconds until the bottom of the frittata is just set.

Remove the skillet from the heat and place it under the broiler for 30 to 40 seconds or until the frittata firms up and lightly browns. Be careful not to overcook or the frittata will become tough and dry.

Remove the pan from the broiler and slide the frittata onto a large warm plate. Pile the chopped tomatoes in the center of the frittata and sprinkle with the torn mint leaves, olive oil and the extra cheese, if desired. To serve, cut the frittata into wedges.

Italian Frittata

$1/4$ red bell pepper
$1/4$ yellow bell pepper
$1/4$ poblano chilli
2 tablespoons olive oil
5 to 6 large eggs
8 basil leaves, torn
6 marjoram leaves, torn
Salt and freshly ground black pepper
4 shiitake mushroom caps, thinly sliced
1 cup spinach leaves, roughly chopped
1 clove garlic, crushed
4 to 6 slices prosciutto
2 tablespoons freshly grated pecorino romano
1 tablespoon extra-virgin olive oil
SERVES 4 TO 6

Preheat the broiler. Rub the bell peppers and the poblano chilli with 1 tablespoon of olive oil. Place them under the broiler skin-side up and cook until the skins are blistered and black. Remove from under the broiler, leaving the grill on, and peel and discard the skins. Thinly slice the peppers and chilli and set aside.

Crack the eggs into a bowl, add the basil and marjoram, season with salt and pepper and beat lightly with a fork.

In a large nonstick skillet with an ovenproof handle, heat 2 tablespoons of olive oil over high heat, spreading the oil around to coat the bottom and sides of the pan. Add the peppers, chilli, mushrooms, spinach and garlic and cook for 45 seconds to 1 minute, stirring. Pour in the egg mixture and scramble gently with a wooden spoon for 30 seconds until the mixture forms small curds. Then leave to cook undisturbed for another 45 seconds until the bottom of the frittata is just set.

Remove the skillet from the heat and place it under the broiler for 30 to 40 seconds or until the frittata firms up and lightly browns. Be careful not to overcook or the frittata will become tough and dry.

Lay out the prosciutto on a large, warm serving plate. Remove the pan from the broiler and slide the frittata onto the plate on top of the prosciutto. Sprinkle with the pecorino and drizzle with 1 tablespoon extra-virgin olive oil. To serve, cut the frittata into wedges.

Vegetable Stew

The spirit of the harvest.

20 chestnuts, fresh, unshelled

1 pound red Swiss chard

4 salsify, peeled, cut into 2-inch pieces and set aside in acidulated water

1 tablespoon lemon juice

3 baby parsnips, washed and peeled

8 baby turnips, washed and peeled, stems retained

15 small Brussels sprouts, trimmed, stems carved with a cross

8 ounces kale leaves, torn into 2-inch pieces

1 pound spinach leaves, torn into 1/2-inch pieces

20 shiitake mushrooms, cleaned and stemmed

4 tablespoons unsalted butter

3 cups Vegetable Stock (see page 210)

1/2 teaspoon sugar

3 tablespoons olive oil

10 to 12 cloves garlic, peeled and left whole

1/2 teaspoon dried red pepper flakes

Salt and freshly ground black pepper

4 medium leeks (white and light green parts only), sliced 1/4 inch thick and washed

1 medium red onion, finely chopped

6 small fresh porcini mushrooms, cleaned, caps only (optional)

2 tablespoons tarragon leaves

2 tablespoons chervil sprigs

2 tablespoons chives, cut into 1-inch pieces

1 tablespoon extra-virgin olive oil

SERVES 6 TO 8

Preheat the oven to 350°F. Carve a cross on the flat side of each chestnut, place them in a roasting pan and bake for 30 minutes.

Meanwhile, remove the Swiss chard leaves from their stalks and discard any that are bruised or discolored. Roughly tear the leaves into 2-inch pieces, wash in several changes of water then set aside. Trim the Swiss chard stalks and cut them into 2-inch pieces. Measure out 1 1/2 cups of stalk, wash and set aside.

Prepare an ice bath. Bring a medium saucepan of salted water to a boil and add the lemon juice. Add the salsify to the pan and boil for 10 minutes, drain and place it in the ice bath. Remove from the ice bath to a baking sheet and set aside.

In a large pot of boiling salted water, blanch separately the following vegetables for the specified time: baby parsnips and turnips 6 to 8 minutes; Brussels sprouts 6 minutes; chard stems 4 minutes; kale 2 minutes; chard leaves 1 minute; spinach 30 seconds; shiitakes 20 seconds. As each batch of vegetables is cooked, remove it from the pot with a slotted spoon, transfer to the ice bath to cool, then remove to the baking sheet, keeping each variety together. Squeeze the kale, chard and spinach leaves dry.

Remove the chestnuts from the oven. When cool enough to handle, peel off the shells and remove any brown skin. In a medium saucepan over a medium heat, melt 2 tablespoons of the butter and add the chestnuts, sugar and 1/2 cup of the vegetable stock. Bring to the boil, then lower the heat and simmer the chestnuts over the heat for 4 to 5 minutes, stirring until dry and glazed.

In a large casserole over medium heat, place 2 tablespoons of the olive oil. Add the garlic and parsnips in one layer and cook until golden brown, for 4 to 5 minutes, stirring occasionally. Stir in the red pepper flakes and 1/2 teaspoon salt. Add the leeks and red onion, stir and cook for 1 minute without letting them brown.

Season all the blanched vegetables with salt and pepper. Pour 1 cup of vegetable stock into the casserole and increase the heat to medium-high. Add 1 tablespoon of butter to the casserole and allow them to cook for 2 to 3 minutes. Add the salsify and stir to combine. Cook for 2 minutes, then add the baby turnips and cook another 2 minutes.

Add the Brussels sprouts and 1/2 cup of the vegetable stock. Stir gently and cook for 1 minute. Add the kale, spreading it evenly into the casserole, and stir gently to combine. Cook for 1 minute, then spread the Swiss chard leaves evenly into the casserole and fold them in gently. Cook for another minute, then add the spinach, spreading it evenly throughout and folding it in gently.

Add another 1/2 cup of vegetable stock to the casserole, cook for 30 seconds then add the chard stems and shiitakes, tucking them in. Cook for 1 minute, then add the chestnuts and another 1/2 cup of vegetable stock.

Remove the casserole from the heat, cover and place in the oven for 20 to 25 minutes. Meanwhile, melt 1 tablespoon of butter in a skillet and lightly sauté the porcini, if using. Remove the casserole from the oven and garnish with the cooked porcini, tarragon, chervil and chives. Drizzle with a tablespoon of extra-virgin olive oil and serve.

Vegetable Tian

A healthy soil produces healthy plants and a healthy dish. Using produce straight from the garden, this tian is baked slowly to allow the vegetables to soak up the flavors of the onion and garlic baste.

FOR THE TIAN

6 cloves garlic, peeled and smashed, plus 1/2 clove garlic for flavoring the baking dish

4 tablespoons softened unsalted butter, plus 3 tablespoons butter, melted

1 potato, peeled, trimmed to a rectangle and covered with cold water

1/4 cup olive oil

2 pounds medium onions, thinly sliced

A bouquet garni made from 4 sprigs of rosemary and 6 sprigs of basil, tied together with string

6 or 7 basil leaves

8 mixed red and yellow bell peppers, cored, seeded and sliced into rounds 1/4-inch thick

1 medium eggplant, thinly sliced into rounds on a mandoline

1 large summer squash, thinly sliced into rounds on a mandoline

1 large zucchini, thinly sliced into rounds on a mandoline

5 beefsteak tomatoes, thinly sliced

A few sprigs of rosemary, to garnish

3/4 cup crumbled soft goat cheese, optional

Salt and freshly ground black pepper, plus extra flaked salt to garnish

FOR THE ROASTED ONION AND GARLIC BASTE

2 medium Roasted Onions (see page 217)

2 heads Roasted Garlic (see page 217)

2 tablespoons olive oil

1/2 cup basil leaves, roughly chopped

1 tablespoon chopped rosemary leaves

1 tablespoon chopped marjoram leaves

1 1/2 teaspoons salt and 1 teaspoon freshly ground black pepper

SERVES 6 TO 8

To make the baste, peel the roasted onions and squeeze the base of each head of roasted garlic to extract the soft cloves. Roughly chop them together. Transfer the onions and garlic to a food processor and purée. Add the olive oil, basil, rosemary, marjoram, salt and pepper and pulse until well combined. Set aside.

To prepare the tian, rub the inside of a 13 x 9-inch ceramic baking dish with the cut clove of garlic, then rub it with 1 tablespoon of the butter.

Preheat the oven to 350°F. To cook the potato, line a baking tin with baking parchment and brush the paper lightly with the melted butter. Sprinkle with salt and pepper. Remove the potato from the water and thinly slice on a mandoline into 9 to 10 slices. Arrange the slices in a single layer on the baking pan. Brush the slices well with more melted butter and sprinkle with a little more salt and pepper. Cover with another sheet of baking parchment and bake for 10 minutes. Remove from the oven and set aside.

Heat the remaining 3 tablespoons of butter and the olive oil in a large shallow saucepan over moderate heat. When the butter has melted and is foaming, add the onions, smashed garlic and 1 1/2 teaspoons of salt. Raise the heat to medium-high and cook, stirring and tossing, for about 8 minutes to brown the onions. Then reduce the heat to low, add the bouquet garni and cook gently for about 15 to 20 minutes or until the onions are well caramelized.

Discard the bouquet garni. Remove the caramelized onions from the pan and transfer to the seasoned baking dish, spreading them out to cover the base. Place a layer of cooked sliced potato over the onions, scatter the torn basil leaves over the top and season generously with salt and black pepper to taste.

Reduce the oven to 300°F. Arrange the prepared vegetables upright in the baking dish, in alternating rows, pressing them together tightly and basting each row with the puréed onion mixture as you go. When the dish is full, baste the top of the vegetables with the remaining onion mixture.

Place the dish on a baking sheet and bake for 2 to 2 1/2 hours until lightly browned on top. Remove the tian from the oven, sprinkle with flaked or sea salt and freshly ground pepper and garnish with the sprigs of rosemary. Let stand for 20 minutes. If using crumbled goat cheese, sprinkle over the tian during the last 15 to 20 minutes of baking.

NOTE

• The roasted onion and garlic baste can be made up to 1 day ahead and can be used for many grilled foods.

Salads & Vegetables

Golden & Red Beet
and artichoke salad

16 baby red beets, washed and leaves removed, reserving 3/4-inch stem
16 baby golden beets, washed and leaves removed, reserving 3/4-inch stem
4 sprigs rosemary
4 sprigs thyme
7 tablespoons olive oil
3/4 cup lemon juice
16 baby artichokes
1 medium onion, chopped
1 carrot, chopped
1 stalk celery, chopped
6 cloves garlic, chopped
Salt and freshly ground black pepper
1 1/2 cups white wine
3 cups Light Chicken Stock or Vegetable Stock (see pages 209 and 210)
A bouquet garni made from 2 bay leaves, 8 sprigs parsley and 6 sprigs mint, folded and tied with string
10 black peppercorns
FOR THE VINAIGRETTE
1 tablespoon Dijon mustard
A pinch of cayenne pepper
2 tablespoons lemon juice
1/3 cup reserved artichoke cooking liquid
1/2 cup olive oil
Salt and freshly ground black pepper
FOR THE GARNISH
16 leaves red oak-leaf lettuce
16 leaves lollo rosso lettuce
16 frisée leaves
4 teaspoons finely chopped chives
4 teaspoons finely chopped flat-leaf parsley
SERVES 4

Preheat the oven to 400°F. Place the beets in a baking dish large enough to allow a little space between them. Place the rosemary and thyme on top of the beets and sprinkle evenly with 3 tablespoons of olive oil, plus some salt and pepper. Cover with foil and place in the oven for about 30 minutes or until easily pierced with a knife. Remove the beets and set them aside until cool enough to handle.

Leaving the stem attached, remove the skin and set aside.

Place the lemon juice in a large bowl with 6 cups of cold water. Peel and trim the artichokes; place them in the acidulated water as you go.

Meanwhile, place the onion, carrot, celery and garlic in a food processor fitted with the steel blade and pulse until finely chopped and thoroughly combined. In a medium saucepan, heat the remaining 4 tablespoons olive oil over medium heat. Add the vegetable mixture and sweat for 5 to 8 minutes.

Lift the artichokes from the acidulated water using a slotted spoon. Add the artichokes to the vegetables in the saucepan and toss to combine, then add 2 cups of the lemon water, the white wine, stock, bouquet garni, peppercorns and 2 teaspoons of salt. Bring to a boil then lower the heat and simmer for 15 minutes. Remove the pan from the heat and set aside for 30 minutes to cool thoroughly. Remove the artichokes from the broth and refrigerate in a large salad bowl. Strain the broth, reserving 1/3 cup of liquid to use in the vinaigrette.

To make the vinaigrette, place the mustard, cayenne, lemon juice and reserved artichoke cooking liquid in a food processor. Process until well combined. With the machine running, drizzle in the olive oil slowly until the mixture emulsifies. Season with salt and pepper.

Remove the artichokes from the refrigerator and pour 4 tablespoons of the vinaigrette over them. Gently arrange 4 artichokes to one side of each of the 4 serving plates.

Combine the golden beets in the salad bowl with 2 tablespoons of vinaigrette, mix, then arrange 4 on each plate opposite the artichokes.

Toss the red beets in the salad bowl with 2 tablespoons of vinaigrette then arrange on the serving plates near the golden beets.

Clean and dry the salad bowl. Combine the lettuce leaves with 4 tablespoons of vinaigrette, tossing gently to combine.

Lay 4 leaves of red oak-leaf lettuce in your hand, slightly overlapping them along the length of your palm. Press 4 lollo rosso leaves into the center then wrap the red oak leaves around to form a bouquet, squeezing tightly at the base. About 1½ inches from the base of the

bouquet, wrap 4 leaves of frisée tightly (like a knot) around to secure it. Use a sharp knife to trim the base flat, then firmly press the base of the bouquet down in the center of one of the serving plates so that the arrangement stands upright.

Make another 3 bouquets from the remaining leaves and arrange on the serving plates. Drizzle 1 tablespoon of vinaigrette over each serving then sprinkle each plate with a teaspoon of chives and a teaspoon of parsley. Serve.

NOTES

• This recipe can be broken down and used in many different ways. The prepared artichokes and beets can be used elsewhere, with a tossed garden salad or on their own as a side dish to any meat, fish or poultry preparation. The vinaigrette can be used in any salad.
• Toasted pine nuts are another good addition to this dish.
• Adding 2 strips of bacon to the artichokes when cooking adds a subtle smoked flavor.

Warm Salad of Braised Celery with Blood Oranges, Persimmon, Toasted Walnuts and Stilton

The tangy-sweet flavor of a completely ripe persimmon is unbelievable. Five different tastes and textures make this a unique dish.

1 cup blood orange juice
6 stalks celery
3 tablespoons lemon juice
3 tablespoons olive oil
6 sprigs thyme
10 black peppercorns
10 coriander seeds
1 garlic clove, cut into thirds
A pinch of dried red pepper flakes
8 walnut halves
3 medium blood oranges
3 persimmons
3 ounces Stilton cheese, at room temperature
Salt and freshly ground black pepper
4 teaspoons extra-virgin olive oil
SERVES 4

Place the blood orange juice in a small saucepan and boil vigorously until reduced in volume to 1/4 cup of liquid. Set aside to cool.

Preheat the oven to 425°F. Cut the celery stalks in half widthwise and trim them for 12 31/2-inch-long pieces. Remove the strings. In a flameproof casserole, place the celery stalks, 3/4 cup of water, the lemon juice, olive oil, thyme, peppercorns, coriander, garlic, 1/4 teaspoon of salt and the red pepper flakes. Bring to a boil, then cover and transfer to the oven for 15 minutes or until the celery is easily pierced. Remove and set aside.

Meanwhile, in a small pan, place the walnuts and toast in the oven for 4 to 5 minutes. Remove and set aside. When cool enough to handle, chop the walnuts roughly. Peel the oranges, cutting away all the pith, then cut them into 1/4-inch-thick slices, flicking out any seeds with the tip of the knife. Trim the ends of the persimmon and peel using a knife. Cut each into 4 to 6 wedges and remove the seeds.

Place several orange slices on each serving plate, alternating them with the wedges of persimmon to form a pinwheel. Crumble the Stilton over the pinwheels, then sprinkle with the chopped walnuts.

Arrange 3 pieces of celery over each plate of salad. Drizzle a tablespoon of the blood orange reduction around each plate, then a tablespoon of the celery's cooking juices, along with a teaspoon of olive oil. Grind some black pepper over the top and serve warm.

NOTE

• Replace the celery in this salad with broiled Wilted Endive (see page 141).

Hummous

Serve this with the children's canapés on page 70.

1/2 cup dried chickpeas
3 tablespoons freshly squeezed lemon juice
2 tablespoons extra-virgin olive oil
4 teaspoons tahini
1 clove garlic, finely chopped, or more to taste
Salt and freshly ground black pepper
MAKES 1 1/4 CUPS

In a medium bowl, soak the chickpeas in 3 cups of cold water overnight.

Next day, drain the soaked chickpeas. In a small saucepan over high heat, place the chickpeas and 2 cups of fresh water. Bring to a boil, then lower heat to a slight simmer and cook for 1 hour 20 minutes or until soft. Drain.

In a food processor fitted with a metal blade, place the chickpeas, lemon juice, olive oil, tahini, garlic and 3 tablespoons of water and process until smooth and well combined. Season to taste with salt and black pepper.

Serve with pita bread cut into strips or as a dip for crudités.

Spring Salad with
Spaghetti Squash and Goat Cheese Croutons

The most awesome and exciting time of the year, spring is a fresh new start, a beginning.

1/2 head radicchio, torn into large pieces

1 head lettuce (bibb or butter), torn into large pieces

1 bunch red leaf lettuce (such as lollo rosso), torn into large pieces

1 bunch watercress, stems removed

1 bunch arugula, stems removed, leaves torn into large pieces

4 radishes, washed and very thinly sliced using a mandoline

1 cup torn basil leaves

1 cup torn flat-leaf parsley

1/2 cup dill sprigs

3 tablespoons snipped chives

1 1/2 tablespoons lemon thyme leaves, with flowers

Salt and freshly ground black pepper

10 mixed edible flowers, torn (optional)

Salt and freshly ground black pepper

FOR THE DRESSING

3 tablespoons freshly squeezed lemon juice

1 tablespoon balsamic vinegar

1 tablespoon sherry vinegar

2 1/2 teaspoons Dijon mustard

1/2 cup plus 2 tablespoons olive oil

FOR THE SUGAR SNAP PEAS (OPTIONAL)

3 cups sugar snap peas, washed and strings removed

2 tablespoons chopped mint leaves

1 tablespoon lemon juice

1 teaspoon olive oil

Salt and freshly ground black pepper

FOR THE SPAGHETTI SQUASH AND GOAT CHEESE CROUTONS

1/2 small spaghetti squash, seeded

2 tablespoons unsalted butter

1 teaspoon olive oil

1 sprig thyme, plus leaves or flowers from 2 sprigs extra to garnish

Salt and freshly ground black pepper

1/2 baguette

1 clove garlic, cut in half

4 ounces fresh soft rindless goat cheese

SERVES 6

To cook the spaghetti squash, preheat the oven to 375°F. Fill the squash with the butter, olive oil, sprig of thyme and some salt and pepper and place cut-side down in a baking dish with 4 tablespoons of water. Bake for 40 to 45 minutes or until tender.

Meanwhile, thinly slice the baguette into 18 slices 1/4 inch thick and grill or toast them until just crisp.

Remove the squash from the oven, leaving the oven on, and use a fork to separate the flesh of the squash from the shell, creating spaghettilike strands.

Rub both sides of the toasted croutons with garlic. Line a baking sheet with greaseproof paper, place the croutons on the baking sheet and crumble some goat cheese evenly over each crouton. Bake until just warm.

Top each crouton with a little spaghetti squash. Return to the oven for about 3 minutes until the spaghetti squash is just warm. Season with salt and pepper and garnish with thyme leaves or flowers. Set aside and keep warm.

In an abundant amount of cold water, wash all lettuces, radicchio, cress and arugula. Dry thoroughly, then combine with the radishes and fresh herbs in a large bowl. Season with salt and pepper and toss.

In a small bowl, whisk together the lemon juice, vinegars and mustard. Slowly whisk in the olive oil to form an emulsion, then season with salt and pepper.

To prepare the sugar snap peas, bring a large saucepan of salted water to the boil. Blanch the sugar snap peas for 3 minutes then drain and refresh under cold running water. Drain the sugar snaps thoroughly then toss with the mint, lemon juice, olive oil, and season to taste with salt and pepper.

Drizzle the vinaigrette over the greens and toss gently. Serve immediately with peas and flowers (if using) and the warm croutons around the salad.

NOTES

• The croutons need not be served with the spring salad. Try them as cocktail party canapés.

• Add some chopped Slow-Roasted Garlic Tomatoes in Olive Oil (see page 216) and torn basil leaves.

Millet and Aduki Bean salad with sheep cheese and tomato oil vinaigrette

6 Slow-Roasted Garlic Tomatoes in Olive Oil (see page 216), plus
3/4 cup oil from the tomatoes
3/4 cup dried aduki beans, rinsed and soaked in water to cover overnight,
then drained
1 cup millet, rinsed
6 ounces (1 cup) fava beans, peeled
1 1/2 cups red chard stems, chopped into 1/4-inch pieces
4 tablespoons red wine vinegar
2 teaspoons salt
Freshly ground black pepper
1 cup fresh peas
1/2 cup finely sliced scallions
1 cup mixed herb leaves, such as basil, chervil, dill, fennel fronds,
nasturtium leaves and Italian flat parsley, torn in half if large
2 ounces hard sheep's cheese, shaved into curls using a vegetable
peeler
3 tablespoons Herb Oil (see page 215), (optional)
SERVES 6

Prepare the Roasted Garlic Tomatoes and cut them in half.

Meanwhile, in a medium saucepan, place the aduki beans and 4
cups of fresh water. Bring to a boil, cover, lower heat to a simmer
and cook for 1 hour or until soft. In another medium saucepan, place
the millet and 4 cups of water. Bring to a boil, immediately lower
heat to a simmer and cook for 6 to 8 minutes. Drain the millet
through a fine-mesh strainer under cold running water then set aside
to drain thoroughly. When the aduki beans are cooked, drain and set
aside.

Bring a large saucepan of salted water to the boil then add the fava
beans and blanch them for 30 to 45 seconds. Remove from the pan
with a slotted spoon, refresh under cold running water and set aside.
Add the red chard stems to the same pan of boiling water and cook
for 4 to 5 minutes before draining and refreshing under cold running
water. Peel beans.

In a small bowl, whisk together the red wine vinegar, tomato oil, salt
and black pepper.

In a large salad bowl, toss together salad ingredients. Arrange on a
platter then garnish with the tomato halves, cheese curls and herb
oil.

NOTE

• If hard sheep's cheese is unavailable, curls of Parmesan can be
used instead.

Lake House Goat Cheese, Eggplant and Asparagus Salad with Hazelnut Vinaigrette and Red Pepper Juice Oil

Warm fresh goat cheese, rich toasted hazelnuts and sweet red pepper juice oil makes an impressive combination.

24 spears asparagus (about 1½ pounds), tough stems removed, trimmed and washed

½ medium eggplant, cut lengthwise

Olive oil, for brushing

3 ounces arugula or watercress

12 ounces fresh goat cheese log, cut into 1-inch discs

½ tablespoon unsalted butter, softened

lamb's lettuce leaves, to garnish

Salt and freshly ground black pepper

FOR THE RED PEPPER JUICE OIL

2 red bell peppers, cored, seeded and cut into 1-inch pieces

3 tablespoons olive oil

FOR THE HAZELNUT VINAIGRETTE

¼ cup hazelnuts

1 tablespoon finely chopped shallot

1½ teaspoons Dijon mustard

2 teaspoons lemon juice

2 teaspoons balsamic vinegar

1½ teaspoons red wine vinegar

½ cup olive oil

½ teaspoon salt

Freshly ground black pepper

2 teaspoons finely chopped chives

2 teaspoons finely chopped tarragon

SERVES 6

Bring a large saucepan filled with lightly salted water to the boil. Tie the asparagus together into 2 equal bundles then lower them into the water and cook for 5 to 6 minutes. Remove them from the pan, untie and refresh under cold running water, dry and set aside.

To make the red pepper juice oil, process the bell peppers in a juice extractor. Transfer the liquid to a small saucepan, bring to a boil and simmer until the volume of liquid has reduced to 2½ tablespoons. Remove the bell pepper juice from the heat and whisk in the olive oil. Set aside.

Leaving the skin on the eggplant, thinly slice it lengthwise on a mandoline into at least 12 slices. Lightly brush each side with olive oil and season with salt and pepper. Heat a grill or broiler to a medium heat and grill the eggplant until lightly browned and soft (not crispy), turning slices 90 degrees on each side to create cross-hatch marks. Set aside. Process the arugula or watercress in a juice extractor and set aside the liquid.

Preheat the oven to 325°F. To prepare the vinaigrette, spread the hazelnuts on a baking sheet and roast for 8 to 10 minutes, stirring once. Remove from the heat and wrap the nuts in a kitchen towel, leaving them to sit for a few minutes. Then use the kitchen towel to "rub" the skins off the nuts. Discard the skins and cut the nuts into thirds.

In a bowl, combine the shallot, mustard, lemon juice, balsamic vinegar, red wine vinegar and the salt and pepper. Gradually whisk in the olive oil to give a thick dressing, then add the hazelnuts. Allow to sit for 10 to 20 minutes at room temperature.

To warm the fresh goat cheese, heat the oven to 400°F. Lightly butter a small baking sheet and place the goat cheese rounds on the baking sheet. Bake for 4 to 5 minutes, until soft and warm but not runny.

To assemble the salad, place 4 asparagus spears on each plate, 2 tips facing one way, 2 tips facing the other, and season with salt and pepper. Stir the herbs into the vinaigrette, then drizzle each plate with 1 tablespoon of the dressing.

Place 2 slices of grilled eggplant lengthwise across the center of the asparagus, extending over the plate and making one end longer than the other. From the oven, using a small metal spatula, place the warm goat cheese directly on the eggplant and asparagus in the center of the plate. Drizzle the goat cheese with 1 tablespoon of vinaigrette then fold the ends of the eggplant up and over the goat cheese, tucking in the ends.

Drizzle 1½ teaspoons of the red pepper juice oil around the plate, then drizzle each plate with 1½ teaspoons of the arugula or watercress juice. Top the eggplant-wrapped goat cheese with a small bunch of lamb's lettuce then drizzle with a final ½ tablespoon of dressing. Repeat with the remaining 5 plates and serve.

Wilted Endive

A beautiful balance of Belgian endive, champagne vinegar and olive oil enhanced by the smokiness of broiling.

3 endive
$1/2$ cup champagne vinegar
$1/2$ cup olive oil
1 tablespoon sugar
Salt and freshly ground black pepper
SERVES 4

Trim the base from the endive and separate the leaves, discarding any that are damaged. Place them in a large bowl with the remaining ingredients and toss together. Set aside to marinate for 10 minutes.

Preheat a broiler. Drain the endive, reserving the excess for another use, then place the leaves on the broiling pan and cook until translucent and limp, turning over halfway through cooking. Remove to a serving dish and top with a few grindings of black pepper before serving.

NOTE

• Serve as a vegetable side dish, or with the burgers on page 115. The excess marinade can be used again, as a quick marinade for fish, or as the basis for a vinaigrette.

Tomato salad with
Fresh Beans and
Basil Vinaigrette

Make this only at the height of summer, preferably in Italy, but Wiltshire will do.

24 green beans, Italian green beans or haricots verts
4 large beefsteak tomatoes, sliced 1/4 inch thick
2/3 cup Basil Vinaigrette (recipe below)
4 green tomatoes, sliced 1/4 inch thick
12 red cherry tomatoes
6 yellow cherry tomatoes, halved
24 arugula leaves
Coarse sea salt and freshly ground black pepper
BASIL VINAIGRETTE
5 tablespoons Pesto (see page 81)
1 1/2 tablespoons red wine vinegar
1/3 cup olive oil
1 tablespoon lemon juice
Water if needed
SERVES 4

In a large saucepan, cook the beans in an abundant amount of boiling salted water until they are just tender to the bite. Drain and refresh under cold running water, then set aside to drain thoroughly.

To make the basil vinaigrette, using a wooden spoon combine the pesto and vinegar in a small bowl. Add the olive oil and mix until thoroughly incorporated. Stir in the lemon juice. Thin with water if necessary.

Forming circles, divide the slices of beefsteak tomato among 4 serving plates. Season with salt and pepper and drizzle each serving with 2 teaspoons of the vinaigrette.

Place the green tomato slices toward the middle, on top of the beefsteak tomatoes. Season with salt and pepper and drizzle those tomatoes with 2 teaspoons of the vinaigrette.

Arrange 6 beans on top of the tomatoes in the center of each plate and drizzle each serving with 1 teaspoon of vinaigrette. Then top each plate with 6 arugula leaves and drizzle each pile with 1/2 teaspoon vinaigrette.

Arrange 3 red cherry tomatoes and 3 halves of yellow cherry tomatoes around the stack of tomatoes, beans and arugula. Season them lightly, then drizzle the remainder of the vinaigrette around the perimeter of each plate and garnish each serving with sea salt and a few grinds of black pepper.

NOTES

• The secret to making this simple salad is using a variety of tomatoes: red, yellow, green, some small, some large, in different shapes. I like to use red cherry tomatoes for their particularly sweet flavor.
• Serve the vinaigrette with some crisp summer greens and a loaf of crusty bread.
• August is the month for tomatoes, when they are particularly sweet and fruity. A walk through the Lake House vegetable garden at this time of year transforms this vibrant vegetable into a work of culinary art.
• Red, yellow, orange, green and even a shade of pinky purple: Numerous types of tomato are available, ancient and modern, in an abundance of shapes and sizes. Heirloom tomatoes, a favorite of mine, are an ancient variety of native seeds that have become depleted simply because they were unsuitable for large-scale production.
• Raw sliced tomatoes splashed with vinaigrette or extra-virgin olive oil and sea salt is the simplest way to serve them but, when slowly poached in olive oil with roasted garlic purée, tomatoes develop an almost unbelievable richness. The essence of the tomato lies in the water it contains, so delicate yet fully flavored, and I use this extraction as the base of many sauces and vinaigrettes.
• To peel fresh tomatoes, use a small, sharp knife to remove the stem and core, then score the opposite end by slicing a cross into the flesh. Drop the tomatoes in boiling water for 30 seconds, then drain under cold running water. The skins will come easily away. To remove the seeds, cut the peeled tomato horizontally in half and gently use your little finger to scoop out the seeds, shaking the remainder free as necessary. Then proceed to slice or chop as required.
• To make a sauce, press the peeled tomatoes through a sieve or food mill fitted with a fine disc . . . or just grate them.
• When making a sauce from whole tomatoes, garden-ripened fresh varieties are my first choice, but when they are out of season I recommend tinned, peeled plum tomatoes from San Marzano, near Naples.

Spring Vegetables with Carrot Ravioli, Truffle Vinaigrette and Parmesan Tuiles

Your entertaining will never be the same after serving this feisty, spring-is-here salad.

4 baby carrots, peeled leaving 1-inch stem attached
1 cup shelled fresh peas
8 spears white asparagus, 3 inches long
8 spears green asparagus, 3 inches long
8 spears wild asparagus, 4 inches long
8 spears purple asparagus, 3 inches long
2 tablespoons unsalted butter
4 ounces chanterelle mushrooms, cleaned and trimmed leaving tender part of stem attached
3 ounces mousseron mushrooms, prepared as above
10 pea shoots with flowers
4 long radishes, finely sliced on a mandoline
1 tablespoon finely chopped fresh herbs, such as chervil, chives or tarragon
Salt and freshly ground black pepper
FOR THE CARROT PURÉE AND RAVIOLI
1 pound carrots, peeled and trimmed
Olive oil, for greasing
A bouquet garni made from 6 sprigs parsley, 4 sprigs thyme, 2 bay leaves, 2 cloves garlic and 8 black peppercorns, tied together in muslin
1 clove garlic, crushed
4 to 5 tablespoons vegetable stock or water
2 tablespoons mascarpone cheese
1 tablespoon grated Parmigiano Reggiano
Freshly grated nutmeg, to taste
Salt and freshly ground pepper
8 wonton wrappers
1 large beaten egg, for brushing
1½ teaspoons marjoram leaves
FOR THE PARMESAN TUILES
1 cup roughly grated Parmigiano Reggiano
FOR THE TRUFFLE VINAIGRETTE
1 tablespoon finely chopped shallot
3 tablespoons lemon juice
2 teaspoons mustard
6 tablespoons olive oil
1 tablespoon truffle oil
2½ ounces black truffle, finely diced
2 tablespoons truffle juice

1 teaspoon thyme flowers
Salt and freshly ground black pepper
SERVES 4

To make the carrot purée, preheat the oven to 300°F. Boil the carrots with the bouquet garni in salted water for about 20 minutes or until tender, then drain.

Spread the drained carrots out on a lightly oiled baking sheet and place in the oven for 15 minutes or until most of the moisture has evaporated. Then remove the carrots from the oven, roughly chop them and place in a food processor. Add the garlic and purée to a slightly coarse consistency, adding 4 to 5 tablespoons of vegetable stock or water to help it blend properly and scraping down the sides of the bowl as necessary.

Transfer the purée to a small saucepan and place over low heat, stirring until you have a thick consistency. Remove from the heat, leave to cool, then stir in the cheeses, nutmeg, salt, and pepper to taste. Set aside.

Place 4 of the wonton wrappers on a lightly floured work surface and brush them lightly with the beaten egg. Place 1 tablespoon of carrot purée in the center of the wrappers (you will have some purée left over, which should be set aside until serving) and then place 1 or 2 tiny marjoram leaves on top of each pile of purée. Cover with the remaining wonton wrappers, pressing your fingers all around the carrot mixture to seal the ravioli.

Take a 3-inch round pastry cutter and press it into each wonton parcel to make a circular ravioli, discarding the excess pieces of wrapper. Line a plate with plastic wrap, place the ravioli on top, cover with more plastic wrap and refrigerate until needed.

To cook the ravioli, bring a medium saucepan of salted water to a boil, add the ravioli, lower the heat and cook for 3 minutes. Remove the ravioli with a slotted spoon, drain, set aside on a lightly oiled plate and cover. Keep at room temperature.

To prepare the vegetables, bring a large saucepan of salted water to a boil and add the baby carrots. Return to a boil and cook for 1 to 2

Remove the cheese from the oven and let it stand for 1 to 2 minutes or just until cool enough to handle. Lift with a flat metal spatula, drape the cheese lengthwise over a rolling pin and leave to cool completely. When they have set, slide the tuiles off the rolling pin and use immediately or store in an airtight container. If necessary, the tuiles can be reheated and reshaped.

To make the vinaigrette, combine the shallot, lemon juice and mustard in a small bowl and whisk in the olive oil to form an emulsion. Whisk in the remaining ingredients, adding salt and pepper to taste.

To finish the vegetables, melt 1 tablespoon of the butter in a small frying pan over a medium heat and gently cook the chanterelle mushrooms until only just soft. Remove from the pan, season with salt and pepper and set aside. Wipe out the pan and melt the rest of the butter in it. Add the pea shoots, toss and cook them gently for 30 to 40 seconds until just softened but not wilted.

To present the salad, place a ravioli in the center of a serving plate. Lay 2 wild and 2 green asparaus spears on one side of the ravioli and 2 white and 2 purple asparagus spears on the other. Take 2 heaped tablespoons of the remaining carrot purée and shape them into quenelles, placing them at opposite ends of the plate near the asparagus. Arrange a small pile of peas near each quenelle and a small pile of each mushroom, placing them stem up. Place a small pile of pea shoots and some sliced radish at one end of the plate. Drizzle one-quarter of the vinaigrette around the edge of the plate and over the asparagus, ravioli and peas. Sprinkle some herbs over the ravioli and sit a Parmesan tuile at the side of the salad. Repeat with the remaining ingredients and serve at room temperature.

NOTES

• The purée, all the vegetables, and the Parmesan tuiles can be prepared the day before, the ravioli 1 or 2 hours before.
• White asparagus, which is grown underground or without any light to prevent it becoming green, is usually much thicker than the green variety. Wild asparagus, which is very thin, has a true flavor of a field. You can just use green asparagus. Don't worry if not all the ingredients are available. Improvise and experiment: That is how this salad originated.
• For a change, I like to use the purple asparagus raw in this dish because of its fresh, new-season taste and the crunchy textural contrast it provides.
• This dish works well with different purées, such as parsnip or fava bean instead of carrot.

minutes or until tender yet still crunchy. Use a slotted spoon to remove the carrots to a colander and refresh under cold running water. Set aside to drain well, leaving the water boiling. Repeat with the peas, setting them aside separately, then season the carrots and peas to taste with salt and pepper.

Tie each variety of asparagus together in a small bunch with string. Add the white asparagus to the pan first and cook for 3 to 5 minutes until al dente. Remove from the pan and drain under cold running water. Set aside to cool. Repeat with the green asparagus, then the wild (cooking it for only 1 1/2 minutes), then the purple variety, draining them all under cold running water, untie and set aside.

To make the Parmesan tuiles, heat the oven to 375°F and line a small baking pan with parchment paper. Form 4 equal shapes of grated Parmigiano Reggiano, measuring about 6 x 2 inches and spaced about 2 inches apart on the parchment paper. Bake the Parmesan for 5 minutes or until slightly browned.

Coco's Curls

The first time we made this mixture of fried potatoes and carrots, Coco was fascinated by the Japanese turning machine and turned all the vegetables herself. We've called them Coco's Curls ever since.

1 1/2 pounds carrots, peeled
2 1/2 pounds potatoes, peeled
1 cup flour
1/4 teaspoon salt
4 cups grapeseed oil
FOR THE BATTER
2/3 cup flour
2/3 cup cornstarch
2 teaspoons baking powder
1/4 teaspoon salt
1/2 cup milk
3/4 cup ice-cold water
SERVES 4

To make the batter, in a bowl place the flour, cornstarch, baking powder and salt. Make a well in the center and add the milk and water, whisking thoroughly to give the batter the consistency of cream. Set aside for 30 minutes before use. Preheat oven to 200°F.

Meanwhile, turn the carrots, then the potatoes, through a turning slicer machine to form curls, keeping the curled vegetables in separate piles.

Heat 2 ounces of the grapeseed oil to 350°F in a large, heavy saucepan. Line a baking sheet with parchment paper. Place the flour in a medium mixing bowl and season with the salt. Take a handful of curled potatoes and drop them in the hot oil. They will form a nest; using a pair of metal tongs, move the curls around so that they do not clump together as much. Turn the curls over to brown the potatoes evenly, cooking for 1 1/2 to 2 minutes in total. Remove the curls from the oil and place them on the prepared baking sheet to drain, shaping them into an attractive pile of curls. Keep the cooked batches warm in a low oven. Repeat with the remaining potatoes.

Take a handful of the carrot curls and toss them in the seasoned flour to coat. Shake off any excess flour then immerse the carrot curls in the batter. Lift them out with your hand, squeezing the curls so that the majority of batter drips back into the bowl. Place the battered carrot curls in the hot oil, swirling to keep the strands as separate as

possible. Fry for 1 1/2 to 2 minutes in total, turning over halfway through cooking to brown the curls evenly.

When cooked, remove the carrot curls from the hot oil and place them next to the potatoes on the prepared baking sheet to drain, shaping them into an attractive pile of curls, keeping them warm in the oven. Repeat with the remaining carrots, then serve warm with the curled potatoes.

Pea Purée

Peas, mint and tarragon is a classic combination of flavors. The Parmigiano ties them all together.

1 cup fresh peas, shelled from about 12 ounces of pea pods
1 sprig tarragon, leaves picked
4 small mint leaves, torn
2 tablespoons heavy cream
2 tablespoons finely grated Parmigiano Reggiano
Salt
MAKES ABOUT 3/4 CUP

In a small saucepan, bring 3 cups of salted water to a boil. Add the peas, tarragon leaves and mint and cook for about 5 to 6 minutes or until the peas are soft.

Prepare an ice bath. Drain the peas, reserving the tarragon and mint. Plunge the peas and herbs into the iced water then drain. Transfer to a blender, add the cream and purée until smooth, scraping down the sides of the blender as necessary.

Stir in the Parmigiano Reggiano then add salt to taste. The purée may be refrigerated for up to 1 day in a covered container.

NOTES

• Serve this with the children's canapés on page 70.
• Makes a great sauce for fried balls of leftover risotto.
• Eliminate the Parmigiano and serve this mixture under steamed cod with dots of Balsamic Glaze (see page 211) to garnish.

Braised Red Cabbage
and Beets

This dish has a kind of poetic sharpness. Beet juice not only gives the cabbage a deeper color but reinforces the mixture's incredibly vibrant flavor.

1 medium red cabbage (about 2^1/$_2$ pounds), quartered and thinly sliced lengthwise using a mandoline
^{3}/$_4$ pound raw beets, peeled and cut into ^{1}/$_4$-inch dice
1 Granny Smith apple, peeled, cored and cut into ^{1}/$_4$-inch dice
6 cups red wine, preferably Burgundy
6 juniper berries, crushed
2 bay leaves, crushed
2 tablespoons olive oil
1 medium red onion, thinly sliced
^{3}/$_4$ cup red wine vinegar
^{1}/$_2$ cup sugar
1 tablespoon salt
1^1/$_2$ cups beet juice
SERVES 6 TO 8

In a shallow, nonreactive dish, combine the cabbage, beets, apple, red wine, juniper berries and bay leaves. Press a layer of plastic wrap over the surface then weigh it down with a plate to completely submerge the cabbage. Marinate overnight in the refrigerator.

Next day, heat the oil in a large pot over medium heat. Add the onion and sauté for about 4 minutes until soft. Add the marinated cabbage mixture, vinegar, sugar and salt, stirring to combine. Briskly simmer the cabbage over medium-high heat for 1 hour, stirring occasionally. If there is still liquid in the pot when the cabbage has finished cooking, increase the heat to high and boil until almost all of the liquid has evaporated.

Add the beet juice to the cabbage, lower the heat to medium-high and cook, stirring, for about 10 minutes or until almost dry. Serve hot or cold.

Fire-roasted
Onions

Serve with grilled chicken skewers on page 107.

2 small red onions, peeled, trimmed and each cut into 6 wedges
3 slices smoked bacon, each cut into 4 pieces crosswise
12 small sprigs marjoram
6 teaspoons olive oil
6 teaspoons balsamic vinegar
Salt and freshly ground black pepper
MAKES 12

Heat the oven to 400°F, or prepare a charcoal grill that is medium-hot. Cut 12 pieces of kitchen foil measuring 8 inches square.

Place 1 wedge of onion, cut-side down, on a piece of foil. Top with a piece of bacon, a few grinds of pepper and a sprig of marjoram. Drizzle with ^{1}/$_2$ teaspoon of olive oil and ^{1}/$_2$ teaspoon of balsamic vinegar. Pull the edges of the foil together to make a generous parcel and seal the edges. Repeat with the remaining ingredients.

Transfer the onion parcels to a baking sheet and cook in the oven for 25 to 30 minutes or until tender. Alternatively, place the parcels directly on the grill of the medium-hot fire and cook until the onions are tender.

Roast Carrot Confit

I usually call this spiked carrots because of the balance of the flavorings to the carrot itself. Drain the juice that remains after cooking and use it as a sauce for any fish or duck preparation. You can add some rice wine vinegar or some pickling spice to the cooking juices and use it as a vinaigrette for a beet and orange salad. Or swirl in some Herb Oil or Tomato Water (see page 211) and have a whole new concept. Can be served as a vegetarian course.

20 thin carrots (about 2^1/$_2$ pounds), peeled and trimmed to a length of about 6 inches.
^{3}/$_4$ cup freshly squeezed orange juice

1/4 cup freshly squeezed lemon juice

2-inch piece fresh ginger, peeled and grated

1/2 cup olive oil

4 cloves garlic, finely chopped

2 teaspoons grated orange zest

2 teaspoons grated lemon zest

1 teaspoon cumin seeds

Salt and freshly ground black pepper

SERVES 4

Heat the oven to 275°F. Combine all the ingredients in a shallow ovenproof dish measuring approximately 11 x 7 inches, spreading the carrots evenly over the bottom. Cover the dish with foil or a lid and bake for about 2 hours, until the carrots are tender.

Roasted Vegetables

Roasted vegetables can be of any combination – this version includes Brussels sprouts and salsify (also know as oyster plant) along with the more usual root vegetables and onions. I have always enjoyed this method of layering the vegetables through the cooking time.

4 medium parsnips, peeled and halved lengthwise, or 3 large parsnips, peeled and cut into quarters

3 medium carrots, peeled and halved lengthwise

8 small red potatoes, halved if large

8 small white potatoes, halved if large

6 small white turnips, halved lengthwise

2 salsify, peeled, cut into 2-inch pieces and set aside in acidulated water

3 tablespoons olive oil

8 white pearl onions, peeled

8 red pearl onions (if available), peeled

8 cloves garlic, trimmed but unpeeled

1 large portobello mushroom, stemmed and cut into eight wedges

10 Brussels sprouts, trimmed and a cross cut in each base

4 green onions (white and light green parts only), trimmed

8 shiitake mushrooms, stemmed

1 1/2 tablespoons unsalted butter, diced

4 teaspoons thyme leaves

1 tablespoon flat-leafed parsley leaves, halved

Salt and freshly ground black pepper

SERVES 8

Preheat the oven to 375°F. In a large bowl, toss the parsnips, carrots, potatoes, turnips and drained salsify with 1 tablespoon of the olive oil, plus a little salt and pepper, until coated. Arrange the vegetables cut-side down on a large baking sheet and roast on the bottom shelf of the oven for 35 minutes or until the vegetables are beginning to brown. Turn the vegetables 2 or 3 times during cooking to prevent burning.

In the same bowl, toss the pearl onions, garlic and portobello mushroom with 1 tablespoon of olive oil, plus a little salt and pepper, until coated. Add this mixture to the baking sheet of vegetables and gently stir to combine. Continue roasting for 10 to 12 minutes.

Meanwhile, bring a small saucepan of salted water to boil and blanch the Brussels sprouts and green onions separately for 1 to 2 minutes each. Drain thoroughly under cold running water. Set aside separately.

In a small bowl, combine the shiitake mushrooms and the Brussels sprouts and toss with 1 tablespoon of olive oil, plus a little salt and pepper, until coated. Add them to the baking sheet of vegetables, stirring to combine. Dot the butter over the vegetables and sprinkle with 2 to 3 tablespoons of water. Roast for another 10 minutes. Add the green onions and roast for 5 minutes more.

Remove the vegetables from the oven and gently mix them with the thyme and parsley before serving.

NOTES

• Acidulated water is a soaking medium that prevents cut raw vegetables and fruits browning. Simply add the juice of half a lemon to about 2 cups of water and place the salsify in it.

• You can remove the skins from the pearl onions easily by placing them in a bowl of warm water for 5 minutes.

• Including some squash in this basic recipe will add another texture to the dish.

• Whenever I prepare vegetables, an overwhelming desire to cook grains and leafy greens occurs. Alongside this recipe, serve some cooked wild rice, Sweet Potato Purée (see page 151), and sautéed spinach, cabbage or Swiss chard, and you have a Lake House Vegetarian Roast.

Lake House
Mashed Potatoes

After one year of making mashed potatoes every night at Coco Pazzo's restaurant in New York, these are their secrets: creamy and rich.

5 or 6 Yukon Gold, Maris Piper or King Edwards potatoes (about 2 pounds), peeled and sliced 1/4 inch thick
1 tablespoon salt
1/2 cup milk
1/2 cup cream
5 tablespoons unsalted butter, cubed
Freshly ground black pepper
SERVES 4 TO 6

Place the potatoes in a medium saucepan and sprinkle in the salt. Cover with cold water and bring to a boil. Reduce the heat and simmer for about 15 to 18 minutes, until the potatoes are fork-tender.

Meanwhile, heat the milk, cream and butter in a small saucepan until the butter melts. Drain the potatoes and pass them through a food mill fitted with a fine disc into a medium bowl, adding the milk mixture as you pass them. Season to taste and serve.

Truffled Mashed Potatoes

Lake House Mashed Potatoes (see above)
1/4 cup unsalted butter
3 shiitake mushroom caps, sliced
4 green onions or baby leeks, trimmed, thinly sliced and washed
1/2 cup cooked wheatberries
1 golf-ball-sized black winter truffle, cut into 1/8-inch dice (optional)
1 tablespoon white truffle oil, more if desired
1 teaspoon finely chopped garlic
Salt and freshly ground black pepper
SERVES 4

Make the mashed potatoes and set aside in a warm place.

In a small saucepan over low heat, melt 3 tablespoons of the butter and cook the mushroom caps slowly for 2 to 3 minutes, adding salt and pepper to taste. Remove and set aside.

Meanwhile, in the same pan over low heat, melt the remaining butter and gently cook the green onions for 2 minutes.

Stir the cooked mushrooms and green onions into the mashed potatoes, then add the wheatberries, black truffle (if using), truffle oil, garlic and more salt and pepper to taste, mixing until thoroughly combined. Serve warm.

NOTE

• Serve with any fish, meat, chicken or game dish.

Sweet Potato purée

The roasting process concentrates the flavors, but the inclusion of carrot makes this purée less dense than one made exclusively from sweet potato.

1 large sweet potato (about 8 ounces)
1 large carrot (about 5 ounces)
1/2 teaspoon olive oil
1/2 tablespoon unsalted butter at room temperature
1 teaspoon honey
A pinch of cinnamon
1/4 teaspoon salt
MAKES 1 CUP

Preheat the oven to 350°F. Prick the sweet potato several times. Rub the potato and carrot with the oil and transfer to a baking pan. Bake for 50 minutes to 1 hour or until soft. Remove from the oven.

When the potato and carrot are cool enough to handle, peel and cut them into 1-inch pieces. Place in a food processor fitted with a steel blade and add the butter, honey, cinnamon and salt. Process until just smooth.

NOTES

• Can be served alone as a side dish but also good as an accompaniment to a roasted chicken and a salad.
• Try with roast duck, some spaghetti squash, and a sauce of Roasted Pepper Purée (see page 218) thinned with some of the duck's cooking juices.
• Perfect with the Children's Veggie Canapés on page 70.

Swiss Chard and
Mushroom—stuffed Onions

Meltingly sublime, the mushroom and chard filling is the perfect foil to the rustic onion shells.

10 medium onions (about 3 inches in diameter), unpeeled
1 ounce dried porcini mushrooms
$1^{1}/_{4}$ pounds Swiss chard
6 cups lightly packed spinach leaves, torn in half
1 ounce unsalted butter
1 tablespoon olive oil
$^{1}/_{2}$ cup finely chopped onions
$^{1}/_{8}$ teaspoon freshly grated nutmeg
$^{1}/_{2}$ cup mascarpone cheese
$^{1}/_{3}$ cup freshly grated Parmigiano Reggiano
1 tablespoon tarragon leaves
Salt and freshly ground black pepper
MAKES 10

Preheat oven to 400°F. Trim the ends of the onions to make them sit flat. Place the onions root-end up in a shallow baking dish. Fill the dish a quarter of the way up with water and transfer it to the oven for 45 minutes, regularly adding more water as necessary. Turn the onions root-end down, and return to the oven for another 45 minutes.

While the onions are cooking, soak the porcini mushrooms in a small bowl with 2 cups of warm water for 30 minutes. Using a slotted spoon, lift the rehydrated porcini mushrooms from the bowl, rinse under cold running water to ensure dirt has been removed, place on a cutting board and roughly chop. Drain the soaking liquid through a fine-meshed sieve, reserving $1^{1}/_{4}$ cups. Set aside.

Meanwhile, remove the Swiss chard leaves from their stalks and discard any that are bruised or discolored. Tear the leaves in half, wash in several changes of water then set aside. Trim the Swiss chard stalks and cut them into $^{1}/_{4}$-inch cubes. Measure out 1 cup of stalks, wash and set aside.

Remove the cooked onions from the oven. Discard the water from the baking dish and leave the onions to cool until they are easy to handle. Gently peel the onions. Using a serrated knife, cut the top quarter from each onion and set these aside to use as lids. With a

teaspoon, remove the center of each onion, leaving the 2 to 3 outside layers intact. Reserve the center sections from 2 of the onions and finely chop them.

Bring a large saucepan of salted water to a boil. Add the Swiss chard leaves and stems and boil for 3 minutes. Add the spinach leaves and boil for another 3 minutes. Drain in a colander and refresh under cold running water. Firmly press the greens inside the colander with your hands to remove any excess water. Chop roughly and set aside.

Lower the oven to 350°F. Combine the butter and olive oil in a large skillet over medium heat. Add the finely chopped onions and cook for about 2 minutes or until translucent, then add the chopped porcini and cook for 1 minute. Stir in the reserved porcini soaking liquid, plus the Swiss chard leaves and stems, spinach, reserved centers of the cooked onions, nutmeg and a little salt and pepper. Cook until the mixture is almost dry.

Remove the mixture from the heat and gently fold in the mascarpone, $^{1}/_{4}$ cup of the Parmigiano Reggiano and the tarragon. Spoon the filling tightly into the shells of the onions, mounding them up. Cover with the onion lids and sprinkle with the remaining Parmigiano Reggiano. Return to the baking dish and roast for 15 to 20 minutes, until heated through. Serve immediately.

Notes

• Any leftover stems of Swiss chard need not be wasted: You can steam them as a vegetable, or add them to soups, stews and salads, such as the Millet and Aduki Bean Salad (see page 139).
• This filling can also be used to stuff filo triangles. Bake them at 350°F for 10 minutes and drizzle with truffle oil before serving. (The filo parcels can be frozen once filled.)
• Try using different hard and soft cheeses.

Potato and
Celery Root Gratin

4 teaspoons unsalted butter

1 clove garlic, cut in half

2 medium onions (about 1¼ pounds in total), thinly sliced

3 cups Light Chicken Stock (see page 209)

A bouquet garni made from 3 sprigs of flat-leaf parsley and 3 sprigs of thyme tied together with string

2 pounds russet potatoes, peeled and very thinly sliced on a mandoline

2 pounds small celeriac, peeled and very thinly sliced on a mandoline

1½ cups grated Gruyère

1 cup grated Parmigiano Reggiano

1 tablespoon thyme leaves

1 tablespoon salt

Freshly ground black pepper

2 cups fresh bread crumbs

SERVES 6 TO 8

Preheat the oven to 375°F. Butter an 8-cup baking dish with a quarter of the butter then rub it with the garlic and set aside.

In a large skillet, combine the onions, 2 cups of the chicken stock, 1 tablespoon of butter and the bouquet garni. Bring to a simmer and cook for about 12 minutes or until the onions are soft.

Transfer the onion mixture to a large bowl. Add the potatoes, celery root, Gruyère, half the Parmigiano Reggiano, thyme, salt and pepper. Stir to combine. Pour the remaining 1 cup chicken stock over to moisten. Toss and transfer the mixture to the prepared dish.

In a small bowl, combine the remaining ½ cup of Parmigiano Reggiano with the bread crumbs, then spread them evenly over the potato mixture. Cover the baking dish loosely with foil and place it on a baking tray in case the gratin bubbles over.

Transfer to the oven and bake for 1 hour, then increase the heat to 400°F, remove the foil and bake for an additional 30 minutes. Remove and cool for 20 minutes before serving.

Notes

• Celery root tastes like a cross between celery and parsley with strong earthy overtones. Use it shredded or grated raw in salads.
• I especially like the way the bread crumbs soak up the combination of cheeses and stock, then dry to form a crust.
• Make this into a soup, without the bread crumbs, by cooking it in a pot. Add some more chicken stock and a little cream and purée the mixture before serving.

Sauté of Fennel,
Artichokes and Carrots

Look, no butter. This particular mix of vegetables does well slightly brown and crispy. The mint leaves bring the flavor up and out.

1 teaspoon fennel seeds
2 small fennel bulbs, washed and trimmed, halved but not cored
12 baby carrots, washed and peeled but stems retained
6 baby artichokes, trimmed, cut in half lengthwise and rubbed with lemon
2 tablespoons olive oil, plus extra-virgin oil to garnish
2 teaspoons tiny mint leaves
Salt and freshly ground black pepper
SERVES 6

In a medium saucepan of salted water, place the fennel seeds; bring to a boil. Add the fennel bulbs and cook for 8 to 10 minutes or until fork-tender. Drain and cool under cold running water. Cut each half of fennel lengthwise into 6 pieces and set aside.

Meanwhile, in another saucepan of boiling salted water, add the carrots and boil for 1 to 2 minutes or until cooked but still crisp. Drain and cool under cold running water. Set aside.

In a medium-large skillet over a medium-high heat, heat 1½ tablespoons of olive oil. Add the artichokes, cut-side down, and fry for 5 to 6 minutes or until crisp, golden and cooked, turning once. Remove them from the pan and set aside in a bowl in a warm place.

Lower the heat to medium-low and if needed add more oil. Add the carrots and cook for 2 minutes, stirring occasionally, until slightly brown, then remove the carrots to the bowl of artichokes. Raise the heat to medium and add more oil if needed.

Cook the fennel cut-side down for about 3 minutes or until crisp and brown, turning once. Remove and toss with the other vegetables. Season with salt and pepper. Remove to a serving dish, garnish with the extra-virgin olive oil and mint leaves then serve.

NOTES

• I like mixed vegetables a little moist so I sometimes add about 4 tablespoons of warm stock or Tomato Water (see page 211) and some dots of Chive Oil (see page 214) around this dish.

• Serve with the Curried Lamb Shanks (see page 113) or as a side dish to the Roast Duck or Roast Pork (see pages 120 and 116). Alternatively, add some roast potatoes and serve with roast chicken.

Achiote Onion Rings

Serve with Lake House Ketchup (see page 212).

3 pounds medium onions, sliced ½ inch thick and separated into rings
4 cups buttermilk
½ cup achiote or annatto seeds
6 cups peanut oil, for frying
2 cups flour
2 cups cornstarch
1 cup fine yellow cornmeal
2 teaspoons salt
1 teaspoon paprika
SERVES 8 TO 10

Combine the onions and buttermilk in a large bowl, carefully stirring to coat the onions in the liquid. Leave to stand for 1 hour.

Meanwhile, heat the achiote seeds and oil in a large, heavy saucepan over low heat for 20 minutes. Remove from the heat and strain. Place the oil back in the saucepan and set aside.

In a large bowl, combine the flour, cornstarch, cornmeal, salt and paprika. Preheat oven to 150°F.

Place the saucepan of achiote-infused oil over a medium heat. When it reaches 350°F. on a deep-fry thermometer, remove the onion rings from the buttermilk and drain them well. Divide the onion rings into 6 batches. Dip in the cornmeal mixture, shaking off the excess.

Cook each batch of onion rings in the hot oil for 2 to 3 minutes or until golden. Remove to a baking tray lined with parchment paper to drain, then transfer the baking tray to the warm oven. Fry the remaining batches, then serve immediately.

NOTE

• Brick-red achiote seeds, otherwise known as annatto, are a natural coloring agent.

Pies, Puddings & Ices

4

Apricot Tart

FOR THE ALMOND NUT CRUST
1/2 cup whole unblanched almonds
1/2 cup plus 2 tablespoons unsalted butter
1/3 cup plus 1 tablespoon sugar
1/4 teaspoon pure almond extract
1 cup plus 1 tablespoon flour
FOR THE PASTRY CREAM
2 egg yolks
2 1/2 tablespoons superfine sugar
1 tablespoon flour
1/2 cup milk
1/4 vanilla bean, split lengthwise and scraped, reserving both the pod and seed
1/2 amaretti cookie, crushed, optional
FOR THE APRICOTS
1 1/3 cups sugar
2 vanilla beans, split lengthwise
3 sprigs mint, folded in half
3 pounds apricots, halved and pitted
SERVES 8

To make the almond nut crust, in the bowl of a food processor fitted with a steel blade, pulse the almonds until chopped. Add the butter, sugar and almond extract and pulse until combined. Add the flour in 3 batches, pulsing for 30 to 40 seconds after each addition. When the dough forms into a ball, transfer it to a piece of plastic wrap, shape into a 6-inch disc, wrap and chill in the refrigerator for 1 hour.

Butter and flour a 10-inch fluted tart tin with a removable base, tapping out any excess flour. Remove the chilled pastry from the refrigerator, unwrap it and place it in the center of the tart tin. With the palm of your hand, press down firmly on the pastry to spread it out over the base and up the sides of the tart tin, making the crust about 1/4 inch thick at the base and sides. Place in the refrigerator for 2 hours.

Meanwhile, make the pastry cream. In a small bowl, place the yolks and half the sugar. Sift in the flour and mix thoroughly. In a medium saucepan over medium heat, place the milk, the remaining sugar and the vanilla bean pod and seed. Bring to a boil, stirring. Remove the pan from the heat and add a little of the hot milk mixture to the egg mixture, stirring constantly. When combined, add the remaining milk mixture and stir well.

Return the pastry cream to a medium saucepan and place over medium heat, whisking constantly until the mixture thickens and bubbles, 1 to 2 minutes. Let it bubble for about 10 seconds then remove the pan from the heat and pass the mixture through a fine sieve into a small bowl. Add the crushed amaretti cookie, if using, then place a circle of plastic wrap on the surface of the pastry cream to prevent a skin forming. Chill over iced water or refrigerate for 20 minutes.

Preheat the oven to 425°F. Remove the pastry case from the refrigerator. Using a fork, prick the bottom of the case 8 times. Completely line the bottom and sides of the pastry case with buttered parchment paper. Fill the lining up to the rim of the pastry case with pie weights. Place the tart case directly on the bottom shelf of the oven and bake for 15 minutes.

Remove the tart case from the oven and leave it to stand for 10 to 20 minutes. Meanwhile, lower the oven temperature to 325°F. Remove the paper and beans from the tart case then return it to the oven for 15 to 20 minutes or until light brown. Remove the tart case from the oven and leave to cool.

Meanwhile, to prepare the apricots, rinse the fruit, pat dry and set aside. In a medium saucepan over medium-high heat, place the sugar and 4 cups of water. Bring to a boil then lower the heat to a gentle simmer and stir until the sugar dissolves, about 2 minutes. Add the vanilla bean pod and mint sprigs.

Place one-third of the apricots in the liquid and poach for 1 to 2 minutes, being careful not to overcook the apricots. They are done when the skin comes away from the flesh easily. Transfer the apricots gently to a colander; set over a bowl to drain. Carefully remove the skin and place the apricots cut-side down on a baking sheet lined with greaseproof paper. Repeat the process with the remaining apricots. Cover and refrigerate for 15 to 20 minutes, reserving 1 cup of the poaching liquid and the liquid drained from the apricots.

To assemble the tart, remove the cooled pastry case from the tart tin and place it on a serving plate. Using a spatula, spread the pastry cream evenly over the bottom of the pastry. Arrange the apricots on top of the pastry cream in a tight circular pattern completely covering the pastry cream.

Just before serving, in a small saucepan, place the reserved apricot poaching liquid and bring to a boil. Cook until the liquid is syrupy and reduced to about 1/4 cup in volume. Brush a thin layer over the apricots and the crust. Serve immediately.

- Make sure the apricots are all of the same size and same degree of ripeness.
- The apricots need to be quite soft, but if they are perfectly ripe, they may not need to be poached. Simply peel the apricots with a small knife, cut them in half, pit and arrange the halves on top of the pastry cream.

English Toffee Tart

Fifteen years ago I converted a house into a bakery business and lived above the kitchen and retail space. I invented a tart combining my two uncontrollable vices, chocolate and caramel. In the middle of the night, I would get out of bed, walk downstairs, eat half a tart, and in the morning wake up with a contented smile.

13$^1/_2$ ounces Pâte Sucrée (half of recipe on page 219)
FOR THE TOFFEE
1$^1/_4$ cups superfine sugar
4 tablespoons unsalted butter
$^1/_2$ cup heavy cream
FOR THE CUSTARD
1 egg plus 2 yolks
$^1/_2$ cup heavy cream
FOR THE GANACHE
6 ounces Valrhona Manjari chocolate, chopped
$^1/_2$ cup crème fraîche
FOR THE FROSTING
1$^1/_2$ cups heavy cream
3 tablespoons grated Valrhona Manjari chocolate
SERVES 10

Butter and flour the bottom and sides of an 11 x 7-inch tart pan with a removable bottom. Roll the dough out into a rectangle measuring about 14 x 10 inches and a thickness of $^1/_8$ inch and use it to line the prepared pan. Chill for 1 hour.

Preheat the oven to 375°F. Line the pastry case with a piece of foil or parchment paper and fill it with pie weights. Bake for 20 minutes or until the pastry is golden brown, then remove from the oven and leave it to cool before removing the pie weights. If the pastry is still a little uncooked, return it to the oven without the pie weights for another 3 to 5 minutes until fully cooked. Leave to cool.

To make the toffee, dissolve the sugar in $^3/_4$ cup of water in a medium saucepan over low heat. Raise the heat to medium, bring to a boil, brushing down the sides of the pan with a pastry brush dipped in water, and simmer for about 30 minutes or until amber and approaching the burned stage.

Remove the pan from the heat. Using a wooden spoon, gradually beat in the butter until it has melted, followed by the cream, stirring constantly for about 2 minutes or until the toffee is smooth. Allow the mixture to cool slightly, but not completely. Set aside.

Preheat the oven to 325°F. To make the custard, whisk the egg, egg yolks and cream in a medium-sized bowl, then stir in 4 tablespoons of the toffee. Pour the mixture into the pastry case and bake for 15 minutes or until it has just set. Remove from the oven and leave to cool.

Reserve 2 tablespoons of the toffee in a small bowl for later use. Lightly rewarm the remaining $^3/_4$ cup of toffee and spread it over the caramel custard in a thin layer. Place in the refrigerator to set for 45 minutes.

Meanwhile, make the ganache. In a heatproof bowl, melt the chocolate and crème fraîche together in the top of a double boiler over barely simmering water, stirring until the chocolate melts and the mixture is thoroughly combined. Let cool for 10 minutes. Pour the ganache into the tart and smooth over the surface. Leave to set for another 10 minutes.

Place the cream for the frosting in the bowl of an electric mixer fitted with a whisk attachment, add the reserved 2 tablespoons of toffee and beat until stiff peaks form, being careful not to overbeat. Transfer the whipped cream to a piping bag fitted with a $^1/_2$-inch star tip and pipe a decorative pattern over the tart. Sprinkle the top with the grated chocolate then chill before serving.

Lemon Tart

A recipe so good you will keep it in your repertoire forever.

FOR THE PASTRY
1$^2/_3$ cups flour, plus extra for dusting
3 tablespoons superfine sugar
$^1/_2$ teaspoon grated lemon zest
A pinch of salt
8 tablespoons unsalted butter, plus extra for greasing
1 large egg
2 tablespoons heavy cream
FOR THE FILLING
6 large eggs, plus 8 large egg yolks
1$^1/_2$ cups superfine sugar
1$^1/_2$ cups lemon juice
Grated zest of 3 lemons
1 cup unsalted butter, softened
FOR THE DECORATION
$^1/_4$ cup superfine sugar

Blueberries
Edible flowers
Fresh mint leaves
SERVES 8

To make the pastry, combine the flour, sugar, lemon zest and salt in a bowl and rub in the butter until the mixture resembles coarse bread crumbs. In a small bowl, whisk the egg and cream together and add them to the flour mixture to make a dough, gradually bringing the mixture into a ball. Remove from the bowl and shape the dough into a 6-inch disc. Cover with plastic wrap and chill for 2 hours.

Meanwhile, butter and flour a 9-inch tart pan with a removable base, measuring 2 inches deep. Remove the chilled dough from the refrigerator and roll it out on a lightly floured work surface to a 16-inch circle, 1/8 inch thick. Use the rolling pin to help you lift the pastry up over the tart pan, pressing it firmly down inside and leaving any excess pastry hanging over the sides of the pan. Chill for 1 hour.

Preheat the oven to 350°F. Prick the base of the pastry case with a fork 8 times. Line the pastry shell with parchment paper and fill the base of the shell with pie weights. Bake for 25 minutes. Remove the tart case from the oven and carefully lift out the paper and weights, then return the tart case to the oven to bake for a further 5 minutes. Remove from the oven and leave to cool for 5 minutes. Using a sharp knife, trim away the excess pastry to give a smooth finish on the rim. Gently remove the tart shell from the pan and set aside on a serving plate to cool completely.

To make the filling, heat a saucepan of water to boiling, then reduce to a simmer. In a metal bowl that fits over the saucepan, place the whole eggs, yolks, sugar, lemon juice and grated zest. Being sure the bowl does not touch the water, place it over the pan of simmering water. Whisk the mixture for 10 minutes or until it thickens and turns bright yellow.

Remove the bowl from the heat and add the butter, a piece at a time, whisking continuously. Pour the mixture into the pastry case and chill for 3 to 4 hours or overnight until set.

Preheat the broiler. Sprinkle the sugar over the top of the set tart and place under the broiler until the sugar caramelizes. Alternatively, caramelize it with a blowtorch. Garnish the tart with blueberries, edible flowers and mint leaves, then serve.

Picnic
Cherry Pies

America is the world's leading cherry producer and this is my version of one of the U.S.A.'s favorite snacks, cherry Pop Tarts.

FOR THE PASTRY
3 1/4 cups white flour
2 tablespoons superfine sugar
1/2 teaspoon baking powder
1/4 teaspoon salt
1/2 cup unsalted butter
4 ounces cream cheese
1/2 teaspoon grated lemon zest
1 large egg, lightly beaten
1/2 tablespoon cold milk (optional)
1 tablespoon heavy cream
1 tablespoon granulated brown sugar
FOR THE CHERRY FILLING
1/2 cup sugar
1 3/4 pounds cherries, stemmed and pitted
2 tablespoons brandy
1/2 teaspoon cinnamon
A pinch of salt
1 tablespoon balsamic vinegar
1 tablespoon cornstarch
1 tablespoon grated lemon zest
MAKES 12 TO 14

To make the filling, place the sugar in a medium sauté pan with 2 tablespoons of water and set over high heat. Allow the sugar to caramelize for about 5 minutes, until it reaches an amber color. Add the pitted cherries and stir with a metal spoon.

Carefully add the brandy, which will ignite, then stir in the cinnamon and salt. Lower the heat to medium and cook for 10 minutes, stirring occasionally. If the caramel sticks to the spoon, scrape it back into the cherry mixture to dissolve.

Stir in the balsamic vinegar and cook for 2 more minutes. Set a colander over a bowl and strain the cherries, collecting the juices. Return the juices to the sauté pan and simmer them over medium heat for 5 minutes. Add any extra juices from the cherries to the simmering liquid.

In a small bowl, mix the cornstarch with 1 tablespoon of water and stir the mixture into the pan. Return the sauce to the boil, stirring constantly, until the sauce is syrupy in consistency, about 1 minute. Strain the sauce over the cherries in the bowl and stir in the lemon zest. Chill the filling for about 1 hour to give a jam consistency.

To make the pastry, in the bowl of a food processor fitted with a steel blade, combine the flour, salt, baking powder and sugar. Add the butter, cream cheese and lemon zest and process until the mixture resembles coarse crumbs. While the machine is still running, add the egg through the feed tube and, if the dough is dry, add the milk. The dough should be sticky.

Turn the pastry out onto a lightly floured surface and shape it into a disc with your hands. Wrap in plastic wrap and chill for 1 hour.

Line two baking trays with baking parchment. To assemble the pies, roll the dough out on a lightly floured surface to a square measuring about 16 inches across and about 1/8 inch thick. Using a 4 1/2-inch plain round cutter, cut out discs of pastry and transfer them to the baking sheets. Chill for 30 minutes.

Remove the discs from the refrigerator and let them stand for 3 to 4 minutes at room temperature until just pliable. Take a heaped tablespoon of cherry filling, allowing most of the juice to drain back into the bowl, then place it in the center of one half of a pastry disc. Brush the complete edge of the disc with cold water and fold the dough over to form a semicircle. Seal the dough edges together with the tines of a fork.

Repeat the process with the remaining dough and cherry filling and place the hand pies on parchment-lined baking trays. Chill for 30 minutes.

Preheat the oven to 375°F. Remove the pies from the refrigerator and using scissors, snip the top of each pie several times to form a decorative row. Brush each pie with cream to glaze and sprinkle with brown sugar. Place them immediately in the oven and bake for 20 minutes. Allow the pies to cool for at least 10 minutes on the baking trays before serving as the cherry filling will be very hot. Can be eaten warm, at room temperature or cold.

NOTES

• Any leftover cherry filling can be served with ice cream, used as a sauce for desserts, or even as the base of a sauce for duck.
• Strawberries, figs and blackcurrants can be substituted for cherries.

Little
Apple Pies

The meltingly soft fruit, nestled against the crispy pastry . . . well, it's only apple pie!

FOR THE PASTRY
1 1/2 cups white flour, plus extra for dusting
1/4 teaspoon superfine sugar
A pinch of salt
6 tablespoon unsalted butter, chilled and diced
1/4 cup vegetable shortening, chilled and diced
FOR THE FILLING
6 Granny Smith apples (about 1 pound), peeled, cored and cut into
1/4-inch cubes (4 cups)
Juice of 1/2 lemon
1 1/2 tablespoons sugar
1/4 teaspoon ground cinnamon
A pinch of ground nutmeg
A pinch of salt
2 tablespoons unsalted butter, finely diced
FOR THE CRUMBLE TOPPING
2/3 cup flour
1/4 cup soft light brown sugar
1/4 cup white granulated sugar
1/4 teaspoon ground cinnamon
1/4 teaspoon ground nutmeg
1/4 cup unsalted butter, chilled and diced
MAKES 12

To make the pastry, place the flour, sugar and salt in the bowl of a food processor fitted with a steel blade and pulse until combined. Add the butter and shortening and process for 20 to 25 seconds, until it resembles coarse crumbs. Slowly add 2 1/2 to 3 tablespoons of iced water while the processor is running and process until the dough comes together and forms a ball. Sprinkle a work surface with 1/2 tablespoon of flour and dust the surface of dough with 1/2 tablespoon of flour. Shape it into a disc, wrap in plastic wrap and chill for at least 1 hour.

Meanwhile, brush 12 muffin-tin cups 2 1/2 inches in diameter and 1 inch deep with 1 tablespoon of melted butter and dust them lightly with flour, tapping out any excess. Remove the chilled pastry from the refrigerator and let it stand at room temperature until soft enough to roll. On a lightly floured surface, roll out the pastry to a thickness of $1/8$ inch. Using a $3^1/2$-inch plain round cutter, cut 12 circles of pastry and fit each circle into the prepared muffin cups, easing the pastry down into the bottom of the cups and up the sides, letting it extend $1/2$ inch above the rim. Refrigerate for 30 minutes.

To make the filling, in a large bowl, combine the apples, lemon juice, sugar, cinnamon, nutmeg and salt, stirring gently until well mixed. Set aside.

To make the crumble, in a smaller bowl, place the flour, brown and white sugars, cinnamon and nutmeg and stir to combine. Use your fingers to rub the pieces of butter into the flour mixture until it has the consistency of rough bread crumbs.

To assemble the pies, remove the muffin tin from the refrigerator. Divide half the apple filling equally between the pastry shells then dot each one with a pinch of butter. Sprinkle each pie with 1 tablespoon of the crumble topping, then divide the remaining apple mixture equally among them, piling it high above the rims of the pastry shells. Sprinkle each pie with 2 teaspoons of the remaining topping. Chill for 30 minutes. Preheat the oven to 400°F.

Remove the pies from the refrigerator and bake for 15 minutes, then lower the heat to 350°F and continue baking for another 40 minutes. Remove the pies from the oven and leave to cool for about 10 minutes in the cups. Using a round-bladed knife, gently ease the pastry away from the cups and lift the pies out. Serve.

Rustic
Open Peach Pie

The topping in this pie sends shock waves through the palate.

FOR THE PASTRY
$2^1/4$ cups flour
2 tablespoons superfine sugar
1 teaspoon salt
1 cup unsalted butter, chilled and diced
$1/4$ cup iced water
1 egg, separated
$1/2$ vanilla bean, split lengthwise and scraped, reserving the seeds
1 tablespoon semolina

FOR THE PEACH FILLING
2 pounds $6^1/2$ ounces peaches (about 10), pitted and each cut into eighths
2 tablespoons flour
2 tablespoons cornstarch
$1/4$ cup superfine sugar
Juice of $1/2$ lemon
2 tablespoons unsalted butter, chilled and diced
FOR THE STREUSEL TOPPING
3 tablespoons unsalted butter
2 tablespoons ground almonds
2 tablespoons flour
2 tablespoons superfine sugar
FOR THE GLAZE
$1^1/2$ tablespoons heavy cream
1 tablespoon superfine sugar
SERVES 8

First, make the pastry. Place the flour in a mixing bowl with the sugar and salt and thoroughly combine. Rub the butter into the flour mixture until the mixture resembles coarse crumbs.

In a small bowl, place the iced water, egg yolk and the scraped seeds of the vanilla bean and mix them together. Pour into the flour mixture and use your hand to gently combine until the pastry comes together to form a ball.

Remove it to a lightly floured surface, flatten the ball into a disc about 6 inches in diameter, wrap it in plastic wrap and chill for 1 hour.

Meanwhile, make the peach filling. Place the peach segments in a bowl and sprinkle over the flour, cornstarch and sugar. Toss together gently with your hands, then pour over the lemon juice. Dot the peaches with the butter and toss again. Cover and set aside in the refrigerator.

To make the streusel topping, mix the butter, almonds, flour and sugar together in a food processor fitted with a steel blade. Pulse until well combined.

Roll the pastry out on a lightly floured surface to a circle about 16 inches in diameter and less than $1/4$ inch thick. Cut the pastry to a diameter of 14 inches, creating a circle. With the aid of a rolling pin, lift the pastry onto a baking sheet lined with parchment paper. Carefully smooth over any cracks in the pastry with your fingers to prevent the pie from leaking when it is cooked.

Brush the pastry with the egg white, leaving a 2-inch gap around the edge, then over the brushed area sprinkle the semolina.

Pile the peaches high in the center of the pastry. Use your hands to bring the edges of the dough up and onto the pile of peaches to create a rim approximately 3 inches high, going around the whole pie and leaving some peaches showing at the top.

Take pinches of the streusel mixture and place them on top of the peaches, using all the mixture. Chill the pie for 2 hours.

Preheat the oven to 400°F. In a small bowl, mix together the cream and sugar to make the glaze and brush it over the pastry. Bake for 40 to 45 minutes, turning once. Leave to cool for 15 to 20 minutes on the baking sheet. Using two large metal spatulas, carefully remove the pie to a serving plate.

NOTE

• Variations on this theme are plentiful: Use the cherry mixture from the Picnic Pies (see page 162), or try plums or nectarines. You can also make the recipe into individual pies.

Winter Fruit Tart

Cooked apples are my favorite. Here they are mixed with pears, cranberries and warming spices for a sensational explosion of sharp and sweet flavors.

1¹/₂ pounds Quick Puff Pastry (see page 219)
¹/₄ to ¹/₂ teaspoon ground ginger
FOR THE FILLING
3 Granny Smith apples, peeled, cored and cut into ³/₄-inch-thick slices
3 McIntosh apples, cored and cut into ³/₄-inch-thick slices
3 Empire apples, cored and cut into ³/₄-inch-thick slices
2 Bartlett pears, cored and cut into ³/₄-inch-thick slices
2 Bosc pears, cored and cut into ³/₄-inch-thick slices
6 tablespoons unsalted butter
³/₄ cup maple syrup
3 star anise
1 vanilla bean, split lengthwise and cut into 3 pieces
9 tablespoons freshly squeezed lemon juice
Salt
³/₄ cup cranberries (optional)

1 egg, lightly beaten
1 cup Riesling wine
1 tablespoon confectioners' sugar
Cinnamon Crème Anglaise, to serve (see page 166)
SERVES 8 TO 10

Dust a large piece of baking parchment lightly with flour. On the paper, roll out the puff pastry into a circle measuring 14 inches in diameter and ¹/₈ to ¹/₄ inch thick. Transfer the paper and pastry to a baking sheet.

Sprinkle a line of ground ginger around the circumference of the pastry about 1 inch in from the edge. Roll the edge of the pastry like a rope over the ginger to make a 12-inch tart case. Chill for 30 minutes.

Meanwhile, prepare the filling. Place a colander over a bowl and set aside. In a large bowl, combine all the apples and pears then divide into three equal batches. In a large skillet over medium heat, melt 2 tablespoons of the butter and, when it is foaming, add ¹/₄ cup of the maple syrup, 1 star anise, 1 piece of vanilla pod, 3 tablespoons of lemon juice and a pinch of salt. Heat through briefly, stirring. Add one-third of the cranberries, if using, then add one batch of the sliced fruit and cook for 5 minutes or until the fruit begins to soften, carefully stirring.

Remove the fruit from the pan with a slotted spoon and place it in the colander to drain. Repeat the process with the remaining butter and two batches of cranberries and other fruit, leaving them to drain thoroughly. Reserve all the liquid to make the sauce.

Preheat the oven to 425°F. Remove the pastry from the refrigerator and prick the base 10 or 12 times. Brush the pastry case with the beaten egg, being careful not to brush any on the baking parchment;

otherwise it will impede the pastry rising. Spoon the drained sautéed fruit – still containing the spices – into the pastry case, piling it high in the center. Bake the tart in the oven for 25 minutes.

When the tart has been in the oven for 25 minutes, dust the top evenly with confectioners' sugar and continue baking at 375°F. for a further 20 minutes.

Meanwhile, place the skillet over medium heat and add the wine, stirring with a wooden spoon to deglaze the pan and incorporate any caramelized cooking juices. Bring the wine to a boil and boil hard until it has reduced by half. Add the drained cooking juices from the fruit to the wine and continue boiling until you are left with 1/2 cup of syrupy sauce. Set aside in a warm place.

Remove the tart from the oven and serve warm or at room temperature with the sauce, and a sauceboat of Cinnamon Crème Anglaise.

NOTES

• If buying ready-made puff pastry, try to find one made with butter, rather than vegetable fat. The puff pastry trimmings can be used to make other desserts or cut into shapes, baked and used as crispy garnishes.
• To make Cinnamon Crème Anglaise, add 1 to 2 teaspoons of ground cinnamon to 2 1/4 cups prepared Crème Anglaise.

Summer
Fruit Noisette

A luxurious but simple tart redolent of summer's bouquet of fruits. The black pepper sparks it beyond the bush.

13 1/2 ounces Pâte Sucrée, chilled (half of recipe on page 219)
1 1/4 pounds fresh raspberries, for decoration
FOR THE FILLING
1 cup unsalted butter, plus extra for greasing
3 large eggs
1 cup sugar
1/2 cup plus 1 tablespoon white flour, plus extra for dusting
1 teaspoon pure vanilla extract
5 ounces fresh strawberries, hulled and halved if large

2$^1/_2$ ounces mixed berries, such as blackberries, halved, blueberries and raspberries
A few grinds of black pepper
SERVES 8

Butter and flour a 10-inch fluted tart pan with a removable bottom. Roll the pastry out on a lightly floured surface to a circle 13 inches in diameter. Use the pastry to line the base and sides of the tart pan and trim off any excess. Prick the base 10 times with a fork and chill for 30 minutes.

To make the filling, melt the butter in a small saucepan over medium heat for about 20 minutes until it is nut brown in color. While the butter is browning, break the eggs into a large bowl and beat them well together with the sugar, flour and vanilla.

Preheat the oven to 350°F. Place the strawberries in the tart case cut-side down. Scatter the mixed berries over the top. Sprinkle with a few grindings of black pepper.

When the butter has turned nut brown, pour it immediately into the egg mixture and whisk until the butter is fully incorporated. Pour the egg mixture into the tart case and bake for 45 to 50 minutes. Remove from the oven and leave to cool in the tart pan.

Carefully remove the side of the tart pan and decorate the tart with the raspberries, placing them in tight circles over the whole tart.

NOTE

• The French term *noisette* refers to the butter, which is cooked to a nut (*noix*) brown.

Berry Cobbler

The combination of different fruits is the real kicker that sets this cobbler apart from others.

10 cups mixed soft fruit, such as blackberries, black currants, blueberries, raspberries and strawberries
6 tablespoons superfine sugar
$^1/_4$ cup flour
1 tablespoon cornstarch
2 teaspoons butter, chilled and diced, plus extra for greasing
2 tablespoons freshly squeezed lemon juice, plus 2 teaspoons lemon zest

FOR THE COBBLER DOUGH
1 cup plain flour
3 tablespoons sugar
2 teaspoons baking powder
$^1/_2$ teaspoon salt
5 tablespoons unsalted butter
$^1/_2$ cup buttermilk
FOR THE GLAZE
1$^1/_2$ tablespoons cream
1 teaspoon superfine sugar
A pinch of cinnamon
Mint leaves, to garnish
SERVES 6 TO 8

Preheat the oven to 375°F and lightly butter a 10-inch round fluted ovenproof dish. In a large bowl, combine the berries with the sugar, flour, cornstarch, butter, lemon juice and zest. Transfer the mixture to the prepared dish.

To make the cobbler dough, place the flour, sugar, baking powder and salt in a large bowl. Rub in the butter until it resembles coarse bread crumbs, then stir in the buttermilk until combined. Using a large spoon, drop the dough onto the surface of the berries in about 10 even spoonfuls, being sure not to cover all the berries.

In a small bowl, combine the cream, sugar and cinnamon for the glaze. With a pastry brush, brush the mixture over the top of the cobbler dough. Place the dish on a baking sheet and transfer it to the oven for 35 to 40 minutes. Remove from the oven and leave to stand for 10 minutes before serving. Garnish with mint leaves and serve with fresh cream.

NOTE

• Don't hesitate to experiment with other fruits in this recipe.

Caramelized Rice
Pudding with Sour Cherry Sauce

The arborio rice is imbued with a wintry creaminess and textural crunch.

4 cups milk
3 cups heavy cream
2 strips lemon zest, each 2 x 1 inch with the white pith removed
2 cinnamon sticks
1 vanilla bean, split lengthwise and scraped, reserving both the seeds and the pod
1½ cups arborio rice
1 teaspoon unsalted butter, softened
¾ cup plus 2 tablespoons superfine sugar
2 large eggs, plus 1 large egg white
FOR THE DRIED SOUR CHERRY SAUCE
½ cup sugar
1 cup dry white wine
½ cup dried sour cherries
2 sprigs mint
½ vanilla bean, split lengthwise and scraped, reserving both the seeds and the pod
SERVES 6 TO 8

To make the cherry sauce, take a heavy, shallow saucepan and combine the sugar with ½ cup of water and heat gently until the sugar dissolves, stirring frequently. Brush any sugar down from the sides of the pan with a wet pastry brush. Bring the mixture to a boil and boil for 5 minutes until just thick.

Add the wine, return to a boil and boil for 8 to 10 minutes until the mixture is syrupy and all the alcohol has evaporated. Add the cherries, mint sprigs, vanilla pod and seeds to the syrup. Leave to cool then cover and infuse overnight. Remove the vanilla pod and mint. Serve warm or cold.

In a large saucepan over medium-high heat, combine the milk, cream, lemon zest, cinnamon sticks and vanilla pod and seeds. Bring to a boil then remove from the heat and leave to infuse for 30 minutes.

Once infused, strain the milk mixture, return it to the saucepan and bring to boil. Stir in the rice, return to a boil, then reduce the heat to low and simmer uncovered for about 25 minutes or until the rice is tender, stirring frequently.

Meanwhile, lightly rub a 6-cup pudding mold or heatproof bowl with the butter. To make the caramel, in a heavy saucepan, combine ⅓ cup of the sugar with 2 tablespoons of water, stirring several times to dissolve the sugar. Bring the mixture to a boil, brushing down the sides of the pan with a pastry brush dipped in water. Lower the heat and simmer, without stirring, until the syrup begins to color and turns a deep amber, 3 to 5 minutes. Immediately pour the caramel into the bottom of the prepared mold.

In a medium bowl, whisk together ½ cup of the sugar with the whole eggs and egg white until well combined. Stir ½ cup of the rice mixture into the egg mixture, then carefully fold in the remaining rice until well combined.
Transfer the mixture to the mold, smooth over the top, cover with a kitchen towel and leave to set for 45 to 60 minutes.

To serve, loosen the edges of the pudding with a knife. Cover the mold with the serving plate, then invert and tap gently to loosen the pudding. If the sides of the unmolded pudding are a little loose, reshape them with a spatula or knife. Serve with the dried sour cherry sauce.

NOTE

• When cherries are in season, substitute 1 cup pitted and halved sour cherries for the dried fruit.

Crème Brûlée
with Kadaifi Discs and Summer Fruit

Inspired by Jacques Torres, pastry chef at Le Cirque restaurant in New York. The ginger and crème fraîche lift the crème brûlée to great heights. The crunch of the kadaifi disc adds just the right texture next to the smooth, snappy crème brûlée.

FOR THE KADAIFI DISCS
6 ounces Kadaifi (see page 87)
1/4 cup Clarified Butter, warmed (see page 215)
1 1/2 tablespoons confectioners' sugar, sifted
FOR THE RASPBERRY SAUCE
1 cup raspberries
1 tablespoon freshly squeezed lemon juice
1/2 tablespoon superfine sugar
1/4 cup Simple Syrup (see page 219)
FOR THE MINT SAUCE
1 cup mint leaves
1/2 cup Simple Syrup (see page 219)
1/2 vanilla bean, split lengthwise and scraped, reserving the seeds
FOR THE MANGO SAUCE
1 ripe mango, peeled and roughly chopped
1 tablespoon freshly squeezed lemon juice
1 tablespoon freshly squeezed lime juice
1/4 teaspoon finely chopped lemongrass
FOR THE CRÈME BRÛLÉE
2 cups heavy cream
1 vanilla bean, split lengthwise and scraped, reserving the pod and seeds
2-inch piece fresh ginger, peeled and sliced 1/4 inch thick
1 large egg, plus 5 large yolks
1/2 cup sugar
A pinch of salt
1/2 cup crème fraîche
1/4 cup raspberries, plus 16 extra to garnish
1/4 cup blueberries, plus 16 extra to garnish
1/4 cup blackberries, plus 16 extra to garnish
SERVES 8

To make the raspberry sauce, combine the raspberries, lemon juice and sugar in a small bowl and leave to stand at room temperature for 30 minutes to macerate. Transfer to a food processor fitted with a

steel blade and process with the syrup until puréed. Strain and refrigerate in a covered container.

To make the mint sauce, bring a small saucepan filled with water to the boil. Add the mint leaves and blanch for 20 seconds, then drain and place immediately under cold running water. Squeeze the mint dry and chop finely. In a blender, combine the mint, syrup and seeds of the vanilla pod and purée for 1 to 2 minutes. Refrigerate in a covered container until needed.

To make the mango sauce, combine the chopped mango, lemon and lime juices and lemongrass in a blender. Purée until smooth – if the sauce is too thick, add some water a tablespoon at a time until a sauce consistency is achieved. Strain the sauce through a fine sieve and refrigerate in a covered container.

To make the crème brûlée, combine the cream, vanilla pod and seeds and ginger in a saucepan over medium heat and bring to the scalding point. Immediately remove the pan from the heat and set aside to infuse for 30 minutes. Strain through a sieve.

Preheat the oven to 275°F. In a medium bowl, whisk together the whole egg and yolks, sugar and salt for 2 minutes or until well combined. Pour a little of the infused cream onto the egg mixture. Mix together then add the rest of the cream and the crème fraîche, whisking to combine. Strain the mixture through a fine sieve.

Scatter the berries in the bottom of a 9-inch square baking dish and pour the custard over the berries. Place the baking dish in a large roasting pan and fill the roasting pan halfway with hot water. Place on the middle rack of the oven and bake for 50 to 55 minutes. Remove the baking dish to a wire rack to cool completely before transferring to the refrigerator to chill.

Raise the oven temperature to 375°F.

To make the kadaifi discs, line two baking trays with parchment. Measure out 1 heaping tablespoon of kadaifi and place it on the parchment, flattening it with your hand and shaping it into a disc measuring 4 inches in diameter and 1/8 to 1/4 inch thick.

Using a pastry brush, dab the discs with the warm clarified butter, then dust with about 1/8 teaspoon of the confectioners' sugar. Repeat the process to give 24 discs, using up all the pastry. Bake for 5 minutes then rotate the baking trays and cook for another 5 minutes or until golden brown. Cool on the baking trays.

To assemble the dish, place a kadaifi disc in the center of a dessert plate. Top with 1¹/₂ heaping tablespoons of crème brûlée. Place a second kadaifi disc on top of the crème brûlée. Add another 1¹/₂ heaping tablespoons of crème brûlée and a final kadaifi disc. Drizzle 1¹/₂ tablespoons of mango sauce around the plate, then a tablespoon of raspberry sauce and a tablespoon of mint sauce. Scatter 6 of the berries you have reserved for a garnish over the top. Repeat with the remaining ingredients and serve.

NOTES

• The mango, raspberry and mint sauces can be used with any dessert you like. They can be refrigerated for up to 2 days or frozen for up to 1 month.
• Alternatively, for a traditional crème brûlée, transfer the custard mixture to 8 3-inch ramekins and bake in a bain-marie until just set. Remove and generously sprinkle the tops with sugar, then caramelize under a broiler or by using a blowtorch.

Chocolate Soufflés
with Chocolate Dog Tuiles

The tuiles for this dessert were inspired by Finbar and Gideon, the two Irish wolfhounds at Lake House, but you could make the tuiles a different shape if you prefer.

FOR THE SOUFFLÉS
¹/₂ cup plus 1 tablespoon unsalted butter, plus extra, melted
¹/₃ cup plus 1 tablespoon superfine sugar, plus extra, for dusting
8 ounces Valrhona Manjari chocolate (64% cocoa solids), chopped or Green 'n' Black's Dark Chocolate (70% cocoa solids)
¹/₄ cup unsweetened cocoa powder
4 eggs, separated
A pinch of salt
³/₄ cup Chocolate Sauce (see page 218)
8 scoops Vanilla Ice Cream (see page 179)
FOR THE TUILES
¹/₄ cup superfine sugar
2 tablespoons unsalted butter
3 tablespoons flour
1 tablespoon honey
1 tablespoon unsweetened cocoa powder
1 egg white

¹/₄ teaspoon pure vanilla extract
SERVES 8

To make the tuiles, in the bowl of a food processor fitted with a steel blade, combine the sugar and butter and process until light and fluffy. Scrape down the sides of the bowl with a rubber spatula, then add the flour, honey, cocoa, egg white and vanilla extract and process for a further 2 minutes.

Using a rubber spatula, transfer the mixture to a clean bowl and chill for 1 hour.

Meanwhile, draw the outline of a dog on a piece of acetate or a large plastic lid, measuring approximately 3 inches from head to paw and 3¹/₂ inches from nose to tail. Use a sharp pair of scissors or a stenciling knife to cut away the center of the drawing to make a stencil.

Preheat the oven to 325°F and line a baking sheet with parchment paper. Remove the tuile mixture from the fridge. Place the stencil over the parchment paper at one corner of the baking sheet. Using a spatula, spread a thin layer of tuile mixture across the stencil to form a dog shape. Carefully lift the stencil away from the paper and repeat with the remaining tuile mixture to make at least 8 tuiles in total.

Bake for 5 minutes then remove from the oven and leave to cool on the baking sheet.

To make the soufflés, butter the interior of 8 4-ounce ramekins measuring 3 inches in diameter and 1¹/₂ inches deep. Dust the bottom and sides with sugar and tap out any excess.

In a double boiler over barely simmering water, melt the chocolate, butter and cocoa powder together, stirring until thoroughly combined. Remove from the heat and set aside to cool for 5 minutes, then stir in the egg yolks, mixing well.

Preheat the oven to 425°F. In a large bowl or bowl of an electric mixer fitted with a whisk attachment, add the egg whites and salt. Beat until just foamy, then add the sugar, 2 tablespoons at a time, beating after each addition. When all the sugar has been incorporated and the whites are stiff, stir a spoonful of the whites into the cooled chocolate mixture to lighten it. Then use a large rubber spatula to carefully fold the chocolate mixture into the whites.

Spoon the soufflé mixture into the prepared ramekins, filling them three-quarters of the way up the sides, and bake for about 8 minutes,

until they have risen slightly and are dry on top but underdone in the center. Meanwhile, reheat the Chocolate Sauce if necessary in a double boiler.

To serve, invert the soufflés onto the centers of 8 serving plates and place a scoop of ice cream next to each one. Drizzle 1 1/2 to 2 tablespoons of warm chocolate sauce around each plate and insert the front paws of each dog-shaped tuile in the ice cream with the back paws on the plate so that the dogs are standing up.

NOTE

• The soufflés can be prepared up to 24 hours in advance, and stored uncooked and covered in the refrigerator. Remove them from the fridge 40 minutes before baking to let them come to room temperature.

Norma's Sticky Toffee Puddings with Sweet Potato

Here an English classic is revised and given an American twist: the richness of sweet potato.

FOR THE PUDDINGS
1 large sweet potato (about 12 ounces)
1/2 teaspoon ground cinnamon
9 1/2 tablespoons unsalted butter, softened, plus extra, melted, for greasing
1 cup hot water
1 cup dried dates, roughly chopped
3 1/2 teaspoons instant coffee
2 1/2 teaspoons pure vanilla extract
1 teaspoon baking soda
1/4 teaspoon salt
7 tablespoons firmly packed light brown sugar
2 large eggs, lightly beaten
2 cups flour
2 teaspoons baking powder
FOR THE SAUCE
1 cup firmly packed light brown sugar
6 tablespoons unsalted butter
3 tablespoons heavy cream
1/2 cup pecans, chopped
MAKES 12

Preheat the oven to 400°F. Prick the sweet potato all over with a fork, place it in a baking dish and bake for about 1 hour or until very soft. When the potato is cool enough to handle, peel and discard the skin and mash the flesh with a fork in a small bowl. Measure out 2/3 cup, saving any remaining sweet potato for another use. Add cinnamon and stir to combine.

Reduce the oven temperature to 375°F. Brush 12 2/3-cup timbale molds with melted butter and line the bases with baking parchment. In a medium bowl, combine the hot water, chopped dates, coffee, vanilla, baking soda and salt.

In the bowl of an electric mixer fitted with the paddle attachment, beat the butter and sugar together until light and fluffy. Gradually add the eggs, mixing to combine. Mix the baking powder and flour together then gradually add the flour mixture and sweet potato mixture to the mixing bowl alternately, beginning and ending with flour, beating to combine.

Using a large rubber spatula, stir in the date mixture until thoroughly combined. Divide the batter evenly among the molds then place the molds on a baking sheet and transfer to the oven. Bake for 20 minutes.

In a small saucepan, combine the sugar, butter, cream and pecans and stir over low heat until the sugar has dissolved, about 5 minutes. Remove the puddings from the oven and leave to stand for 5 minutes.

Turn the puddings out onto serving plates, remove the baking parchment, and turn top-side up. Serve immediately with the warm sauce over the puddings.

Rhubarb and
Strawberry Crumble

FOR THE CRUMBLE
1/2 cup walnuts
1 cup flour
1/3 cup light brown sugar
1 tablespoon granulated sugar
1/8 teaspoon ground cinnamon
A few scrapings of nutmeg
A pinch of salt
1/2 cup unsalted butter, softened, plus extra for greasing
FOR THE FILLING
1 3/4 to 2 1/4 pounds rhubarb, trimmed and chopped into 1/2-inch pieces (6 to 7 cups)
4 cups strawberries, hulled and sliced
1 cup superfine sugar
1/2 cup flour
8 mint leaves, torn, plus extra sprigs to garnish
FOR THE SAUCE
1 cup heavy cream
3 tablespoons superfine sugar
1/2 cup mascarpone cheese, softened
SERVES 6 TO 8

To make the topping, preheat the oven to 350°F and toast the walnuts in a small baking pan for 5 minutes or until lightly browned. Remove them from the oven and cool before chopping them coarsely. In a medium bowl, mix together the walnuts, flour, sugars, cinnamon,

salt and nutmeg and work in the butter until the mixture is crumbly and holds together somewhat.

Prepare the filling in a large bowl by tossing the rhubarb and strawberries together with the sugar, flour and mint leaves.

Raise the oven temperature to 375°F. Rub a 2-quart baking dish with 1/2 teaspoon of butter. Evenly add the fruit to the dish. Spread the crumble over the top leaving a border of 1 inch around the outer edge. Bake for 40 minutes or until you can easily insert a skewer into the rhubarb.

Meanwhile, make the sauce. In a large cold bowl, whisk the cream for about 2 minutes or until slightly thickened. Add the sugar and whisk for another couple of minutes, then add the softened mascarpone and mix until smooth. Chill then serve alongside the warm fruit crumble, each garnished with a sprig of mint.

NOTE

• Try serving with Vanilla Ice Cream (see page 179) if preferred.

Pears with Filo

FOR THE PRALINE FILLING
3 tablespoons unsalted butter at room temperature
2 tablespoons granulated sugar
3 tablespoons Hazelnut Praline (see page 218)
1 large egg, beaten
1 tablespoon flour
1 teaspoon dark rum
A pinch of salt
FOR THE PEARS
6 large ripe Comice pears with stems
Juice of 1 lemon
9 sheets filo pastry, each measuring 16 x 11 inches
6 tablespoons unsalted butter
1/2 cup confectioners' sugar
MAKES 6

To make the praline filling, place the butter and sugar in a medium mixing bowl and beat with an electric mixer until creamy and fluffy. Beat in the praline, egg, flour, rum and salt. Refrigerate until cold, about 15 minutes.

Slice 3/4 to 1 inch from the top of each pear and brush the cut side with lemon juice. Reserve the tops. Using a small melon baller, scoop out along the length of the core, working from the top down through the pear, leaving the base intact and retaining as much of the pear flesh as possible.

Brush the inside of each pear with a little lemon juice to prevent discoloration. Fill the cavity of each pear with 2 to 3 teaspoons of the praline filling, then set the tops back on top of each pear and stand them upright on a baking sheet.

Using a sharp knife, halve the filo pastry crosswise to give 18 rectangles measuring 8 x 11 inches each. Place them together under a damp kitchen towel to prevent the pastry drying out.

In a small saucepan, gently melt the butter. Place the confectioners' sugar in a sieve. To assemble each pear, place a sheet of filo on a clean work surface and lightly brush it with melted butter. Sprinkle with a little confectioners' sugar, then repeat with another 2 sheets of filo, buttering and sprinkling with sugar.

Place a pear in the center of the pastry and bring the corners up to the stems, gently pressing the pastry onto the body of the pear to seal while decoratively folding back the edges at the stem. Brush the outside of the parcel with more butter and place it on a parchment-lined baking sheet. Repeat with the remaining pears and pastry then place the packaged pears in the refrigerator to chill for 30 minutes.

Preheat the oven to 325°F. Dust the pears with confectioners' sugar and bake for 35 to 40 minutes until the pears are tender when pierced with a skewer and the pastry is golden brown and crisp. Allow to cool for 10 minutes before serving.

Black Currant Sorbet

3 1/2 cups black currants
1/2 cup plus 1 tablespoon superfine sugar
6 tablespoons crème de cassis
MAKES 3 CUPS

If necessary, place the bowl of your ice cream machine in the freezer to chill.

Pick over the black currants, removing any bits of stem or bruised fruit. Place them in a saucepan with the sugar and 1 cup plus 2

tablespoons of water and slowly bring to the boil, stirring occasionally until the sugar is dissolved. Boil for 5 minutes, then remove the pan from the heat and leave the black currant mixture to cool completely. Refrigerate until very cold, at least 2 hours.

Remove the mixture from the refrigerator and stir in the crème de cassis. Pour the mixture into the bowl of the ice cream machine and freeze according to the manufacturer's instructions. When the sorbet is thoroughly churned, remove it to a chilled stainless steel mixing bowl or a plastic container with a lid. Serve immediately or cover and place in the freezer.

NOTES

• This is best made just prior to being eaten.
• The exact amount of sugar required depends on how sweet or ripe the fruit is: Use less if necessary.
• Serve the sorbet with Biscotti (see page 184).

Vanilla Ice Cream

What makes this recipe are the ingredients straight from the Lake House farm.

3 1/4 cups milk
10 large egg yolks
1 1/4 cups sugar
1 teaspoon pure vanilla extract
2 1/2 cups heavy cream
MAKES 2 QUARTS

If necessary, place the bowl of the ice cream machine in the freezer to chill.

Place the milk in a medium saucepan and bring to a simmer over medium-high heat. Meanwhile, in a large bowl, beat together the egg yolks, sugar and vanilla until well combined.

Once the milk has simmered, remove it from the heat and pour a little onto the yolk mixture, beating well. Add the rest of the milk then return the custard to the saucepan and place the pan over low heat, stirring continuously for about 10 minutes until the custard thickens and coats the back of a spoon.

Strain the custard into a clean bowl and chill for about 2 hours or until cold. Then stir in the cream and pour the mixture into the ice cream machine. Freeze following the manufacturer's instructions.

Neon Lime
Jelly

Jelly is not just for juveniles: Grown-ups like this too.

1¹/₂ cups superfine sugar
³/₄ cup freshly squeezed lime juice
30 jelly letters or other jelly candies
4 tablespoons unflavored gelatin
SERVES 10/MAKES 30

Place the lime juice in a small bowl and sprinkle over the gelatin. Set aside to soften for 10 minutes.

Meanwhile, place 8 cups of water in a large pan with the sugar and heat gently, stirring occasionally, until the sugar dissolves. Bring to a boil and boil for 5 minutes.

Lower the heat to a simmer. Using a rubber spatula, thoroughly remove all the gelatin from the bowl and add to the syrup. Whisk the mixture for 2 minutes over low heat until the gelatin has completely dissolved.

Line a fine-mesh sieve with wet cheesecloth and use it to strain the jelly mixture. Pour half the jelly mixture into a dish measuring approximately 11 x 7 inches and at least 2¹/₂ inches deep. Transfer the dish to the refrigerator to chill for 1 hour. Leave the remaining jelly mixture at room temperature.

When the jelly in the refrigerator has just set, place the jelly letters at regular intervals on the surface and return to the refrigerator for 15 minutes. Then pour over the remaining jelly mixture and chill for at least 4 hours until thoroughly set. Leave the jelly to set overnight, if desired.

To remove the jelly from the dish, line a clean cutting board with greaseproof paper or plastic wrap. Dip the underside of the dish into a bowl or sink filled with hot water for 30 seconds, ensuring no water enters the dish. Invert the jelly onto the cutting board, remove the dish and return the jelly to the refrigerator for 30 minutes.

Remove and cut the jelly into 30 squares ensuring there is a jelly letter in the center of each piece. To serve, stack the jellies in two large glass containers, or on individual serving plates.

Toffee Apples

For this recipe you will need twelve 7-inch wooden liquorice sticks, sharpened at one end (so that you can pierce the apples easily) and a sugar thermometer.

12 small McIntosh apples
2¹/₂ cups superfine sugar
³/₄ cup golden syrup or ¹/₂ cup dark corn syrup plus ¹/₄ cup light corn syrup
Grapeseed oil, for greasing
MAKES 12

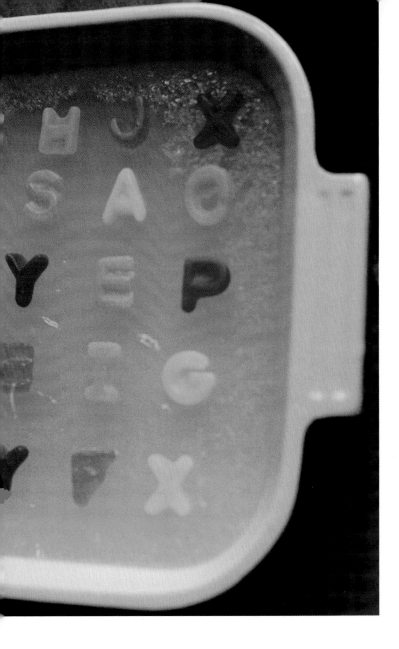

Thoroughly wash and dry the apples and insert a stick into the stem end of each.

Combine the sugar, syrup and 1 1/2 cups of water in a deep, heavy saucepan and place over low heat, stirring until the sugar dissolves. Brush down the sides of the saucepan with a wet pastry brush to dissolve any sugar crystals. Clip a sugar thermometer onto the side of the saucepan and raise the heat to high. Cook the syrup, without stirring, until it starts to turn amber (310°F) which will take about 30 minutes.

Meanwhile, line a baking sheet with aluminum foil and lightly brush it with grapeseed oil.

When the toffee has reached the right temperature and color, immediately remove the saucepan from the heat and, working quickly, dip one apple at a time into the hot toffee to coat completely, letting any excess toffee drip back into the pan. Transfer to the foil-lined baking sheet. Repeat with the remaining apples. Leave until set.

Cookies, Cakes & Breads

5

Biscotti

1³/₄ cups flour
²/₃ cup sugar, plus 1 teaspoon extra for glazing
Generous ¹/₃ cup whole almonds, with skins
2 tablespoons sliced almonds
1 tablespoon cornmeal
2 teaspoons anise seeds
³/₄ teaspoon baking powder
A pinch of salt
¹/₄ cup unsalted butter, softened
1 large egg, plus 1 egg white extra for glazing
¹/₂ tablespoon vanilla extract
¹/₂ tablespoon Pernod
MAKES 30 TO 35

Preheat the oven to 350°F and line a baking sheet with baking parchment. Combine the flour, sugar, almonds, cornmeal, anise, baking powder and salt in the bowl of an electric mixer fitted with the paddle attachment. Mix at low speed until all the ingredients are well combined. Add the butter and process until the mixture resembles wet sand.

In a separate bowl, lightly beat together the whole egg, vanilla and Pernod and add them to the butter mixture. Mix for about 1 minute to give a soft dough.

Transfer the dough from the mixer to a lightly floured surface and shape it into a log measuring about 15 inches long and 1¹/₂ inches in diameter. Place the dough on the parchment-lined baking sheet.

In a small bowl, lightly beat the egg white for the glaze and brush it over the dough. Dust the log with 1 teaspoon of sugar and bake for 30 minutes. Remove from the oven and cool to room temperature on the baking sheet. Leave the oven on.

When the log is cool, transfer to a cutting board and, using a serrated knife, cut the log diagonally into ¹/₄-inch slices to give approximately 30 biscotti. Lay each biscotti flat on the baking sheet and put them back in the oven for 8 minutes or until lightly browned. Turn the biscotti over and bake for another 8 minutes. Immediately transfer the biscotti to a wire rack and cool. Store the biscotti in a parchment-lined airtight container for up to 1 week.

Black Cat Chocolate
Shortbread Cookies

Don't cross this cat's path! This shortbread dough makes a great cookie.

2 cups flour
¹/₂ cup unsweetened cocoa powder, plus 2 tablespoons extra for dusting
¹/₂ teaspoon baking powder
A small pinch of salt
1 cup unsalted butter, softened
1 cup plus 3 tablespoons superfine sugar
²/₃ cup semi-sweet chocolate chips or good-quality plain chocolate, chopped
Angelica, cut into 28 tiny pieces
MAKES 14

Sift the flour, cocoa, baking powder and salt together and set aside. In an electric mixer fitted with the paddle attachment, cream the butter and sugar together until light and fluffy. Add the flour mixture and beat at low speed until just combined. Fold in the chocolate chips by hand, then wrap the dough in plastic wrap and chill for at least 1 hour.

Meanwhile, draw a cat shape measuring approximately 4 inches from head to paw and head to tail on a piece of acetate or a large plastic lid. Cut it out to use as a template for the cookies. Line a baking sheet with baking parchment and set aside.

On a lightly floured surface, roll the chilled dough out to ¹/₄ inch thick. Place the cat template in one corner of the dough and cut around it with a small, sharp knife. Repeat until all the dough is used up – you will have about 14 cookies in total – then transfer the cookies to the baking sheet using a metal spatula and chill for 1 hour.

Preheat the oven to 275°F. Bake the cookies for 20 minutes, then remove from the oven and cool on the baking sheet for 5 minutes

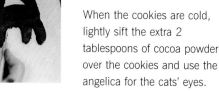

before transferring to a wire rack to cool completely.

When the cookies are cold, lightly sift the extra 2 tablespoons of cocoa powder over the cookies and use the angelica for the cats' eyes.

Chocolate Chip
Cookies

Children and adults love these chewy, chunky cookies.

1 cup unsalted butter
3/4 cup plus 1 tablespoon granulated sugar
3/4 cup plus 1 tablespoon soft light brown sugar
2 large eggs
1/2 tablespoon pure vanilla extract
2 cups flour
3/4 teaspoon baking soda
1 1/2 cups walnuts, chopped
1 cup semi-sweet chocolate chips, or good-quality plain chocolate, chopped
MAKES 18

In the bowl of an electric mixer fitted with the paddle attachment, beat the butter and sugars and cream until light and fluffy. Add the eggs one by one at low speed, scraping down the sides of the bowl with a rubber spatula, then add the vanilla and beat until combined. Slowly beat in the flour and baking soda until well combined. Remove the bowl from the machine and, using a rubber spatula, fold in the walnuts and chocolate chips.

Place the cookie mixture in the fridge to chill for 30 minutes, then divide the dough into 18 balls and chill for a further 30 minutes.

Preheat the oven to 325°F. Line two baking trays with parchment and place the balls on them, spaced about 3 inches apart. Bake for 18 minutes, rotating the baking sheets halfway through the cooking time.

Remove the cookies from the oven and leave them on the baking sheets for 3 to 5 minutes before transferring to a wire rack to cool completely.

NOTE

• You can double the recipe if desired, roll into large balls and freeze. Then, just defrost enough to shape and bake.

S'Mores

The graham cracker was called a health food in the 1830s. This popular snack is usually rectangular and made from whole wheat, sweetened with honey and spices. Roast the marshmallows over a fire and sandwich them between the prepared graham crackers. You'll always want s'more!

FOR THE MARSHMALLOWS
Grapeseed oil, for brushing
Confectioners' sugar, for dusting
2 tablespoons unflavored gelatin
1 3/4 cups granulated sugar
1/2 cup light corn syrup (or liquid glucose)
1/4 teaspoon salt
1 teaspoon pure vanilla extract
FOR THE GRAHAM CRACKERS
1 1/2 cups all-purpose flour
1 cup plus 2 tablespoons rye flour
1 cup plus 2 tablespoons whole-wheat flour
1 1/2 teaspoons baking powder
3/4 teaspoon cinnamon
1/2 teaspoon nutmeg
1/2 teaspoon salt
1/3 cup unsalted butter, softened
1/2 cup plus 1 tablespoon light soft brown sugar
1 large whole egg plus 1 yolk
1/2 cup honey

1¹/₂ tablespoons molasses
FOR THE CHOCOLATE PRALINE GANACHE
6 ounces Valrhona Manjari chocolate (64% cocoa solids)
¹/₂ cup crème fraîche
¹/₂ cup Hazelnut Praline (see page 218)
MAKES 12

First make the marshmallows. Brush a 9 x 5 x 3-inch glass loaf pan with oil, then dust generously with finely sifted confectioners' sugar. In the bowl of an electric mixer, place ¹/₂ cup of water and sprinkle the gelatin evenly over the surface, leaving it to soak.

Combine the granulated sugar, corn syrup, salt and 7 tablespoons of water in a heavy medium-sized saucepan. Place over low heat and stir until the sugar has dissolved. Clip on a candy thermometer and raise the heat to high. Cook the syrup without stirring until it reaches 240°F., or the soft ball stage, then immediately remove the pan from the heat.

Using the whisk attachment of the mixer, beat the gelatin on high speed, adding the hot syrup slowly until the mixture is white, fluffy and stiff, about 10 minutes. Add the vanilla, whisking for 30 seconds.

Pour the marshmallow mixture into the prepared pan. Brush a spatula with oil and use it to smooth over the top, brushing it with oil again as necessary. Let stand uncovered, at room temperature for 10 to 12 hours.

Turn out onto a work surface dusted generously with sifted confectioners' sugar. Sift sugar over the top of the marshmallows. Coat a sharp knife with oil and cut into 12 squares. Roll the squares in sifted confectioners' sugar to coat on all sides. Set aside.

Preheat the oven to 325°F. To make the graham crackers, sift the flours, baking powder, cinnamon, nutmeg and salt together. In the bowl of an electric mixer fitted with the paddle attachment, combine the butter and sugar, beating on medium speed until light and fluffy, scraping down the sides of the bowl with a rubber spatula. Add the egg and yolk and beat until well combined. Add the honey and molasses then, very slowly, add the sifted dry ingredients, mixing well between additions. If you are making the dough by hand, knead it for 5 to 10 minutes on a well-floured surface until smooth.

Line the bases of two 15 x 10 x 1-inch jelly-roll pans with parchment. Divide the dough in half and roll each piece out to a rectangle large enough to line the base of each pan, at a thickness of around ¹/₈ inch. Transfer the dough to the pans, trim off any excess dough at the edges, and score each pan into 12 rectangles measuring 3³/₄ inches across. Using a fork, prick each 6 times at regular intervals.

Bake the crackers for 9 minutes in the middle of the oven until just firm. Allow to cool briefly then remove one set of crackers from the pan to cool completely and leave the other set in the pan.

Meanwhile, make the ganache. Break the chocolate into a heatproof bowl set over a pan of simmering water. Add the crème fraîche and cook for 8 to 10 minutes, stirring until the mixture is smooth. Remove the bowl from the pan and stir in the praline. Chill for 20 minutes or until the mixture is spreadable but not runny. Spread the chocolate ganache evenly on the graham crackers remaining in the pan, and chill for 20 minutes.

Preheat the broiler. To assemble the S'mores, remove the chocolate-coated graham crackers from the fridge and allow to stand for 15 minutes to return to room temperature. Top each piece with a marshmallow and broil for 1 to 2 minutes until golden. Separate the remaining graham crackers and use them to sandwich the marshmallows. Serve immediately.

NOTES

• The marshmallows can be made up to 2 days ahead.
• If you like, buy the graham crackers to save time.

Jane's Shortbread
Cookies

These are ethereal with the perfume of butter and a specialty of my colleague, Jane. For this recipe you will need a 2¹/2-inch-diameter shortbread mold.

1¹/2 cups unsalted butter
¹/3 cup superfine sugar
¹/2 cup confectioners' sugar
3 cups flour, plus extra for dusting
³/4 cup rice flour
²/3 cup cornstarch
Grapeseed oil, for greasing
MAKES 16

Cream the butter and both sugars together in the bowl of an electric mixer fitted with the paddle attachment until light and fluffy. Gradually add the flours and cornstarch beating until smooth.

Remove the mixture from the bowl and roll it into a cylinder 8 inches long and 2¹/2 inches in diameter. Wrap the dough in plastic wrap and chill for 30 minutes, or freeze for use later.

Remove the dough from the fridge and slice it into 12 circles about ¹/2 inch thick. Lightly flour a work surface and lay the circles of dough on it. Grease a shortbread mold lightly with oil then dust it with flour. Press the mold very firmly down onto one of the circles with the palm of your hand. Repeat the process with the remaining shortbread, greasing and flouring the mold for each one.

Place the shortbread on parchment-lined baking sheets, spacing them 2 inches apart. Chill for 20 minutes.

Preheat the oven to 325°F. and bake the shortbread for 25 minutes. Remove from the oven and leave to cool on the baking sheet for a few minutes before transferring to a wire rack to cool completely.

Sugar Cookies

FOR THE COOKIES
4 cups flour
$1/2$ teaspoon salt
$1/2$ teaspoon baking powder
$1/4$ teaspoon ground cloves
1 cup unsalted butter, softened
$1^3/4$ cups superfine sugar
2 large eggs, lightly beaten
2 teaspoons freshly squeezed lemon juice
2 teaspoons grated lemon zest
FOR THE THICK PIPING ICING
1 large egg white
1 tablespoon freshly squeezed lemon juice
$2^1/3$ cups confections' sugar, sifted
Food coloring
FOR THE THIN PIPING ICING
2 large egg-whites
$3^1/2$ cups plus 2 tablespoons confectioners' sugar, sifted
$1/4$ cup freshly squeezed lemon juice
Food coloring
MAKES 12 TO 14

To make the cookies, sift the flour, salt, baking powder and ground cloves into a large bowl and set aside.

Using an electric mixer fitted with the paddle attachment, cream the butter and sugar until light and fluffy. Gradually beat in the eggs followed by the lemon juice and lemon zest. With the mixer at low speed, gradually beat in the flour mixture to form a soft dough.

Turn out the dough mixture onto a lightly floured surface and knead for 3 to 4 seconds until smooth. Wrap in plastic and chill for 1 hour.

Divide the dough into 6 equal pieces. Using one piece at a time, knead each piece until smooth and, using a well-floured rolling pin, roll them out on a lightly floured surface to $1/8$ inch thick.

Using a selection of large cookie cutters measuring 7 to 8 inches at the largest points, stamp out 12 to 14 shapes, rerolling the trimmings after cutting the first six cookies. Place the cookies on baking sheets lined with parchment paper and chill for 1 hour. Preheat the oven to 325°F.

Bake each tray of cookies in the middle of the oven for 18 minutes until the edges are just brown. Leave to stand on the baking sheets for 10 minutes after baking to allow them to crisp up, then transfer to a wire rack and leave until cold.

To make the thick piping icing, place the egg white in a bowl with the lemon juice and beat gently to combine. Gradually beat in the confectioners' sugar until smooth.

Spoon half the icing into a pastry bag fitted with a fine writing tip and pipe the icing around the edge of each cookie. Leave to set. Color the remaining icing with a color of your choice, place it in another pastry bag with the same writing tip and set aside.

Make the thin piping icing in the same way as the thick icing, coloring it as desired, and spoon it into a piping bag fitted with a 1/8-inch plain tip. Pipe 2 to 3 tablespoons of icing on each cookie inside the lines you have already piped and spread it with a knife.

Alternatively, spoon the icing onto each cookie and then spread it out. Set the cookies aside for the icing to set completely.

To finish, decorate each cookie with the reserved colored icing.

NOTE

• Unfortunately I have not been able to find organic food coloring as yet, but I would hope that it will become available for the ever-growing market of organic consumers.

DECORATING SUGAR COOKIES

Fun, festive sugar cookies can be used to add a flash of color to any special event. Choose the shape of the cookie cutters and the patterns and colors of the icing to suit the theme of the occasion: witches and masks for Halloween, stars and Christmas ornaments for December, a dog or cat for a child's birthday – the only limiting factor is the cook's imagination, so explore your talents, and mix and match colors and techniques to bring your ideas to life.

Make things easy for yourself by allowing plenty of space to work on. Line some baking sheets with paper towels so that the cookies may be left to dry flat and undisturbed while you are working. You will need a pastry bag for each color of icing you intend to use, plus a selection of small tips, choosing the size and shape of the tips to match your decorative idea.

To ensure your icing has the right consistency, lift the spatula and allow the mixture to flow back into the bowl: It should disappear by a count of five. Always use edible colorings to tint your icing, adding a little at a time until you reach the desired shade.

Different icing effects can be achieved by altering the manner in which you add the icing to the cookie. For a smooth flat finish, outline the cookie with your desired color then immediately fill in the outline with more icing by piping a generous amount around the interior and spreading it to meet the outline. You can then pipe a contrasting color onto the iced cookie while it is still wet, allowing the piped icing to sink smoothly into the first layer. Set the cookie aside to dry completely.

Alternatively, for a raised pattern, allow the first layer of icing to dry completely and then pipe your contrasting color or colors on top.

Sanding sugar or Sugartex, available from specialist cake decorating shops, can be used to give a flocked effect to the icing. Sprinkle it on while the icing is still wet, then tap off the excess and set the cookie aside to dry completely. When the icing has set completely, any stray crystals can be lightly removed with a pastry brush.

Lake House
Chocolate Torte

This is a rich and simple cake.

14 ounces bittersweet 70% chocolate, finely chopped
1 cup unsalted butter, plus extra for greasing
7 large eggs, separated
1 cup superfine sugar
6 tablespoons flour, plus extra for dusting
SERVES 8 TO 10

Preheat the oven to 325°F. Butter a 9-inch springform cake pan and dust with flour, tapping out any excess.

In the top of a double boiler set over simmering water, place the chocolate and butter and allow them to melt, stirring occasionally to combine. Remove from the heat and set aside.

In a medium bowl, whisk the egg yolks with 3/4 cup sugar until pale and fluffy, about 1 minute.

In the bowl of an electric mixer beat the egg whites just until frothy. Add 2 tablespoons of the sugar and continue beating for 3 minutes, then add the remaining 2 tablespoons of sugar and beat just until soft peaks form, being careful not to overbeat.

Whisk the flour into the egg yolks then, using a rubber spatula, fold the reserved chocolate mixture into the egg yolk mixture. Fold 1/4 of the egg whites into the chocolate mixture to lighten it, then gently fold in the remaining egg whites. Transfer the batter to the prepared pan and bake for 50 to 55 minutes, until the top is cracked and the cake has shrunk away from the side of the pan.

Remove the cake from the oven and leave in the cake pan to cool to room temperature, during which time the cake will sink and crack. Remove from the pan and serve.

NOTES

• The cake freezes for up to 2 weeks if well wrapped.
• Serve with an espresso-flavored crème anglaise, crème Chantilly or crème fraîche.
• Omit the flour, cook, and you have a fudge torte.

Brownies

For best results, eat between 2 and 3A.M.

6 ounces Valrhona unsweetened chocolate, chopped
1 1/2 cups unsalted butter, plus extra for greasing
6 large eggs
2 1/2 cups packed soft light brown sugar
1/2 tablespoon pure vanilla extract
1/2 cup flour, sifted, plus extra for dusting
MAKES 18

Preheat the oven to 325°F. Butter and flour a 12 x 8 1/2-inch baking pan.

Melt the chocolate and butter together in the top of a double boiler over barely simmering water. When smooth, remove from the heat and leave to cool for 15 minutes.

In a large bowl, beat the eggs, sugar and vanilla together until thoroughly combined. Fold the melted chocolate mixture into the egg mixture, then fold in the flour.

Pour the batter into the prepared pan, smoothing over the top. Bake for 35 minutes to give a fudgy texture or, for a drier texture, until a skewer inserted in the center comes out clean.

When completely cool, cut into 18 squares. The brownies may be stored in an airtight container for up to 1 week.

NOTE

• Freeze and serve frozen with Vanilla Ice Cream (see page 179) and a hot Chocolate Sauce (see page 218).

Buttermilk Scones

1¹/₂ cups plus 2 tablespoons plain white flour

2 teaspoons baking powder

¹/₂ teaspoon salt

¹/₄ cup unsalted butter, diced

¹/₃ cup currants or raisins

¹/₄ cup supefine sugar

¹/₂ cup buttermilk

Beaten egg, to glaze

MAKES 6

Preheat the oven to 450°F. Sift the flour, baking powder and salt into a large mixing bowl. Rub the butter into the flour mixture until it resembles coarse bread crumbs. Add the currants or raisins and the sugar and stir to combine. Make a well in the center then stir in just enough buttermilk to form a soft dough.

On a lightly floured work surface, turn out the dough and knead lightly. Roll the dough out to 1 inch thick and cut into rounds with a 2¹/₂-inch plain cutter. Transfer the rounds to a baking sheet lined with baking parchment. Using a pastry brush, brush the tops of the scones with beaten egg. Bake for 7 to 10 minutes, until risen and golden brown on top. Serve hot or cold.

Chocolate Mousse
Cake

When I owned a bakery in Connecticut, every week, on Monday, I would drive into New York and purchase cakes from a grand pâtissier to resell in my shop. Early one week a gentleman came into the shop and purchased a chocolate mousse cake, went home, loved it, came back on a Friday and ordered one for Saturday. I had no more cakes in the freezer. I panicked, and that night I invented this cake. Fifteen years later I am still making it and receiving tremendous kudos.

FOR THE CAKE

2 ounces Valrhona unsweetened chocolate, chopped

1 cup sugar

3 tablespoons unsalted butter, chilled and diced

1 large egg

A pinch of salt

1 cup flour

¹/₂ teaspoon baking soda

1 tablespoon pure vanilla extract

FOR THE MOUSSE

2 ounces Valrhona Manjari chocolate, chopped

³/₄ cup unsalted butter, diced

3 tablespoons brandy

5 eggs, separated

¹/₄ cup superfine sugar

A pinch of salt

FOR THE DECORATION

4 ounces Valrhona Manjari chocolate, chopped

8 ounces good-quality plain chocolate chips, or plain chocolate, chopped

SERVES 8

Preheat the oven to 325°F. Lightly butter and flour two 8-inch round cake pans, tapping out any excess flour. Line the bottom of each pan with parchment.

To make the cake, bring 1 cup of water to a boil in a medium, heavy saucepan. Immediately turn the heat to low and add the unsweetened chocolate. With a wooden spoon, stir until the chocolate has melted, then add the sugar and butter and continue stirring until dissolved. Remove from the heat, pour into a bowl and refrigerate until cool.

In a medium bowl, using a whisk, mix together the egg and salt. Add the cooled chocolate mixture and combine. Add the flour and baking soda and stir until combined, being careful not to overmix. Using a rubber spatula, scrape down the sides of the bowl and add the vanilla. (If the mixture is lumpy at this stage, sieve it as necessary.)

Divide the mixture evenly between the two cake pans and bake for 20 minutes. Remove from the oven and cool the cakes in the pans. When cool, remove the cakes from the pans, wrap well in plastic and freeze overnight on a flat surface.

Make the mousse. In a double boiler set over simmering water, melt together the chocolate, butter and brandy, stirring occasionally and being careful that the bowl is not touching the water. When melted and combined, remove from the heat and leave to cool slightly. Add the egg yolks, one by one, to the chocolate mixture, stirring until combined.

In a large bowl, whisk the egg whites and salt until frothy, then add the sugar in two batches, whisking until the whites are stiff but not dry. Using a plastic spatula, fold a spoonful of the egg whites into the chocolate mixture to lighten it, then fold the chocolate mixture into the egg whites. Cover and chill in the refrigerator for about 2 hours or until set. The mousse can be left overnight; if doing so, remove the mousse from the refrigerator about 30 minutes prior to assembling the cake and leave it to stand at room temperature until the mousse is just soft or of a frosting consistency.

Place one of the frozen cakes on a large plate and top it with two-thirds of the chocolate mousse, spreading it out evenly to give a layer 1½ to 2 inches thick. Place in the freezer for 20 minutes until set. Remove from the freezer and place the second cake on top of the mousse. Frost the top and sides of the cake with the remaining mousse, being careful not to press down too hard on the top of the cake. Transfer the frosted cake to the refrigerator to chill for at least 2 hours, until firm.

When the mousse cake has set, make a chocolate band for the decoration. Melt the Manjari chocolate in a double boiler set over simmering water. Meanwhile, with a flexible tape measure, measure the circumference and height of the cake (approximately 27 x 5 inches). Cut a piece of baking parchment 1 inch longer than the measured circumference but exactly the same height. Lay the paper on a clean work surface. Once the chocolate has melted, pour all of it onto the center of the strip of parchment, spreading it evenly with a metal spatula and being careful not to go over the edges.

Take the chocolate mousse cake out of the refrigerator. Holding the chocolate strip at the ends, lift and place it immediately around the outside of the cake, with the paper side facing outward. Attach the strip very carefully all the way around. Where the edges come together, cut off any excess of the chocolate-covered parchment to give a perfect seam. Return the cake to the refrigerator to set for 15 to 20 minutes.

Remove the cake from the refrigerator and, taking a top corner of the baking parchment, carefully peel away the paper leaving the chocolate band attached to the cake. Return the cake to the refrigerator.

To make chocolate curls for the decoration, melt the chocolate chips in a double boiler set over simmering water. Preheat the oven to 225°F then switch it off and place a clean baking sheet measuring 17 x 11 inches in the oven for 5 minutes until it is quite warm but not so hot you cannot touch it. Place the baking sheet upside down on the work surface. Once the chocolate has melted, pour it onto the baking sheet and use a metal spatula to spread it out, covering the entire area. Refrigerate the chocolate for 30 minutes or until hard.

Remove the baking sheet of chocolate from the refrigerator to a work surface with a wall and leave it to stand at room temperature for a few minutes. Set the baking sheet against the wall to help hold it steady. Take a new paint scraper with a beveled edge and hold it at a 45° angle to the baking sheet. Pushing away from you, and easing the paint scraper around in a semicircle, scrape the chocolate in strips to make large curls: If the chocolate does not curl easily, roll it with your fingertips. If the chocolate is too cold it will chip; let it stand for another 2 to 3 minutes at room temperature.

Carefully transfer the chocolate curls to the top of the cake, piling them in the center, and store the cake in the refrigerator until ready to serve.

NOTES

• It is important to use the specified grades of chocolate for this recipe: They create textural and taste differences that are experienced with each bite.
• Incorporate a paint scraper and an offset spatula into your baking equipment.

Peanut Butter
Cupcakes with
Chocolate Truffle Filling

If you like peanut butter and chocolate you'll love these – soft and chewy with a surprise in the middle. For Halloween, we decorated them with orange sanding sugar and a stencil in the shape of a pumpkin.

FOR THE TRUFFLE FILLING
1/4 cup heavy cream
2/3 cup good-quality milk chocolate, finely chopped
FOR THE CUPCAKES
4 tablespoons unsalted butter
1 cup light brown sugar
1 large egg
1 teaspoon pure vanilla extract
1/2 cup chunky peanut butter
1 cup flour
1 teaspoon baking powder
1/2 teaspoon salt
Plastic stencil, for decorating, optional
Orange sanding sugar, for decorating, optional
MAKES 18

To make the truffle filling, heat the cream in a small saucepan over medium heat. Place the chocolate in a heatproof bowl and pour the hot cream over the chocolate, stirring until the mixture is completely smooth. Chill until firm, which will take at least 1 hour.

Working quickly, form the chilled truffle mixture into 18 balls using a melon baller about 3/4 inches in diameter. Place them on a small baking sheet and transfer the truffles to the freezer until firm, about 20 minutes.

Preheat oven to 300°F. Take two 2¹/2-inch muffin pans and fill them with 18 cupcake papers. Fill any empty holes half-full with water to keep the cupcakes moist.

In a small saucepan, melt the butter and leave it to cool slightly.

In the bowl of an electric mixer fitted with a paddle attachment, cream the melted butter and light brown sugar together on medium speed until combined. Add the egg and continue beating until combined. Add the vanilla extract and peanut butter and mix well, scraping down the sides of the bowl with a rubber spatula.

Mix together the flour, baking powder and salt in a small bowl. Add the dry ingredients to the peanut butter mixture and beat until just combined.

Place about a tablespoon of batter in the bottom of each cupcake paper, and smooth over to cover the base. Then place a truffle into each cup and divide the remaining batter among the cupcake papers, pressing it down to completely surround and seal in the truffles. Smooth tops.

Transfer the cupcakes to the oven and bake until golden brown, about 35 to 40 minutes. Remove to a wire rack to cool completely. As the cupcakes cool, they will sink slightly.

Serve as is or decorate if desired. To decorate, carefully peel the cupcake papers from cupcakes and return the cupcakes, bottom-side up, to a wire rack set over a baking sheet. Place a stencil on one cupcake and sprinkle the sanding sugar over the stencil. Carefully remove the stencil and transfer the decorated cupcake to a serving platter. Repeat with remaining cupcakes.

NOTE

• Sanding sugar is a coarse colored sugar used to decorate cakes and cookies. It is available from specialist cake decorating shops.

Brioche Rolls and Buns

Use these rolls and buns with Mini Goat Cheese Burgers (see page 115) and Lamb and Herb Sausages (see page 114).

3 cups white bread flour, plus extra for dusting
1¹/₂ teaspoons active dried yeast
1¹/₂ teaspoons sugar
4 large eggs, plus 1 extra, beaten, for glazing
1 teaspoon salt
¹/₄ cup plus 2 tablespoons unsalted butter, softened, diced
1 teaspoon poppy seeds
1 teaspoon sesame seeds
1 teaspoon cumin seeds
MAKES 1 POUND 14 OUNCES DOUGH/ABOUT 20 ROLLS AND BUNS

To make the sponge, in the bowl of an electric mixer, place 1 cup of the flour, the yeast and sugar. In a small bowl, place the eggs and ³/₄ cup of water and whisk to combine. Make a well in the center of the flour mixture, add the egg-water mixture and, using a fork, mix to give a sticky sponge. Cover loosely with a cloth and stand at room temperature for 30 minutes.

To complete the dough, using the dough hook of an electric mixer, add the remaining 2 cups of flour and the salt to the sponge. Mix at medium speed for 20 minutes, adding another 2 to 3 tablespoons of flour if necessary to help the dough come together.

After 20 minutes, change the dough hook to a flat paddle. With the mixer at low speed, add the softened butter to the dough a piece at a time, waiting until each piece has been absorbed before adding the next. Adjust the speed to high and beat for 20 to 30 seconds until all the butter is fully incorporated. Scrape the dough from the sides of the bowl; it will be very shiny and elastic.

Remove the dough from the bowl to a floured surface and knead for 1 to 2 minutes. The dough may be sticky, so add more flour as necessary. Place the kneaded dough in a bowl, cover with a cloth and leave to rise at room temperature for 45 minutes to 1 hour or until it has doubled in size.

Punch the dough down then remove it from the bowl and knead again briefly before shaping as required.

To make mini-loaves and rolls of brioche, turn the dough out onto a lightly floured surface and cut it in half. Cover and set one half aside. Shape the other half into a long sausage, then cut it into ten equal pieces. Shape them into loaves and place them on a baking sheet lined with parchment paper. With a very sharp knife, slash the tops of the rolls lengthwise being sure not to cut the ends.

Divide the remaining portion of dough into ten pieces and roll them into balls with the palms of your hands. Place them on the baking tray near the mini-loaves then cover the tray with a kitchen towel. Leave the dough to rise at room temperature for about 45 minutes to 1 hour or until the loaves have doubled in size.

Preheat the oven to 375°F. Brush the tops of the loaves and rolls with beaten egg. Sprinkle the poppy seeds among 7 pieces of the brioche. Sprinkle the sesame seeds over another 7 pieces, and the cumin seeds over the remaining 6 pieces. Bake for 25 minutes until golden brown on top. Serve hot or at room temperature.

NOTE

• Do not make in a hot room or the butter will weep from the dough.

Brioche Bresse

The sourness of the crème fraîche and the sweetness of the brioche make this a brunch staple. Halving the brioche dough recipe won't work: You must make the full amount, use half and either freeze the rest or make a loaf.

15 ounces brioche dough (half of the recipe above)
¹/₂ cup plus 2 tablespoons crème fraîche
1 tablespoon superfine sugar, for sprinkling
1 large egg, beaten
SERVES 6 TO 8

Preheat the oven to 375°F. Roll the dough out to a 12-inch circle about ¹/₄ inch thick. Place it on a baking tray lined with parchment paper and prick several times with a fork. Cover with a kitchen towel and let rest for 20 minutes.

Brush the dough with beaten egg, leaving a 1-inch border. Spread the crème fraîche over the egg and sprinkle with sugar. Transfer to the oven and bake for 20 minutes, then remove from the oven and serve warm or at room temperature, cut in wedges.

Carta Di Musica

A crackly flat bread. The thin unleavened leaves resemble the lines of a musical staff, hence the name "music sheet."

1/2 star anise
1/4 teaspoon cloves
1/4 teaspoon coriander seeds
1/4 teaspoon cumin seeds
2 pinches dried red pepper flakes
2 cups whole-wheat flour, plus extra for dusting
2 cups semolina, plus extra for dusting
1 1/2 teaspoons salt
1/4 teaspoon freshly grated nutmeg
4 pinches paprika
1 1/3 cups lukewarm water, plus more if necessary
MAKES 8

In a dry skillet, toast the star anise, cloves, coriander and cumin for about 30 seconds until fragrant and lightly toasted. Remove from the heat, cool, then transfer the spices and red pepper flakes to a spice mill and finely grind.

Stir together the flour, semolina, salt and all the spices in a large bowl. Slowly add enough lukewarm water to form a moist dough then knead in the bowl until the dough is no longer sticky.

Transfer the dough to a lightly floured work surface and knead for 8 to 10 minutes until smooth. Cover the dough with plastic wrap and let it rest at room temperature for at least 20 minutes, and up to 1 hour.

Preheat the oven to 500°F. Dust a baking sheet very lightly with semolina. Divide the dough equally into 8 pieces. Pat 1 piece into a 6-inch disc, while keeping the others covered with plastic.

Using whole-wheat flour, lightly dust a work surface and roll out the dough to a circle 12 inches in diameter, lifting and rotating the dough frequently to prevent sticking. Transfer the round to the prepared baking sheet and bake for 2 1/2 to 3 minutes or until the edges begin to curl. Turn the dough over and bake for another 3 1/2 to 4 1/2 minutes until bubbles form and golden spots appear on the surface.

Transfer the flat bread to a wire rack to cool. Repeat with remaining dough. The Carta di Musica may be stored at room temperature for up to 3 days in an airtight container.

NOTES

• Rolling this bread very thinly makes it crispy. Toasting and grinding the seeds enhances the flavor.
• Leave the baking sheet in the oven and work by transferring the cooked flat bread and replacing it with uncooked simultaneously, redusting with semolina as you go along.

Lake House Bread

When I first started cooking, I was hired as a prep person for a caterer in Connecticut. They owned a bakery but were secretive about teaching the recipes to anybody. I befriended the evening baker and after work I would go in at midnight to learn bread making. I liked all the breads they made but didn't love them, because the loaves were forced to rise too quickly and therefore lacked character. It was Steve Sullivan's Acme Bakery that led me in the right direction. I went to San Francisco and begged the Acme Bakery to let me work for them for free but they said no. So I begged them for some of their starter dough – which they finally gave me, and I ran back to my hotel to place it in the freezer immediately. I took it back to Connecticut, read and practiced some more and finally came up with this favorite loaf. It is inspired by the Acme Bakery, but dedicated to Lake House.

1^{1}/$_{2}$ tablespoons active dried yeast
6 to 6^{1}/$_{2}$ cups white bread flour
2^{2}/$_{3}$ cup whole-wheat flour
1^{1}/$_{2}$ cups rye flour
^{3}/$_{4}$ cup raw wheat germ, toasted
^{3}/$_{4}$ cup cooked wheatberries
^{3}/$_{4}$ cup sunflower seeds
^{3}/$_{4}$ cup quick-cooking oats
1^{1}/$_{2}$ tablespoons malt extract
1^{1}/$_{2}$ tablespoons salt
Egg white, to glaze
Butter, for greasing
MAKES 3 LOAVES

Place 2^{3}/$_{4}$ cups of room-temperature water in a medium bowl then add the yeast, 2 cups of the white bread flour and ^{2}/$_{3}$ cup of the whole-wheat flour. Whisk to combine. Cover with a kitchen towel and set the mixture aside for 30 minutes to 1 hour until it is bubbly and looks like a sponge.

Transfer the yeast mixture to the bowl of an electric mixer fitted with a dough hook. Add the remaining 2 cups of whole-wheat flour plus another 1^{1}/$_{2}$ cups of room-temperature water then add the rye flour, toasted wheat germ, wheatberries, sunflower seeds, oats, malt extract, salt and another 2 cups of white bread flour. Turn the mixer on to medium speed and mix to combine. Gradually add 2 cups of white flour, or until the dough forms a tight ball, adding another ^{1}/$_{2}$ cup if needed. Mix for 10 minutes. Knead the dough on a lightly floured surface for 5 minutes, adding more flour if necessary.

Place the dough in a clean bowl, cover with a kitchen towel and leave to rise at room temperature for about 1 hour or until doubled.

Punch the dough down and divide it into 3 equal pieces. Roll them into loaves and place in three buttered 9 x 5 x 3-inch loaf pans. Cover and leave to rise at room temperature for 50 minutes or until doubled in size.

Preheat the oven to 450°F. Brush the tops of the loaves with the egg white. Spray the walls of the oven with water. Bake for 15 minutes then spray again and reduce the oven to 400°F. Bake for another 10 minutes, then spray again and bake for a further 20 minutes.

Remove the bread from the pans, place them directly on the oven rack and bake for a final 10 minutes. Remove the bread from the oven and cool on a wire rack.

Focaccia with Robiola Cheese and Truffle Oil

This is one of Trudie's favorite breads. It is also a signature dish of Le Madri Restaurant in New York City. The olive oil and water technique ensures a rich, soft, yet crispy dough.

Flour, for dusting
1^{1}/$_{4}$ pounds Focaccia Dough (half the recipe on page 220)
1^{1}/$_{2}$ tablespoons extra-virgin olive oil
^{3}/$_{4}$ teaspoon salt
8 ounces Robiola cheese, or mild soft goat cheese
1^{1}/$_{2}$ tablespoons white truffle oil
SERVES 6

Preheat the oven to 450°F. Lightly dust a baking sheet with flour. Roll out the dough to a 10-inch circle, place it on the baking sheet and use a fork to prick over the entire surface of the dough. Cover with a kitchen towel, set aside and let rise for 20 minutes or until almost doubled.

In a small bowl, mix together the olive oil, salt and ^{1}/$_{3}$ cup of water. Brush one-third of the olive oil mixture over the top of the dough. Bake in the center of the oven for 18 to 20 minutes, brushing with the oil mixture twice during cooking, until lightly browned. Remove

from the oven (leaving the oven on, if making all at once) and set aside for 15 to 20 minutes, or until cool enough to handle.

When cool, place the focaccia on a cutting board and, using a long serrated knife, cut the dough in half horizontally. Spread the cheese over the bottom half of the focaccia, replace the top half and return to the oven for 5 minutes or until the cheese is just soft.

Remove the focaccia from the oven, brush the surface with the truffle oil, cut into wedges and serve warm.

NOTE

• Serve as a starter with an arugula salad.

Rosemary Focaccia

3 tablespoons extra-virgin olive oil
2$^{1}/_{2}$ pounds Focaccia Dough (see page 220)
2 or 3 sprigs fresh rosemary
2 teaspoons coarse sea salt
MAKES 1

Use 1 tablespoon of the olive oil to grease an 18 x 13$^{1}/_{2}$-inch baking pan. Transfer the dough to the center of the baking pan and then use your fingertips to begin stretching the dough to the edges of the pan. Flip the dough over in the pan so that both sides are well oiled and continue to stretch the dough as evenly as possible to cover the bottom of the pan. Do not try to smooth the top of the dough: Your fingertips should make indentations in it to give a rustic, dimpled look.

Cover the dough with a kitchen towel and leave to rise for about 1 hour or until doubled in size.

Preheat the oven to 450°F. Stud the rosemary leaves into the dough intermittently and sprinkle the surface with sea salt. Bake for 20 to 25 minutes until golden then remove from the oven and drizzle with the remaining 2 tablespoons of the olive oil. Serve immediately.

Herb-brushed
Polenta Bread

6$^{1}/_{2}$ tablespoons unsalted butter, plus extra for greasing
1 cup plus 2 tablespoons flour, plus extra for dusting
1 cup plus 2 tablespoons yellow cornmeal
1$^{3}/_{4}$ tablespoons sugar
3$^{1}/_{2}$ teaspoons baking powder
2 teaspoons salt
4 eggs, lightly beaten
1 cup plus 2 tablespoons buttermilk
4$^{1}/_{2}$ tablespoons heavy cream
FOR THE HERB BRUSHES (MAKES 6)
1 cup olive oil
6 cloves garlic, roughly chopped
4 branches bay, 6 to 8 inches long
4 sprigs rosemary, 6 to 8 inches long
4 sprigs sage, 6 to 8 inches long
4 sprigs savory, 6 to 8 inches long
4 branches thyme, 6 to 8 inches long
4 sprigs tarragon, 6 to 8 inches long
MAKES ONE 2-POUND LOAF

Melt the butter and let it cool. Meanwhile, butter a 2-pound loaf pan, line the bottom with greaseproof paper and dust the sides with flour, tapping out the excess. Preheat the oven to 400°F.

In a medium bowl, combine the flour, cornmeal, sugar, baking powder and salt. In another bowl, combine the eggs, buttermilk, cream and the cooled melted butter, stirring.

Pour the egg mixture into the flour mixture and fold gently until just combined. Pour into the prepared pan and bake for 40 to 45 minutes until a metal skewer inserted in the center comes out clean. Allow to cool in the pan for 10 minutes. Loosen the sides with a small metal spatula or round-bladed knife and invert it onto a wire rack.

Meanwhile, in a small saucepan, gently warm the olive oil then remove from the heat and add the garlic. Set aside to infuse for 30 minutes. Tie each variety of herb together securely at the base to resemble a wicker broom. Leave them to macerate in the garlic oil.

When the bread is cool, cut it into $^{1}/_{2}$-inch slices. Dip one of the herb brushes into the garlic-flavored oil and use it to brush each side of three slices of bread. Repeat using the other herb brushes on the remaining bread.

Preheat the grill or broiler and lightly toast the oiled bread on both sides before serving.

NOTES

• The loaf will freeze for up to 1 month wrapped in plastic wrap.
• At the height of the tomato season, take a handful of cherry tomatoes, squeeze them in your hands and place over the slices of hot grilled polenta bread. Brush with olive oil and sprinkle with flaked or coarse salt. Delicious.
• The herb brushes and garlic oil can be used to accentuate barbecued foods such as chicken, fish and steaks.
• Use either winter or summer savory – summer is milder.
• Use the garlic and flavored oil as a dip for the bread.

Stilton Bread

1 tablespoon plus 2½ teaspoons honey
1 tablespoon unsalted butter, softened
2 teaspoons active dry yeast
5½ to 6 cups white bread flour
2 teaspoons salt
½ cup milk powder
1 large egg, lightly beaten
1 pound (4 cups) Stilton cheese, grated
Freshly ground black pepper
MAKES 3 LOAVES

In the bowl of an electric mixer fitted with a dough hook, combine the honey, butter and yeast with 2 cups of room-temperature water and stir until well combined. Meanwhile, combine the flour, milk powder and salt in a medium-sized bowl. Slowly add the flour mixture to the mixer. Beat together on medium speed until a ball of dough forms around the hook. Knead for 8 to 10 minutes.

Remove the dough from the mixer and transfer to a floured surface. Knead for 5 minutes or until a smooth, silky dough is formed. Cover with a kitchen towel and leave to rise at room temperature until doubled in size.

On a lightly floured surface, divide the dough into 3 equal balls, approximately 1 pound each. Roll each ball into a 10-inch circle

about ½ inch thick. Lightly brush the dough with some of the beaten egg then, leaving a 1-inch border, cover the surface of each circle with 1 cup of the grated Stilton and grind some pepper over.

Bring the edges of each circle up into the shape of a ball, being sure to completely enclose the cheese. Place the 3 loaves on a parchment-lined baking sheet and cover with a kitchen towel. Let rise at room temperature for 30 to 40 minutes. Meanwhile, heat the oven to 375°F.

Brush the risen loaves with the remaining egg. Divide the rest of the Stilton among the tops of each loaf, placing it in the center. Bake for 25 to 30 minutes or until golden brown. Cool on a rack.

NOTES

• Make this bread without the Stilton and you have Lake House Milk and Honey Bread. You could also replace the Stilton with Cheddar, if you prefer. Either way, you can't lose.

6

Basics

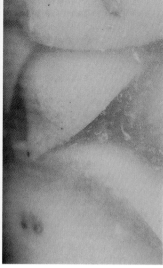

PICKLES & PRESERVES

Marinated Cherries

2³/₄ pounds sour cherries such as Red Montmorency or Red Morella,
picked over
1 cup superfine sugar
Ground nutmeg
3 cinnamon sticks
3¹/₂ to 4 cups grappa
MAKES 2¹/₄ QUARTS

First, sterilize a 2¹/₄-quart glass jar. Fill with water a pot large enough
to take the whole jar comfortably. Bring to a boil, then, using a pair of
tongs, lower the jar gently into the boiling water until it is completely
submerged. Ensure the jar simmers continuously in the water for 10
minutes.

Use the tongs to lift the jar out of the pot then dry the jar carefully
with a clean cloth, being careful not to touch the inside of the jar.

Divide the cherries into three batches and place one batch in the
bottom of the jar, still ensuring you do not touch the inside of the
glass. Sprinkle with 6 tablespoons of the sugar and a pinch of
nutmeg. Repeat using the second batch of cherries, another 6
tablespoons of sugar and a pinch of nutmeg.

Without touching the glass, poke the cinnamon sticks down the side
of the jar between the cherries and the glass, then add the remaining
cherries, sugar and a final pinch of nutmeg. Pour the grappa over the
cherries, making sure they are well covered, and seal the jar tightly.
Turn the closed jar upside down and shake it to dissolve the sugar, then
set the bottled cherries aside for 3 days. If bubbles start to appear, the
cherries have begun to ferment, so open the jar and add more grappa.
The cherries will keep for up to 2 years.

NOTES

• Cherries are one of the last truly seasonal fruits, very difficult to find
in markets outside their growing season, but this recipe means you
can not only enjoy their flavor year-round, but over several years.
• Serve the cherries and their syrup over ice cream, with rice pudding
(see page 168), or as an accompaniment to game.

Pickled Chillies

1 pound 2 ounces chilli peppers such as Fresno, Jalapeño or Serrano
FOR THE PICKLE
2 cups rice vinegar, or more if necessary

³/₄ cup sugar
4 tablespoons salt
4 cloves
2 teaspoons black peppercorns
2 teaspoons mustard seeds
3-inch piece fresh ginger, thinly sliced
4 sprigs lemon verbena
MAKES 1¹/₂ QUARTS

In a small saucepan, combine the rice vinegar, sugar and salt with 1
cup of water and bring to a boil, stirring until the sugar and salt
dissolve. Remove from heat, and add the cloves, black peppercorns
and mustard seeds.

Sterilize a 1¹/₂-quart pickling jar, dry then tightly pack the chillies,
ginger and verbena inside it. Pour the pickling liquid over the chillies.
If the chillies are not completely covered with the pickle, then warm
some more rice vinegar and add it to the jar.

When the pickled chillies are completely cold, cover and store for 3
days before eating. They can be kept for up to 3 months.

NOTE

• For a change, you can use the pickling liquid in this recipe to
preserve beets (see below) and the pickling liquid for the beets to
preserve these chillies.

Pickled Beets

1¹/₂ pounds raw beets, washed and trimmed
1¹/₂ tablespoons olive oil
3 cloves garlic, peeled
2 small dried chillies, halved, with seeds
6 whole black peppercorns
2 bay leaves
6 sprigs dill

Salt and freshly ground pepper
FOR THE BRINE
2¹/₂ cups cider vinegar, plus extra as necessary
¹/₂ cup sugar
1¹/₂ tablespoons English mustard powder
1¹/₂ tablespoons yellow mustard seeds
1¹/₂ tablespoons ground turmeric
MAKES 4¹/₃ CUPS

Preheat the oven to 400°F. Season the beets and toss with the olive oil, then wrap them in foil and tightly seal the ends to form an envelope. Place on a baking tray and cook in the oven for 1 hour or until the beets are tender when tested with a skewer. Set the beets aside to cool then peel and thinly slice them.

To make the brine, heat the vinegar, sugar, mustard powder, mustard seeds and the turmeric in a large noncorrosive saucepan just until the sugar dissolves, stirring occasionally.

Place half the sliced beets in the base of a sterilized 1¹/₄-quart jar then add the garlic, chillies, peppercorns, bay leaves and dill. Top with the remaining beets and pour in the brine, making sure the beets are well covered and adding more vinegar if necessary. Leave the beets to cool to room temperature before sealing. Store for 3 days before eating. Use within 3 months and store in a cool, dark, dry place. After opening, place in the refrigerator.

Ν ο τ ε

• Serve with shots of ice-cold vodka, Potato Salmon Fritters and Stuffed Red and Yellow Cherry tomatoes (see pages 72 and 71).

Preserved Lemons
6 whole thin-skinned lemons, plus the juice of 14 extra lemons
7¹/₂ tablespoons kosher salt
MAKES 8³/₄ CUPS

Thoroughly wash the whole lemons. Stand 1 lemon on its end on a cutting board and visually divide it lengthwise into three slices. Make a vertical cut one-third of the way in from one side of the lemon, cutting almost all the way through to create a flap. Stand the lemon on its opposite end and repeat, but this time make the slice on the other side of the lemon, creating a second flap. Remove the stem with a paring knife, then repeat with the remaining lemons.

Sprinkle 1¹/₂ tablespoons of the salt in the bottom of a sterilized 2¹/₄-quart jar with a flat, tight-fitting, nonreactive lid. Place 1¹/₂ teaspoons of salt under each lemon flap, placing the lemons in the jar as you go.

Pour in the lemon juice, ensuring it covers the lemons completely, and adding more if needed. Store the lemons at room temperature for 30 days, upturning the jar every other day. After 30 days, transfer the jar to the refrigerator to store, using the lemons as needed.

To use the lemons, remove one from the jar and use a small, sharp knife to cut away and discard the flesh and pith. Slice and use the lemon rind according to each recipe's instructions. The leftover portion of each lemon may be returned to the jar if necessary.

Ν ο τ ε s

• It is important that the lemons are fully covered with salt and lemon juice, and that you wait 30 days before using them.
• These salted lemons are traditionally used in Moroccan dishes. A simple way to flavor couscous is to stir some diced preserved lemon through it.
• Add some finely chopped preserved lemon to oil and vinegar to make a vinaigrette.
• Try combining a little of the lemon rind with fresh coriander, paprika and water in a poaching liquid for fish.

BOTTLING AND PRESERVING

When you open a jar, in winter, of a home-made garden chutney or summer fruit jam, it gives a tremendous feeling of independence, of sovereignty over the seasons. And the results are produced and directed by you, whether you prefer a traditional relish, a pickle inspired by North African or Asian cuisines, a French-style soft set preserve or a jam so thick with fruit you can stand a spoon in it.

It is important to use sterilized preserving jars, not just clean ones. Place the clean jars in a deep pot, making sure they do not touch each other, then cover them with water and bring to a boil. You need to simmer the jars for 10 minutes. Using metal tongs, lift the jars out of the pot and drain them upside down on a clean kitchen towel. Turn the jars right side up and set them aside to dry while you immerse all the lids, rubber seals and any corks in the boiling water for a few seconds, again being careful not to touch them with your hands.

Apricot Jam
I like jam to be soft set with a natural flavor.

4 pounds underripe apricots
2 pounds superfine sugar
MAKES 5 POUNDS

Rinse the apricots under cold running water and drain. Pat dry with a clean kitchen towel. Using a small paring knife, remove any soft or dark patches. Cut the apricots in half and remove the pit.

In a wide, low-sided large saucepan over medium heat, place the sugar with 1 cup plus 2 tablespoons of water and cook, stirring occasionally, until the sugar dissolves and the mixture is of a syrupy consistency. Bring to a boil, add the apricots and simmer for 10 minutes, skimming off any froth with a metal slotted spoon.

Put a small plate in the refrigerator to chill. Place a sugar thermometer in the jam and lower the heat slightly. Stirring constantly to prevent scorching, continue boiling for about 45 minutes, until the jam reaches a temperature of 220°F. and thickens. To test the jam, remove the chilled plate, place some hot jam on it and return to the refrigerator for 10 minutes – the jam is set if it wrinkles when pushed with a finger. If it does not wrinkle, continue cooking for another 3 to 4 minutes and try again.

Remove the pan from the heat and leave it to stand for a few minutes. Using a funnel, ladle the jam into sterilized jars within $1/4$ inch of the rim. Screw the lids on the filled jars.

To sterilize the filled jars, place a rack in the bottom of a large lidded pot. Fill halfway with water and bring to a boil over high heat. Set the filled jars on the rack, making sure they do not touch each other and that they are covered with water by about 1 inch. Cover, bring the water back to a boil and boil for 15 to 20 minutes. Uncover the pot and, using metal tongs, remove the jars and set aside to cool for at least 8 to 10 hours. Store in a cold, dark, dry place for 6 months to 1 year.

DRINKS & GARNISHES

Marinated Melon Kebabs

The epitome of a drink garnish and a great dessert for children. For this recipe you will need 24 wooden skewers or long toothpicks (3 to $3^{1}/2$ inches long).

$1/4$ galia melon
$1/4$ cantaloupe melon
$1/4$ charentais melon
48 applemint leaves
FOR THE MARINADE
$1/2$ cup freshly squeezed orange juice
$1/4$ cup freshly squeezed lemon juice
2 tablespoons freshly squeezed lime juice

1 tablespoon fresh ginger juice
1 tablespoon light brown sugar
A pinch of salt
MAKES 24

Peel and seed the melons and cut the flesh into $3/4$- to 1-inch pieces. Place them in a ceramic dish. Combine all the ingredients for the marinade in a bowl, stirring until the sugar is dissolved. Pour the mixture over the melon, turning the cubes gently in it to coat them thoroughly. Cover with plastic wrap and place in the fridge to macerate for 1 hour, turning frequently.

Thread a piece of galia melon onto a skewer, then a mint leaf, followed by a piece of cantaloupe, then a mint leaf, then a piece of charentais. Repeat until all the melon and mint leaves have been used and serve the kebabs chilled with fresh fruit juices.

NOTES

• You can make the ginger juice easily by crushing a piece of fresh ginger through a garlic press.
• Any melons can be used in this recipe.

Blood Orange Punch with Ice Hands

8 cups unfiltered apple juice
$5^{1}/2$ cups freshly squeezed blood orange juice (about 15 oranges)
$3/4$ cup freshly squeezed lemon juice (about 2 lemons)
$1/2$ cup freshly squeezed lime juice (about 4 limes)
1 cup sparkling spring water
MAKES $8^{1}/2$ CUPS

To make the ice hands, fill some latex gloves with water. Securely enclose the wrists with rubber bands or tie them in a knot. Place them in the freezer on a flat surface until solid.

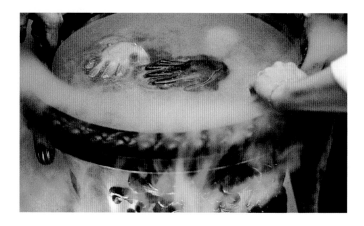

Place the apple juice in a large saucepan over a medium-high heat and simmer for 1 hour or until the volume of liquid has reduced to 1 cup.

In a caldron, combine the citrus juices with the reduced apple juice. Just before serving, stir in the sparkling water. Remove the ice hands from the freezer, peel off the latex and float the hands on top of the punch.

NOTES

• The reduced apple juice sweetens the punch, eliminating the need for sugar.
• For a ghoulish experience, place the caldron in a large container of dry ice.
• The latex gloves can be filled with black water by using black food coloring.

Elderflower Cordial

50 heads elderflowers
2 oranges
2 lemons
6 tablespoons cream of tartar
5³/4 to 6 cups sugar
MAKES 9³/4 CUPS

Wash and carefully dry the elderflowers, then place them in a large basin. Remove the zest, then the white pith, from the oranges and lemons. Reserve the zest, discard the white pith and slice the fruit.

In a large saucepan, place the sugar with 7¹/2 cups of water and slowly bring to a boil, stirring until the sugar has dissolved. Pour the sugar syrup over the flowers and stir in the cream of tartar.

Add the orange and lemon zests and the sliced fruit, then cover and leave to stand for 24 hours.

Line a strainer with two layers of muslin then strain the elderflower mixture through it. Pour the cordial into sterilized bottles and store in a cool dark place for up to 1 month.

NOTES

• You can use the cordial to make sorbet.
• For an elderflower ice cream soda, use sparkling water to make up the cordial and add a scoop of vanilla ice cream.
• Elderflowers have long been a favorite ingredient in drinks. The British make "champagne" from them, and they are used to flavor the popular Italian liqueur Sambucca. Elderflowers themselves also make excellent fritters.

Lemon Verbena Lemonade

³/4 cup light brown sugar
¹/2 cup honey
2 cups lemon juice
pinch of salt
1 lemon, cut into 8 wedges
10 lemon verbena leaves
Begonia ice cubes (see page 208)
MAKES 2¹/2 QUARTS

Put the sugar and honey into a large saucepan with 7¹/2 cups water and place over medium-high heat, stirring to dissolve. Bring to a boil, remove from the heat and transfer to a large pitcher to cool completely.

Stir in the lemon juice and salt, add the lemon wedges and lemon verbena leaves and leave to infuse for 1 hour. Serve over the ice cubes.

Mango Apple Juice

When I prepare juices I often add, depending on how the person is feeling, some sort of remedy, such as a little vitamin C, liquid echinacea, ginseng, bee pollen or primrose oil. Whatever the concoction, everybody ends up with a feeling of balance. Or maybe it's the yoga? This concoction is like an exotic hybrid fruit.

¹/2 pineapple, peeled and cored, or 1 cup pineapple juice
5 Granny Smith apples, or 3¹/2 cups apple juice
3 ripe mangoes, peeled and cut into ¹/2-inch pieces
¹/2 cup freshly squeezed lime juice
2 cups spring water
¹/2 cup light brown sugar
Ice cubes, to serve
Marinated Melon Kebabs, to decorate (see page 206)
MAKES 2 QUARTS

If using fresh pineapple, pass it through a juice extractor to give 1 cup of juice. If using fresh Granny Smiths, pass them through a juice extractor to give 3½ cups.

Place the mango flesh in a blender and purée it. Transfer the mango to a large pitcher and stir in the pineapple and apple juices, spring water and sugar until well combined. Serve the drink over ice, garnishing the glasses with the Marinated Melon Kebabs.

NOTES

• I highly recommend using fresh pineapple and apples.
• Stir in some fresh passionfruit for flavor and texture.
• A usual brunch at Lake House includes fresh carrot juice, apple and ginger juice, and a juice made of spinach, celery, turnip, beets, garlic, carrots and cabbage juice (said to be the healthiest juice on the planet), and freshly squeezed orange juice.

Watermelon and Ginger Juice
With Begonia ice cubes and toasted coconut.

FOR THE JUICE
2 to 3 lemons
2 to 3 limes
5½-inch piece fresh ginger
½ cup granulated brown sugar
3 pounds watermelon flesh
FOR THE GARNISH
Spring water
Begonia flowers
FOR THE TOASTED COCONUT STRIPS
1 coconut
MAKES ABOUT 6 CUPS

To make the begonia ice cubes, fill ice cube trays halfway up with the water and place in the freezer. When the water is only just frozen on top, crack the ice and slip a begonia flower into each cube. Return to the freezer until firm, then fill the trays with more water and freeze until solid.

Meanwhile, juice the lemons and limes. Set aside. Pass the ginger through a juice extractor.

To make the toasted coconut strips, using a hammer and nail, pierce three holes at one end of a coconut. Drain the liquid, reserving it for another use.

Wrap the coconut in a kitchen towel and use the hammer to crack the coconut at its center. Separate the coconut meat from the shell.

Using a vegetable peeler, remove the brown skin surrounding the coconut meat then continue peeling to make thin strips of coconut flesh.

Preheat the oven to 400°F and line a baking sheet with waxed paper. Place the coconut strips in a single layer on the baking sheet and bake for 5 to 10 minutes or until just toasted. Remove from the oven, cool and store in a covered container for up to 3 days.

In a medium saucepan over medium-high heat, combine the lemon, lime and ginger juices. Add the sugar and bring to a boil, stirring to dissolve the sugar. Remove the pan from the heat and leave to cool.

Pass the watermelon flesh through the juice extractor, then strain the juice through a fine-mesh sieve. Transfer the watermelon juice to a large pitcher and add the citrus-ginger syrup to taste. Stir and add the begonia ice cubes. Garnish with toasted coconut strips and serve.

NOTE

• Try this syrup technique for other fresh-fruit drinks.

Mulled Wine
A winter solace.

2 whole allspice
A pinch of grated nutmeg
¼ teaspoon mace blades or ground mace
3 cinnamon sticks, about 6 inches long, each broken into 2-inch pieces
5½ cups red wine, preferably Burgundy
1½ cups tawny port
1 cup brandy
1¼ cups sugar
54 cloves
18 small lady apples or crab apples
FOR THE GARNISH
12 cinnamon sticks, about 6 inches long
SERVES 12

Tie the allspice, nutmeg and mace together in a cheesecloth bag and place it in a large pot with the 3 broken cinnamon sticks, the red wine, tawny port, brandy, sugar and 2 cups of water. Bring to a boil, reduce the heat and barely simmer the mixture for 1 hour. Meanwhile, stick 3 cloves into each apple. After the mulled wine has been simmering for an hour, add the apples and continue simmering for another 30 minutes.

Just before serving, remove the spice bag. Serve the mulled wine warm with an apple in each mug and decorated with a stick of cinnamon.

STOCKS

Brown Chicken Stock
This stock has a medium caramel color with a sweet honey taste.

5 to 6 pounds chicken bones, legs, necks, thighs and wings, skinned and cut into 3-inch pieces
6 cloves garlic, unpeeled
2 to 3 medium carrots (about 6 ounces), cut into 1-inch pieces
2 onions (about 1 pound), cut into 1/2-inch pieces
3 stalks celery, with leaves, cut into 1/2-inch pieces
1 tablespoon tomato paste
1 cup white Burgundy wine
1 bouquet garni made from 4 sprigs thyme, 2 sprigs rosemary, 3 sprigs parsley and 2 bay leaves, tied together with string
1 teaspoon peppercorns
MAKES 8 TO 10 CUPS

Preheat the oven to 425°F. Put the chicken in a baking pan large enough to fit it all in one layer. Place the pan on the bottom of the oven and roast for 45 minutes, rotating the baking pan and stirring the chicken halfway through cooking.

After 45 minutes, stir the garlic, vegetables and tomato paste into the pan and continue cooking for another 30 minutes.

Using a slotted spoon, remove the chicken and vegetables to a stockpot. Pour the fat off from the baking pan then place it over medium-high heat on the stove top. Add the white wine to the pan and bring it to a simmer, stirring vigorously with a wooden spoon to scrape up the caramelized cooking juices on the base of the pan.

Pour the wine mixture from the deglazed pan into the stockpot, add the bouquet garni and peppercorns and 12 cups of water. Bring the mixture to a boil and skim the surface to remove any foam. Lower the heat and simmer the stock for 45 to 50 minutes or until the volume of liquid has reduced by half.

Add another 4 cups of water to the stockpot and simmer briskly for another 25 to 30 minutes. Strain, cool and remove any fat before use. Refrigerate or freeze the stock in batches as necessary.

NOTE

• This is the backbone of sauce and casserole making in this book. We don't use veal bones or beef bones – particularly veal, because of the way they are raised.

Light Chicken Stock
A fiesty bouquet of herbs and aromatic vegetables with a fresh and light chicken taste.

8 pounds chicken bones, wings, legs and necks, skinned and cut into 3-inch pieces
4 medium carrots (about 1 pound), cut into 1-inch pieces
2 medium leeks (white and light green parts only; about 8 ounces), chopped
3 stalks celery, cut into 1-inch pieces
2 medium onions (about 1 pound), peeled and cut into 1-inch pieces
1 medium white turnip (about 8 ounces), cut into 1-inch pieces
1 head garlic, excess paper removed, cut in half crosswise
1 1/2 teaspoons black peppercorns
4 whole cloves
8 sprigs parsley
6 sprigs thyme
6 sprigs tarragon
2 bay leaves
MAKES 4 TO 5 QUARTS

Rinse the chicken pieces under cold running water until the water runs clear. Place the chicken in a medium stockpot, cover with cold water by about 7 inches and add the vegetables, garlic, peppercorns and cloves. Bring to a boil then reduce the heat to low and simmer uncovered for 2 hours, skimming the foam from the surface as necessary.

Remove the pot from the heat, add the herbs and leave to stand for 30 minutes. Pour the stock through a fine sieve, pressing hard on the solids to extract their juices. Chill the stock to 40°F. in an ice bath before transferring to the refrigerator for at least 2 hours. When a layer of fat has hardened on the surface, discard it.

The stock may be refrigerated for up to 5 days in a covered container, bringing it to a boil if using after 2 days. Or it will keep for up to 3 months in the freezer.

Mussel or Clam Juice

1 teaspoon olive oil
1 clove garlic, sliced lengthwise into thirds
A small pinch of dried red pepper flakes
1 1/2 pounds mussels, well scrubbed and beards removed, or cherrystone clams, well scrubbed
MAKES 1 1/2 TO 2 CUPS

Heat a stockpot over high heat. Add 1/2 teaspoon of the olive oil and, after a few seconds, add the garlic and cook until it just begins to sizzle and brown. Add the red pepper flakes, shellfish and 2/3 cup of water. Cover the pot tightly and cook the mussels for 2 to 3 minutes, or the clams for 5 to 8 minutes, shaking the pot occasionally until the shellfish just open.

Remove the pot from the heat and strain the contents through a fine sieve, being careful not to drain the sediment in the bottom of the pan. Reserve the cooked mussels or clams for another use.

Leave the mussel or clam juice to cool then store in the refrigerator for up to 3 days, or freeze for 1 month in ice cube trays.

Notes

• I like to soak clams and mussels in cold salted water for a couple of hours to rid them of any sand.
• This could be a great base for a pasta dish. Pick the shellfish meat, add some chopped parsley and garlic, a pinch of red pepper flakes, some extra-virgin olive oil and the mussel or clam juice and toss with hot cooked pasta. Or use this combination of flavors in a risotto, or a crisp green salad with a few heirloom tomatoes.

Vegetable Stock

4 leeks, washed (light green and white parts only), coarsely chopped
3 small onions, washed, coarsely chopped
5 stalks celery, washed, including leaves, coarsely chopped
1 celery root, washed (about 12 ounces), peeled and coarsely chopped
2 carrots, washed, peeled and coarsely chopped
2 small fennel, washed, coarsely chopped
1 rutabaga (about 1 pound), washed, peeled and coarsely chopped

10 button mushrooms, washed and halved
2 whole heads garlic, excess skin removed and halved crosswise
2 teaspoons coriander seeds
2 teaspoons black peppercorns
2 bay leaves
6 sprigs tarragon
5 sprigs thyme
4 sprigs flat-leaf parsley
MAKES ABOUT 7 CUPS

In a large pot, place the leeks, onions, celery, celery root, carrots, fennel, rutabaga, button mushrooms, garlic, coriander, peppercorns and bay leaves. Add cold water to about 3 or 4 inches above the vegetables. Bring to a boil, uncovered, over high heat, then lower the heat and simmer for 1 hour, skimming if needed.

Remove the pot from the heat and add the tarragon, thyme and parsley. Let stand for 30 minutes to infuse. Strain through a fine sieve, pushing hard on the solids. Return the stock to the pot and boil over a high heat until reduced to about 7 cups.

Remove the stock from the heat and let cool to room temperature for a few hours, or cool rapidly by placing it in a bath of iced water. Divide the stock into plastic containers with lids and freeze until needed, or refrigerate for up to 3 days.

Lobster Fumet

2 lobsters (1 1/2 pounds each, killed according to the Paella recipe, page 91), tails removed and reserved for another use
1 tablespoon olive oil
1 medium onion, chopped
4 cloves garlic, smashed
2 plum tomatoes, chopped
1 tablespoon tomato paste
1/2 cup cognac
A pinch of cayenne
1 cup dry white wine
4 sprigs tarragon
1 bay leaf
1/2 teaspoon coarse salt
A pinch of freshly ground black pepper
MAKES 4 TO 5 CUPS

Clean the lobsters, separate the claws from the bodies, remove the grainy sac from behind the head and take off the outer shell. Using a cleaver, chop the lobster body and claws into 2-inch pieces. Wash in plenty of cold water.

In a large stockpot, heat the olive oil, onion, garlic and lobster pieces over medium-high heat, smashing frequently with a wooden spoon to break up the lobster shells. Cook until the lobster shells have turned bright orange, about 15 minutes.

Stir in the tomatoes and tomato paste, then add the cognac and cayenne. Simmer for about 5 minutes or until the cognac has evaporated. Pour in the white wine and cook for 10 minutes. Add 6 cups of water and the remaining ingredients, apart from the salt and pepper, and simmer for 40 minutes, skimming occasionally.

Strain the fumet through a fine sieve, pushing hard on the solids with a wooden spoon. Season with the salt and pepper. The fumet may be refrigerated for up to 3 days or frozen for up to a month in a covered container.

NOTE

• To reinforce this stock, add the solids back into the fumet and cook for 20 minutes. Strain and use.

Corn Stock

The sweet richness of this stock is both light and luscious. In the summer I often use corn stock as a substitute for lobster stock.

14 ears corn, husks removed and cleaned
4 thin basil stems
4 sprigs tarragon
MAKES 4 TO 6 CUPS

Holding each ear of corn upright on a cutting board, use a small sharp knife to cut down the side of each ear to remove the kernels from the cobs. Reserve 2 cups of kernels and cut the cobs into 2-inch pieces.

In a large pot, combine the corn cobs, reserved corn kernels, and 12 cups of cold water. Bring to a boil, reduce the heat and simmer for 1 hour.

Strain and return the stock to the pot. Boil over medium-high heat until the volume of liquid has reduced to 4 to 6 cups. Remove from the heat, add the basil stems and tarragon and set aside to cool and infuse for 10 minutes. Remove the herbs from the stock before use or storage. The stock may be refrigerated up to 5 days in a covered container or up to 3 months in the freezer.

NOTES

• Reduce to 4 cups for a more intense flavor for dishes such as pea sauce or risotto or when using it in place of Lobster Fumet. Reduce it to 6 cups for soups, when a lighter flavor is required.
• This is a good way to use up the stems of basil when you have used the leaves in another dish.
• Try using the stock in a mushroom sauté.

Tomato Water

8 beefsteak tomatoes, cored and roughly chopped
1 teaspoon salt
MAKES 3 1/2 CUPS

Place half the tomatoes in the bowl of a food processor fitted with a steel blade and pulse on and off just until the tomatoes break up. Transfer to a bowl and set aside while you repeat with the remaining tomatoes. Stir the salt into the bowl of tomato pulp.

Place the pulp in the center of a double layer of cheesecloth and tie with kitchen string to form a bundle. Tie the bundle to a wooden spoon and hang it over a bowl to catch the tomato water. Leave until liquid ceases dripping, about 3 to 4 hours, or leave to drip overnight in the refrigerator. Do not squeeze the bag in an attempt to extract the water any faster. Tomato water can be stored for up to 4 days in the refrigerator or frozen in ice cube trays and used accordingly.

SAUCES

Balsamic Glaze

1 cup balsamic vinegar
1/2 cup Worcestershire sauce
MAKES 1/3 CUP

In a medium saucepan, bring the vinegar and Worcestershire sauce to a boil. Lower to a medium heat and simmer for about 25 minutes until the mixture thickens and has reduced to a volume of 1/3 cup. The sauce may be refrigerated for up to 2 weeks in a covered container.

NOTE

• Can be used as a garnish for most fish, chicken or duck dishes, in addition to another sauce. I drizzle it in a circle or dot it around .

BBQ Sauce

A versatile sauce with character and depth.

1 tablespoon coriander seeds
1 tablespoon cumin seeds
4 dried New Mexican chillies, or 1/3 cup New Mexican chilli powder
1/4 cup olive oil
2 medium onions (about 1 pound), roughly chopped
10 cloves garlic, peeled and roughly chopped
2 canned chipotle chillies in adobo sauce, or 2 strips bacon, chopped
3 tablespoons dry mustard
3 28-ounce cans whole tomatoes with juice
2 bay leaves
1/2 cup packed light brown sugar
1/2 cup red wine vinegar
6 drops Tabasco sauce
1/4 cup freshly squeezed lemon juice
1/2 cup Worcestershire sauce
1/4 cup tomato paste
2 tablespoons salt
1/2 cup honey
MAKES 7 CUPS

In a dry cast-iron skillet over medium heat, toast the coriander and cumin seeds until fragrant. Remove to a spice mill or mortar. In the same skillet, toast the New Mexican chillies according to the instructions at right. Add them to the toasted spices and grind finely. If using chilli powder as a replacement, stir it into the ground spices.

Place the onions and garlic in a food processor fitted with a steel blade and finely mince. In a medium saucepan, heat the olive oil over medium-low heat. Add the onion and garlic mixture and cook until translucent, 10 to 15 minutes. Add the chilli mixture, chipotles or bacon, and mustard and cook for 5 minutes, stirring.

Meanwhile, put the canned tomatoes and their juices through a food mill. Increase the heat to medium and add the puréed tomatoes and bay leaves. Cook, stirring frequently, for 1 hour or until reduced by half.

Reduce the heat to medium-low and stir in the brown sugar, red wine vinegar, Tabasco, lemon juice, Worcestershire sauce, tomato paste, salt and honey. Cook, stirring frequently, for about 1 hour or until the volume of sauce has reduced to 7 cups. Cool before storing in batches as necessary. The sauce will keep for up to 1 week covered in the refrigerator and can be frozen for up to 3 months.

Toasting dried chillies brings out and broadens their flavor. To toast the chillies, tear them into flat pieces and remove the seeds before adding them to the skillet. Using a flat metal spatula, press them against the hot surface for a few seconds, until they begin to blister, crackle and change color. Then flip and repeat on the other side. Remove and break the toasted chilli pieces into a small bowl, then place them in a spice mill and grind to a powder.

Alternatively, you can make an adobo from the toasted chillies by pouring boiling water over them and soaking for 20 minutes. Drain, then tear the reconstituted chillies into small pieces, place in a blender with some roasted garlic and purée. You can marinate chicken in this mixture before grilling or make a chilli aïoli by adding the paste to some mayonnaise.

Lake House Ketchup

Every Saturday night we have fish and chips served with this ketchup.

1 dried chilli, such as a New Mexican chilli
4 14-ounce cans peeled plum tomatoes, roughly chopped
1 cup sugar
3/4 cup cider vinegar
1 clove garlic, smashed
2 fresh bay leaves
1 cinnamon stick, about 2 inches long
1 tablespoon dry English mustard powder
1/2 teaspoon ground coriander
3 cloves
Juice of 2 limes
2 1/2 tablespoons finely chopped cilantro (optional)
MAKES 2 CUPS

In a dry skillet, toast the chilli until crisp (see above). Place the flesh in a spice mill and grind finely.

In a large heavy stockpot, combine the ground chilli, chopped tomatoes, sugar, cider vinegar, garlic, bay leaves, cinnamon, mustard powder, coriander and cloves and bring to a boil. Reduce the heat to medium-low and cook the mixture for 1 hour, stirring occasionally.

Pass the mixture through a food mill fitted with a medium disc and transfer the sauce back to the same pot. Cook over a medium-low heat for about 45 minutes or until the sauce has reduced and thickened.

Remove the sauce from the heat and let cool. Stir in the lime juice and cilantro if using. The ketchup may be refrigerated for up to 1 week in a covered container.

NOTE

• Instead of chopping the tomatoes by hand, you can pulse them in a food processor in 2 batches.

Mayonnaise

1 cup grapeseed oil
1 cup olive oil
2 large egg yolks
4 teaspoons freshly squeezed lemon juice
1 1/2 teaspoons Dijon mustard
1/2 teaspoon salt
A pinch of freshly ground black pepper
MAKES 2 CUPS

Combine the oils together in a glass measuring cup.

In the bowl of a food processor fitted with the steel blade, place the egg yolks and 3 teaspoons of the lemon juice and process until pale yellow in color.

Add the mustard, salt and pepper then, with the machine running, begin adding the oil slowly through the feed tube. When one-third of the oil has been added, add 4 teaspoons of water to the mixture. Continue adding the oil very slowly and, when half of the remaining oil has been incorporated, add another 4 teaspoons of water.

Add the remaining oil then another 3 teaspoons of water and 1 teaspoon of lemon juice. The mayonnaise may be refrigerated for up to 3 days in a covered container.

NOTES

• For roast lamb or chicken, add some roasted mashed garlic, red chile paste and black pepper.
• Mash together some soft white bread, garlic and salt then stir the paste into the mayonnaise to make a grand aïoli for boiled vegetables.
• Peel and chop some horseradish. Purée it with rice wine vinegar. Mix it into the mayonnaise, add a little cream, and you have a sauce for a rib roast.

Red Wine Reduction

A concentrated, full-flavored red wine reduction that really sparks up other sauces and provides a satisfying balance.

1 1/2 tablespoons finely diced shallots
1 tablespoon finely diced carrot
1 tablespoon finely diced red bell pepper
1/2 cup red wine
1/2 cup port
1/3 cup red wine vinegar
1 tablespoon butter, chilled and diced
Salt and freshly ground black pepper
MAKES 2 TO 3 TABLESPOONS

In a medium saucepan over high heat, place the shallots, carrot, red bell pepper, wine, port and vinegar. Bring to a boil, then lower the heat slightly and simmer for 18 to 20 minutes or until the mixture has reduced to a volume of about 2 1/2 tablespoons. Strain and return the sauce to the same pan.

Set the pan over low heat and whisk in the butter gradually to give a smooth, glossy sauce. Remove the sauce from the heat and season to taste with salt and pepper.

NOTES

• The sauce can be made up to 20 minutes in advance, or 3 hours in advance without adding the butter.
• This is particularly good with fish – I swirl it or dot it around the plate when serving cod (see page 98).

Sweet Chilli Sauce

2 cups sugar
1 tablespoon light corn syrup
4 ounces shallots, peeled and finely chopped
3 mild red chillies, about 3 1/2 inches long, deseeded and finely chopped
1 ounce fresh ginger, peeled and finely chopped
1 clove garlic, finely chopped
1 1/2 tablespoons cider vinegar
1 tablespoon soy sauce
1 tablespoon finely chopped fresh cilantro
MAKES 1 1/2 CUPS

In a small saucepan over high heat, place the sugar, corn syrup and 1 cup of water, stirring to dissolve. Bring the mixture to the boil and boil for about 15 minutes, or until the liquid is amber in color and has reduced by about half in volume.

Remove the sauce from the heat and leave it to cool for 5 minutes. Stir in the shallots, chillies, ginger, garlic, vinegar and soy sauce, then transfer to a small bowl. Just before serving, stir in the fresh cilantro. The sauce may be refrigerated for up to 1 week in a covered container.

NOTES

• Broil scallops or shrimp and serve with the sweet chilli sauce, crème fraîche and arugula salad.
• This sauce also goes well with oily fish, chicken and barbecued food: Use it as a baste when grilling, and serve with lemongrass sauce (see page 87).

FLAVORED OILS

Parsley Oil

This oil, and the ones that follow, make plates look appealing and enhance the complexities of each dish.

1 cup parsley leaves
1/3 cup grapeseed oil
1/4 cup olive oil
MAKES ABOUT 1/2 CUP PLUS 2 TABLESPOONS

Prepare an ice bath. Bring a pan of salted water to a boil. Add the parsley to the boiling water and cook for 15 seconds. Drain, then lay the herbs on top of the iced water without submerging.

When cool, remove and coarsely chop the parsley. Place in a kitchen towel and twist to squeeze out the excess water. Transfer to a blender, add the oils and purée for 2 to 3 minutes. Do not strain before use. Pour into a container, cover and refrigerate for up to 2 days.

NOTE

• If I have this around, I'll use it to enhance brown sauces, red sauces, or Roast Chicken with Corn, Fava Beans and Tomatoes (see page 118).
• You can add some lemon juice and cayenne to the oil, brush it over brochettes of seafood or chicken then broil or barbecue.
• For a good Moroccan-style baste, mince some preserved lemon (see page 205) and garlic, and add them to the oil with a little paprika and lemon juice.

Dill Oil

This is a beautiful vibrant green. I like to leave the herb in the oil and achieve a broken effect.

1 cup dill
1/4 cup grapeseed oil
1/4 cup olive oil
MAKES 1/2 CUP

Prepare an ice bath. Bring a pan of salted water to a boil. Add the dill to the boiling water and cook for 15 seconds. Drain, then lay the herbs on top of the iced water without submerging.

When cool, remove and coarsely chop the dill. Place in a kitchen towel and twist to squeeze out the excess water. Transfer to a blender, add the oils and purée for 2 to 3 minutes. Do not strain. Pour into a container, cover and refrigerate for up to 2 days.

NOTES

• Just dot this around some grilled salmon and you don't need anything else, except maybe a bowl of brown rice and some crispy shallots.
• Add some lemon juice, seasoning and a shallot or two to the dill oil and fold the mixture into rices and grains to bring them up a notch.

Chive Oil

1 1/2 cups chives
1/4 cup grapeseed oil
1/2 cup olive oil
MAKES ABOUT 3/4 CUP

Prepare an ice bath. Bring a pan of salted water to a boil. Add the chives to the boiling water and cook for 15 seconds. Drain, then lay the herbs on top of the iced water without submerging.

When cool, remove the chives and coarsely chop. Place in a kitchen towel and twist to squeeze out the excess water. Place in a blender, add the oils and purée for 1 to 2 minutes. Pour into a container, cover and refrigerate for up to 2 days.

NOTE

• This is used in Red Snapper with Basmati Rice and Spiced Saffron Curry Sauce (see page 92). It works well with lamb, summer grilled foods or salads.

Herb Oil

1 cup basil leaves
1/4 cup tarragon leaves
1/4 cup flat-leaf parsley leaves
2 cloves garlic, peeled and sliced
1/4 cup grapeseed oil
1/4 cup extra-virgin olive oil
MAKES 1/2 CUP

Bring a large saucepan of salted water to a boil and add the herbs. Blanch for 30 seconds, then strain and drain under cold running water. Coarsely chop, then place the herbs in a kitchen towel and squeeze out the excess water.

Place the herbs in a blender with the remaining ingredients and purée until well combined. Pour into a container, cover and store in the refrigerator for up to 2 days.

NOTE

• Can be used as an accompaniment to any of the fish preparations. Try combining it with spiced saffron sauce (see page 92) along with dots or swirls of the Red Wine Reduction (see page 213).

Lemongrass Oil

1 cup grapeseed oil
4 tablespoons chopped lemongrass
MAKES 1 CUP

In a small saucepan, combine the oil and lemongrass and heat gently for 10 minutes. Remove the pan from the heat and let the oil and lemongrass infuse for at least 2 hours or overnight. Strain, then use or store, refrigerated for up to 1 week in a covered container.

USING HERBS

Herbs are cool. I find them awe inspiring, highly sensuous yet robust and use them a lot in my dishes, cooked and raw, as a focal point, as a backdrop to other ingredients, and, of course, as a garnish. Placing a chervil sprig on a bowl of fresh steamed peas seems such a natural, obvious thing, I do it without thought.
There's always an herb to bring a different dimension to a dish, whether I'm looking for very aggressive flavors, or simply want to hint at its presence. An intense chive oil, pesto or basil vinaigrette leaves one in no doubt of its nature and purpose; it's the same with an arugula salad. One of my favorite techniques, however, is to use herbs as an infusion where their flavor adds merely a layer of taste and the leaves and stems may not appear in the final dish at all. I

often, for example, put tarragon in a stew at the very end of cooking, let it provide some spark and backbone, then take it out before serving. A similar effect is achieved by using herbs to brush food during cooking, leaving traces of their flavor and aroma behind, or employing the tough stalks as skewers for grilled brochettes.

The secret to using herbs successfully is to separate them into strong, medium and smooth categories. Strong herbs are the ones you would not want to swallow raw. Smooth herbs are those you can nibble on, while medium herbs are between the two and strongly flavored herbs you can eat without spitting them out! The herbs in each category tend to work well with others in that group. Avoid strong herbs in salads but look to them first for infusions and brushes. Medium herbs, such as sage, and the sturdier smooth herbs, such as parsley, can be used for deep-frying and can stand up to strong flavors like garlic. Choose tender, smooth herbs for eating raw and subtly flavoring delicate sauces, vegetables or fish.

If starting a garden, my first choice of herbs would be green and purple basil, chervil, rosemary, lemon thyme, lemon verbena and summer and winter savory. And I'd get a bay tree instead of a rubber plant. The next stage would be to add pineapple sage, kaffir lime leaves and some exotic mints.

You'll notice that dried herbs are rarely mentioned in this book. The only ones I would consider using are bay leaves, oregano and thyme.

EXTRAS

Clarified Butter

2 1/2 cups unsalted butter, diced
MAKES 1 1/2 TO 2 CUPS

In a small, deep saucepan over low heat, place the butter and melt it slowly. Using a spoon or small ladle, skim the foam that rises to the surface and discard.

Once the butter has melted, increase the heat to medium-low and cook for 10 to 15 minutes, allowing the liquid to bubble slightly and continuing to skim the surface until the butter is clear. The sediment at the bottom of the pan will have browned slightly and there will still be some foam on top of the liquid.

Remove the pan from the heat and let it cool for about 5 minutes. Line a sieve with cheesecloth and strain the butter into a glass jar, leaving the solids behind in the saucepan. The clarified butter may be refrigerated up to 1 month, covered.

• Use this for ghee.

Crispy Shallot Rings

1 large shallot, thinly sliced into rings with a mandoline
1 cup grapeseed oil
3 tablespoons flour
Salt and freshly ground black pepper

Separate the shallots into rings and lay them on a small baking sheet lined with parchment paper. Heat the oil in a small saucepan over medium-high heat to 350°F. Place the flour in a small bowl and season with salt and pepper.

Divide the shallots into 5 batches. Toss each batch in the seasoned flour, then transfer to a fine sieve and shake to remove the excess flour. Carefully add the shallots to the hot oil and fry for about 1 minute or until golden. Drain on a baking sheet lined with a kitchen towel. Repeat with remaining shallots.

Use immediately or leave to cool and store at room temperature in a container lined with parchment paper for up to 3 days.

NOTE

• These deep-fried crispy sweet shallots make a useful backdrop or garnish to fish or rice dishes. I use them in the Grilled Scallops with Herb Sauce (see page 74).

Fried Parsley

1 1/2 cups vegetable oil
4 to 6 sprigs flat-leaf parsley, mostly leaves (not stems)
Salt and freshly ground black pepper
SERVES 4 (AS A GARNISH)

In a medium heavy pot over moderate heat, place the grapeseed oil and heat to 350°F.
Carefully add half the parsley and fry for 10 to 15 seconds until crisp but not brown. Remove with a slotted metal spoon and set aside on a small baking pan lined with a kitchen towel. Repeat with the remaining parsley. Season with salt and pepper.

NOTE

• The parsley sprigs can be fried up to 2 hours before use.

Moroccan Spices

1/4 cup whole hazelnuts
1/4 cup blanched almonds
5 teaspoons sesame seeds
2 1/2 teaspoons coriander seeds
2 1/2 teaspoons cumin seeds
1 1/4 teaspoons sumac
MAKES ABOUT 3/4 CUP

Preheat the oven to 350°F. Spread the hazelnuts and almonds on a baking sheet and toast for 8 to 10 minutes until brown. Cool, then rub the hazelnuts in a clean dish towel to remove the skins.

In a food processor fitted with a metal blade, place the nuts and finely grind. Remove and place them in a small bowl.

Toast the sesame, coriander and cumin seeds in a dry skillet over medium heat until fragrant, about 2 to 3 minutes. Transfer the seeds to a spice mill and grind them finely. Combine the seeds thoroughly with the nuts and stir in the sumac. Store in a covered container in the refrigerator for up to 1 month.

NOTE

• We use this spice mixture as a rub for fillets of cod, halibut, monkfish and salmon. Press into both sides before sautéeing.

Slow-roasted Garlic Tomatoes in Olive Oil

1 cup olive oil
5 whole garlic cloves, peeled
8 plum tomatoes
1/2 teaspoon salt
Freshly ground black pepper
3 sprigs fresh thyme, leaves removed
MAKES 16

Preheat the oven to 250°F. Place the olive oil and garlic cloves in a medium saucepan and fry over a medium heat for 8 to 10 minutes or until well browned, turning once during cooking. Remove and set aside to cool.

Meanwhile, using a sharp paring knife, core the tomatoes and cut them in half lengthwise. Remove some of the seeds with your finger. Place the tomatoes cut-side up in a baking dish and season them with the salt and pepper.

Remove the garlic from the oil and place on a cutting board. With the back of a knife, mash it to form a paste. In a small bowl mix the garlic paste and oil together. Pour the garlic-oil mixture evenly over the tomatoes. Sprinkle with the thyme leaves. Transfer to an oven and bake for 2 1/2 to 3 hours or until a deep red color.

Leave the tomatoes to cool in the oil. When cool enough to handle, remove the skins. Using a slotted spoon, lift the tomatoes out of the oil and use accordingly. Strain the oil and reserve for another use. If not using immediately, store the tomatoes covered with the oil in an airtight container for up to 1 week.

NOTE

• The excess oil can be saved and used in vinaigrettes and mayonnaise or to garnish fish dishes.

Tomato Petals

3 plum tomatoes or 2 beefsteak tomatoes, stemmed and cored
1/2 teaspoon olive oil
1/8 teaspoon sugar
1/8 teaspoon coarse salt
A pinch of freshly ground black pepper
4 sprigs thyme
MAKES 12 TO 16

Using a small sharp knife, mark a cross in the base of each tomato. Bring a medium saucepan filled with lightly salted water to the boil. Add the tomatoes and blanch them for 20 to 30 seconds.

Drain the tomatoes, refresh under cold running water then peel off and discard the skins. If using plum tomatoes, cut them into quarters lengthwise and use a knife to cut out the seeds and pith, leaving a neat petal of tomato flesh. If using beefsteak tomatoes, do the same but cut each tomato into 8 pieces.

Preheat the oven to 225°F. or the lowest setting. In a small bowl, combine the tomato petals, olive oil, sugar, salt and pepper. Toss and place the tomatoes skin-side down on a parchment-lined baking sheet and top with the sprigs of thyme.

Bake for 1 to 1 1/2 hours or until the tomatoes are deep red in color and most of the moisture has evaporated.

Roasted Onions

4 small onions, unpeeled
2 tablespoons olive oil
1 tablespoon unsalted butter, diced
6 sprigs thyme
Salt and freshly ground black pepper
MAKES 4

Preheat the oven to 350°F. Place the onions in a baking dish and drizzle with the olive oil. Divide the butter over the onions, top with the thyme sprigs and season. Cover with foil and roast for 1 1/2 hours. Refrigerate in a plastic container for up to 5 days. Peel and proceed with recipe.

NOTE

• The roasted onions can be puréed and added to soups, stews, sauces or combined with some roasted garlic and rosemary and served as an accompaniment to lamb or chicken.

Roasted Garlic

4 heads garlic
2 tablespoons olive oil
1 tablespoon unsalted butter, diced
6 sprigs thyme
Salt and freshly ground black pepper
MAKES 4

Heat the oven to 350°F. Remove the excess paper from around the heads of garlic but leave the cloves unpeeled. Cut away 1/4 inch of

each head of garlic then place them in a baking dish and drizzle with the olive oil. Divide the butter evenly over the heads, top with the thyme sprigs and season.

Cover with foil and roast for 1 hour. Store in covered plastic container for up to 5 days in the refrigerator.

NOTES

• Roasted garlic is used as an ingredient several times in this book, however it can also be served as a side dish with black olives and extra-virgin olive oil.
• Try squeezing the roasted garlic over bruschetta or grilled polenta bread.
• Mash a few cloves with some salt and cayenne and stir the paste into mayonnaise, or purée and use to thicken sauces.

Roasted Pepper Purée

3 red or yellow bell peppers (about 1¹/₂ pounds total)
1 teaspoon olive oil
Salt and freshly ground black pepper
MAKES 1 CUP

Preheat the oven to 400°F. Trim the stems from the bell peppers so that the stem end is reasonably flat and they can sit upright. Brush each pepper with oil and place in a small baking dish, stem-end down. Sprinkle with salt and pepper then transfer to the oven and roast the peppers for about 45 minutes or until they have softened and the skins are blistered and dark.

Let the peppers cool slightly then use a paring knife to cut them in half and remove the skins, cores and seeds. Purée the flesh of the peppers in a blender or food processor until smooth. If not using the purée immediately, store in an airtight container in the fridge for up to 4 days or freeze in small batches for up to 1 month.

NOTE

• I use this a lot in my cooking, as a garnish and as an ingredient. Its color and sweetness really balance a dish, such as Shrimp with Pesto (see page 95).

SWEET THINGS

Chocolate Sauce

8 ounces semisweet chocolate or good-quality plain chocolate, such as Green 'n' Blacks, chopped
3 tablespoons unsalted butter
4 teaspoons cocoa powder
¹/₂ cup milk
¹/₄ cup heavy cream
MAKES 1¹/₂ CUPS

In the top of a double boiler over low heat, melt the chocolate, butter and cocoa powder together, stirring occasionally to combine.
In a small saucepan, heat the milk and heavy cream over low heat then slowly add it to the melted chocolate mixture, stirring until smooth.

Use immediately or cool and store covered in the refrigerator for up to 1 week. Reheat in a double boiler.

NOTES

• A versatile chocolate sauce that can be used for desserts such as Chocolate Soufflés with Chocolate Dog Tuiles (see page 172), poured over ice cream or used to make chocolate milk.
• If not using semisweet chocolate, add sugar to the milk mixture to taste. Place over a low heat and stir till dissolved.

Hazelnut Praline

1 cup hazelnuts
Oil, for brushing
²/₃ cup sugar
¹/₈ teaspoon freshly ground black pepper
MAKES 1¹/₂ CUPS

Preheat the oven to 350°F. Place the hazelnuts on a baking sheet and toast in the oven for 8 to 10 minutes. Place the nuts in a kitchen towel and rub off the skins of the nuts.

Brush a clean baking sheet with oil. Put the sugar in a heavy saucepan with ¹/₂ cup water and heat gently until the sugar dissolves. Bring to a boil and boil for 8 to 10 minutes until the caramel is dark brown and begins to smell burned. Quickly stir in the hazelnuts and black pepper then pour onto the baking sheet.

Allow the praline to cool for 20 minutes then roughly break it into large pieces and place in a food processor fitted with a steel blade. Pulse until the praline is finely ground. Store in a covered container at room temperature for up to 3 weeks.

NOTES

• Praline is delicious sprinkled over ice creams, as well as used in S'Mores (see page 185) and English Toffee Tart (see page 160).
• You can replace half the hazelnuts with almonds.
• Store raw nuts in the freezer.

Simple Syrup

1 cup sugar
MAKES 1¹/₂ CUPS

In a small saucepan over medium heat, combine the sugar and 1 cup of water, stirring to dissolve. Bring the liquid to a boil then remove from the heat and cool to room temperature. The syrup may be refrigerated for up to 10 days in a covered container.

PASTRIES & BREADS

Pâte Sucrée

2³/₄ cup plus 2 tablespoons flour

¹/₃ cup superfine sugar

1 cup plus 1 tablespoon unsalted butter, chilled and diced

2 large egg yolks

¹/₄ cup heavy cream, plus extra if needed

MAKES 1³/₄ POUNDS OR TWO 10-INCH TARTS

Put the flour into a bowl with the sugar and use your fingertips to rub in the butter until the mixture resembles coarse crumbs.

In a small bowl, mix together the egg yolks and cream then stir them into the flour mixture until the pastry comes together in a ball. If the dough is still too dry, add an extra tablespoon of cream. Wrap the pastry in plastic wrap and chill for at least 1 hour before use.

NOTES

• This pastry can also be made in a food processor fitted with a metal blade or in an electric mixer fitted with a paddle attachment, but I prefer making it by hand for a flakier crust.
• The recipes in this book require only a portion of this pastry, so if you are not using it all at once, freeze the remainder for up to 1 month.

Quick Puff Pastry

2³/₄ cups all-purpose flour

1 cup white pastry flour

1 teaspoon salt

2¹/₂ cups unsalted butter, chilled and cubed

1 cup ice-cold water

MAKES 2 POUNDS 13 OUNCES

In the bowl of a food processor fitted with a metal blade, place both flours and the salt and pulse briefly to combine. Add the butter and pulse again until there are still small (¹/₄-inch) pieces of butter present. Slowly add the water and process until the dough is barely combined.

Transfer the dough to a lightly floured work surface and knead until the dough just comes together. Form it into a 9 x 8-inch rectangle, wrap in plastic wrap and freeze for 15 to 18 minutes.

Remove the pastry from the freezer and unwrap it. Allow it to come back to room temperature so that it is a pliable consistency for rolling. On a lightly floured surface, roll the dough into a 20 x 8-inch rectangle. Fold the right-hand end over by a third, covering the center third. Then fold the left-hand side over the top to give three layers of pastry. Turn the pastry clockwise by 90° and roll out again to a rectangle measuring 20 x 8 inches, dusting with more flour as required. Fold in thirds as above then brush away any excess flour with a pastry brush. Wrap the pastry in plastic wrap and refrigerate for 30 minutes.

Remove the pastry from the refrigerator and on a lightly floured surface roll it out to a rectangle measuring 20 x 8 inches, lifting the pastry occasionally and dusting with flour to prevent sticking. Fold into thirds, turn clockwise by 90° then roll out again to 20 x 8 inches. Fold the pastry into thirds, wrap in plastic wrap and chill for 1 hour before use. The pastry will keep for up to 2 days in the refrigerator and 3 months in the freezer.

Pita Bread

2 tablespoons olive oil, plus extra for greasing

1 teaspoon active dry yeast

3 cups white bread flour

1 cup plain whole-wheat or chapati flour, plus extra for dusting

1¹/₂ teaspoons salt

MAKES 14

In the bowl of an electric mixer fitted with a dough hook, combine the oil, yeast and 1¹/₂ cups of room-temperature water. Add the flours and salt and mix for 10 minutes.

Turn the dough out onto a lightly floured work surface and knead for 2 to 3 minutes. Lightly oil a mixing bowl, add the dough, cover with a kitchen towel and leave to rise for 1 hour or until the dough has doubled in size.

Punch down the dough then remove it from the bowl and, on a surface lightly dusted with whole-wheat flour, shape it into a roll 14 inches long. Dust a baking sheet with whole-wheat flour.

Preheat the oven to 500°F. and place a cast-iron griddle or pizza stone on the bottom shelf of the oven. Cut the dough into 1-inch-thick rounds, which will weigh 2 to 2¹/₂ ounces each. Evenly roll each portion into ¹/₄-inch-thick circles and place on the baking sheet. Cover with a kitchen towel and set aside to rise for 20 minutes. Place 2 to 3 pitas on the preheated griddle and bake them for 2¹/₂ to

Remove the towel and, using a wooden spoon, mix in the remaining 1 cup of tipo '00' and all the bread flour to give a very soft, but not wet, dough.

Remove the dough from the bowl and place on a lightly floured work surface, or transfer to an electric mixer fitted with a dough hook, and knead for 8 to 10 minutes.

Return the dough to an oiled bowl, cover and leave to rise until doubled in size, about 45 minutes. Then punch down the dough, cover and leave to rise again until doubled, about 45 minutes.

The dough is now ready to use as desired. You can roll it out in batches to the required size or sizes or wrap in plastic and freeze it for up to 1 month. Remove from the freezer and allow to thaw and rise again.

Notes

• Mixing tipo '00' flour with bread flour creates a crispness to this dough that sets it a world apart from others. Tipo '00' is a fine flour made from wheat. It is available from Italian specialty shops and some supermarkets and is traditionally used in cakes.
• I like dough to rise slowly to develop character and a bit of sourness. This dough is different because I add the salt to the yeast water, which deadens it a bit and creates a sour flavor.
• The dough's rising can vary depending on the temperature of the room and the day it is made, so wait until it doubles.
• The recipe for Focaccia with Robiola Cheese and Truffle Oil (see page 198) requires only half this mixture while Rosemary Focaccia (see page 200) requires the whole batch.

3 minutes or until they puff up like pillows. Remove from the oven and place under a preheated grill if you want to brown the other side.

Wrap the cooked pitas in a damp towel. Repeat with the remaining breads. Rewarm them under the grill before serving.

Note

• The wholewheat flour gives the bread a rustic texture.

Focaccia Dough

5 tablespoons olive oil, plus extra for greasing
1 tablespoon active dry yeast
1¹/2 teaspoons salt
2¹/2 cups tipo '00' flour or pastry flour or all-purpose flour
2¹/2 cups bread flour
MAKES 2¹/2 POUNDS

In a large mixing bowl, whisk together 2 cups of tepid water, the olive oil, yeast, salt and 1¹/2 cups of the tipo '00' flour until combined. Cover with a kitchen towel and set aside in a draft-free place for 1 hour, until the mixture is bubbling and looks like a sponge.

Menus for Spring & Summer

Al Fresco Dinner Party
Pea Soup
Spring Vegetables with Carrot Ravioli and Truffle
  Vinaigrette
Roast Chicken with Corn, Fava Beans
  and Tomatoes
Summer Fruit Noisette

Family Lunch
Shrimp with Mediterranean Shrimp Sauce and
  Basil and Parsley Pesto
Tagliatelle with Tomato Sauce or Gnocchi with
  Pesto
Berry Cobbler

Quick Kitchen Supper
Dover Sole with Sun-dried Tomatoes and Capers
Rhubarb and Strawberry Crumble

Family Brunch
Brioche Bresse
Italian Frittata
Zucchini Blossom Frittata

Picnic
Focaccia with Robiola Cheese and Truffle Oil
Millet and Aduki Bean Salad with Sheep Cheese
  and Tomato Oil Vinaigrette
Stuffed Red and Yellow Cherry Tomatoes
Lake House Crab Cakes with Almond Aïoli
Pita Bread
Picnic Cherry Pies
Chocolate Chip Cookies
Elderflower Cordial

Do-ahead Dinner Party
Spring Salad with Spaghetti Squash and Goat
  Cheese Croutons
Vegetable Tian
Buttermilk Fried Chicken
Roasted Garlic
Sauté of Fennel, Artichokes and Carrots
Lake House Bread
Black Currant Sorbet and Biscotti

Paella Party
Paella
Golden and Red Beet and Artichoke Salad
Biscotti and Shortbread

Vegetarian Kitchen Garden Party
Garden Risotto
Tomato Salad, Fresh Beans and Basil Vinaigrette
Platter of Stuffed Zucchini Blossoms; Sauté
  of Fennel, Artichokes and Carrots;
  Hummous; Roast Carrot Confit
Rhubarb and Strawberry Crumble
Vanilla Ice Cream with Chocolate Dog Tuiles

Cocktails and Finger Food Party
Chicken Wishbones "Frogs' Legs" Style
Stuffed Zucchini Blossoms
Spaghetti Squash and Goat Cheese Croutons
Lake House Crab Cakes with Almond Aïoli
Potato Salmon Fritters

Children's Tea Party
Children's Veggie Canapés
Buttermilk Fried Chicken
Coco's Curls
Neon Lime Jelly
Watermelon and Ginger Juice
Mango and Apple Juice
Marinated Melon Kebabs
Sugar Cookies

Boathouse Party
Grilled Scallops with Roasted Red and Yellow
  Tomatoes, Crispy Shallots with a Herb Sauce
Lake House Goat Cheese, Eggplant and
  Asparagas Salad with Hazelnut Vinaigrette
Trout Duxelles with Fingerling Potatoes, Corn
  and Fava Beans and a Pea Sauce
Crème Brûlée with Kadaifi Discs and Summer
  Fruit

Down by the Beach
Chicken Wishbones "Frogs' Legs" style
Shrimp with Pesto
Cape Cod Fish Stew
Rosemary Focaccia
Lemon Tart

Barbecue
Duck "Ham" Skewers
Grilled Chicken Sticks with Fire-roasted Onions
Mini Goat Cheese Burgers with Brioche Buns
Lamb Sausages with Brioche Rolls
Tomato Salad, Fresh Beans and Basil
  Vinaigrette
Spaghetti Squash and Goat Cheese Croutons

Menus for Autumn & Winter

Family Lunch in the Kitchen
Spaghetti al Aglio e Olio
Vegetable Stew
Little Apple Pies

Afternoon Tea
Stuffed Red and Yellow Cherry Tomatoes
Chocolate Chip Cookies
Jane's Shortbread Cookies
Watermelon and Ginger Juice with Begonia
  Ice Cubes

Halloween Party
Baby Pumpkins Filled with Black Spaghetti and
  Meatballs
Black Thai Rice Witch Hats
Achiote Onion Rings
Turkey Sticks with Orange Cheese Sauce
Peanut Butter Cupcakes with Chocolate Truffle
  Filling
Sugar Cookies
Black Cat Chocolate Shortbread Cookies

Cold Weather Picnic
Chicken Stew with Matzo Ball Dumplings
Stilton Bread
Sticky Toffee Puddings
Mulled Wine

Festive Dinner
Spiced Squash Soup
Warm Salad of Braised Celery with Blood Oranges,
  Persimmon, Toasted Walnuts and Stilton
Roast Pork with Prune and Quince Stuffing
Butternut Squash and Mango Chutney
Sauté of Fennel, Artichokes and Carrots
Potato and Celery Root Gratin
Caramelized Rice Pudding with Sour Cherry Sauce

Fireside Party
Curried Lamb Shanks with Yellow Dhal
Roast Duck
Vegetable Tian
Baked Beans
Herb-brushed Polenta Bread

Vegetarian Dinner Party
Swiss Chard and Pearl Barley Soup
Herb-brushed Polenta Bread

Roasted Vegetables
Crispy Grains with Portabella Mushrooms
Swiss Chard–stuffed Onions
Sweet Potato Purée
Pea Purée

Quick Kitchen Soup-er
Tomato Garlic Bread Soup
Spiced Squash Soup
Rosemary Focaccia

Do-ahead Dinner Party
Roast Duck
Roast Carrot Confit
Fingerling Potatoes
Lake House Chocolate Torte

Children's Dinner Party
Children's Veggie Canapés
Buttermilk Fried Chicken
Coco's Curls
Brownies with Vanilla Ice Cream

Simple French Food
Burgundian Beef Stew
Vegetable Stew
Spiced Potato Pancakes
Winter Fruit Tart with Cinnamon Crème
   Anglaise

British Supper
Lamb and Herb Sausages
Lake House Mashed Potatoes
Braised Red Cabbage and Beets
English Toffee Tart

New York Loft Party
Sea Bass with Sautéed Wild Mushrooms and
   Roast Carrot Confit
Truffled Mashed Potatoes
S'Mores

Index

Acknowledgments

Rachael Skinner
Kitty Percy
Page Marchese-Norman – stylist
Gordon Maskery – head gardener
Albert Stevens
Ben Paulley – assistant gardener
Bryan Wilson
Andy Dubberley
Mark Clayton
Mick Davies
Andy Powell
Nick Hamer
Taff Hanks
Jane Martin – assistant recipe tester, special thanks

Eric and Anna Martin-Ienco
Noel Hart
Judy Maynard
Lil Stevens
Sunnyfields Organic Farm, special thanks
Ian Nelson
West Country Fine Food
Cove Shellfish
Theresa Lowrey Greene
Katie Knight
Dorothee Inderfurth
Abigail Williams
Louisa Swanton
Andrew Wylie
Olivier Lepetit

Alain Mertens
Lindsay Galt
Susie Theodorou
Kori Turribiate
Wendy Cromer
Mrs. D
Tanya
Norma Farrelly
Darren
Luis Conceicao
Isabel Almeida
Marina Black
John Stammers
Graham Parrish
Beata Bishop
Mark Houghton-Brown